BENNY GOODMAN'S FAMOUS 1938
CARNEGIE HALL JAZZ CONCERT

BENNY GOODMAN'S FAMOUS 1938 CARNEGIE HALL JAZZ CONCERT

CATHERINE TACKLEY

OXFORD
UNIVERSITY PRESS

Oxford University Press is a department of the University of Oxford.
It furthers the University's objective of excellence in research,
scholarship, and education by publishing worldwide.

Oxford   New York
Auckland   Cape Town   Dar es Salaam   Hong Kong   Karachi
Kuala Lumpur   Madrid   Melbourne   Mexico City   Nairobi
New Delhi   Shanghai   Taipei   Toronto

With offices in
Argentina   Austria   Brazil   Chile   Czech Republic   France   Greece
Guatemala   Hungary   Italy   Japan   Poland   Portugal   Singapore
South Korea   Switzerland   Thailand   Turkey   Ukraine   Vietnam

Oxford is a registered trade mark of Oxford University Press in the UK and certain other countries.

Published in the United States of America by
Oxford University Press
198 Madison Avenue, New York, New York 10016

Library of Congress Cataloging-in-Publication Data
Tackley, Catherine.
Benny Goodman's famous 1938 Carnegie Hall jazz concert / Catherine Tackley.
p.   cm.—(Oxford studies in recorded jazz)
Includes bibliographical references and index.
ISBN 978-0-19-539830-4 (hardcover: alk. paper)—ISBN 978-0-19-539831-1 (pbk.: alk. paper)
1. Goodman, Benny, 1909–1986—Performances—New York (State)—New York.   2. Goodman, Benny,
1909–1986—Criticism and interpretation.   3. Jazz—New York (State)—New York—1931–1940—History
and criticism.   4. Carnegie Hall (New York, N.Y.)   I. Title.
ML422.G65T33 2011
781.65092—dc23   2011030910

1 3 5 7 9 8 6 4 2

Printed in the United States of America
on acid-free paper

FOR DAN

SERIES PREFACE

THE OXFORD STUDIES IN Recorded Jazz series offers detailed historical, cultural, and technical analysis of jazz recordings across a broad spectrum of styles, periods, performing media, and nationalities. Each volume, authored by a leading scholar in the field, addresses either a single jazz album or a set of related recordings by one artist/group, placing the recordings fully in their historical and musical context, and thereby enriching our understanding of their cultural and creative significance.

With access to the latest scholarship and with an innovative and balanced approach to its subject matter, the series offers fresh perspectives on both well-known and neglected jazz repertoire. It sets out to renew musical debate in jazz scholarship, and to develop the subtle critical languages and vocabularies necessary to do full justice to the complex expressive, structural, and cultural dimensions of recorded jazz performance.

JEREMY BARHAM
SERIES EDITOR

ACKNOWLEDGMENTS

I would like to thank Jeremy Barham for initiating the Studies in Recorded Jazz series and inviting me to contribute to it. At Oxford University Press, Suzanne Ryan has been fantastically supportive. Adam Cohen, Caelyn Cobb and Madelyn Sutton have also been extremely efficient and helpful.

The conception of this book coincided with my move to the Open University, where I was welcomed warmly by my colleagues in the Music Department and supported during the gestation stages of this project. I would like also to thank the members of the What Is Black British Jazz? team, drawn from Music and Sociology—Jason Toynbee, Byron Dueck, Mark Banks and Mark Doffman—for their lively and informed discussions about jazz and for their understanding as I juggled work on these two projects. Outside the OU, Tony Whyton remains a great personal and "critical" friend, and I thank him for his continued support. Andy Simons has been extremely generous with his time and resources, Nigel Haslewood of Sadman Records has been invaluable in helping to obtain rare records, and Cody Coyne kindly assisted with music processing. Susan Satz at the Goodman estate has efficiently ensured my access to resources. Adam Fairhall, Tom Sykes, Claire Troth and Abigail Dolan all contributed useful advice on various aspects. The comments by two anonymous readers on the book proposal and draft manuscript have been extremely helpful to me. Various parts of this book were presented at the Performance Studies Network International Conference at the University of Cambridge in July 2011, the Watching Jazz conference at the University of Glasgow in February 2011, the Royal Musical Associa-

bio-discographical volumes have been invaluable and more recently continued by David Jessup, there is yet to be a detailed analytical study of this sort focused on Goodman.

In Part One, I consider the context for the 1938 concert. In recent times, grand claims have been made for the concert as a "first" that can be qualified and moderated by consideration of precedents for the presentation of jazz and popular music in the concert hall, as well as for development of a listening audience for jazz. More specifically, even before a note was heard, a rich context for the concert performance had been created through promotion and the program, both in terms of content and its presentation in print. Goodman performed at Carnegie Hall with his full orchestra and his Trio and Quartet; the concert also included a series of five numbers entitled "Twenty Years of Jazz" and a "Jam Session." The latter two items included members of Count Basie and Duke Ellington's bands as well as Goodman's own.[1] The context for each of the main elements included in the 1938 program will be established with particular reference to the musicians and choice of repertoire. In Part Three: Representation, I explore the reception and impact of the concert as a live event in 1938 and subsequently on the release of the recording in 1950. This involves consideration of the immediate repercussions of the concert on the performers, the circumstances surrounding production of *The Famous 1938 Carnegie Hall Jazz Concert* and the subsequent tendency to re-create the concert in live and recorded forms.

I hope this book will contribute to development of the study of recorded sound, and in particular the study of jazz recordings, but also that it sheds new light on the performances of Benny Goodman and other musicians at the height of the swing era. There is surprisingly little literature, scholarly or otherwise, on Goodman; but I am indebted to James Lincoln Collier (1989a) and Ross Firestone (1993) for their well-researched biographies, which include important interviews that would otherwise now, sadly, be impossible to obtain. During my research I discovered that a compatriot, Jon Hancock, was about to publish a book after years of researching and collecting every aspect of the concert, and this has also been useful to me (Hancock 2008). But the last word must go to Otis Ferguson, whose writing on Goodman is without question the most evocative I have read. In his introductory comments to the section "Music and Musicians" in the Ferguson reader *In the Spirit of Jazz*, Malcolm Cowley writes:

The unpublished pieces were excerpted from two unfinished book manuscripts. *Benny Goodman: Adventures in the Kingdom of Swing* was to be a biography of Goodman, a description of his band and how it functioned, and a critical evaluation of his music. After Ferguson had drafted a few chapters, he discovered that the publisher wanted a first-person, I-Benny Goodman treatment. As he believed that such a book would be "bogus" and could not be objective about either the man or his music, he abandoned the project [Ferguson, Chamberlain, and Wilson 1997: 1].

Ferguson's extant pieces permit a tantalizing glimpse of what might have been and are a source of inspiration for this book. In particular, his assessment of the performances in question provides a sobering starting point for this investigation:

Their average work is what was heard at Carnegie Hall. The superlative work, which just happens and over which they have no control, is done elsewhere and will be done again. It may be in Hollywood or in the Hotel Pennsylvania; it may even be on some morning when they recorded. But most likely it comes when the hall is full and the air is thick and the acoustics are bright and good, when they can feel the audience listening, the people they are playing for right there in sight, giving their confidence and appreciation in return for the music [78–79].

CONTENTS

BENNY GOODMAN'S FAMOUS 1938
CARNEGIE HALL JAZZ CONCERT

FIGURE 1.1   Billboard outside Carnegie Hall. MSS 53, the Benny Goodman Papers in the Irving S. Gilmore Music Library of Yale University.

PART ONE

Context

> ...it is advertised as "the first swing concert in the history of Carnegie Hall." In fact, it is.
>
> —ARCHETTI 1938a: 362

PRECEDENTS: JAZZ CONCERTS AND AUDIENCES

ALTHOUGH THE CLAIM, in a publicity flyer, that Benny Goodman's 1938 concert was 'the first concert of swing music in the history of Carnegie Hall' was completely accurate, there were a number of important precedents for an event of this type. As Scott DeVeaux states in his seminal article "The Emergence of the Jazz Concert, 1935–1945," "Goodman's Carnegie Hall debut was less an isolated event than a crest of a wave" (De-Veaux 1989: 6). Opened in 1891, Carnegie Hall was the main concert venue in New York City until the Lincoln Center was completed in the 1960s, and it was also bound up with the early history of the jazz concert. In 1910 James Reese Europe and other leading black musicians and composers founded the Clef Club to provide "a central union, a clearing house, and booking agency for the employment of black musicians anywhere in New York and to oversee their contracts and guarantee their professionalism" (Badger 1989: 50). In addition to these practical functions, the Clef Club Orchestra brought the organization and its members to wider public attention. The orchestra consisted entirely of black musicians and was usually over one hundred strong. The instrumentation was unusual, being dominated by plucked strings, reflecting contemporary trends in popular black music performance. The Clef Club Orchestra initially performed at the Manhattan Casino in Harlem with programs of light classics, popular songs, marches, and ragtime (Charters and Kunstadt 1962: 29). But in 1912, when the orchestra appeared at Carnegie Hall in a concert to raise funds for the newly established Music School Settlement for Colored People, the program was focused on traditional spirituals and compositions by black composers. Although the concert was considered to be "the first organized attempt...to show to the public of New York what the Negro race has done and can do in music," Lester A. Walton, reviewing the concert in the *New York Age*, was struck by the wider social implications of the event that anticipated integration *on* the Carnegie Hall stage in 1938:

> The concert was unique in many respects. Some of the leading white citizens sat in evening dress next to some of our highly respectable colored citizens, who were also in evening clothes. No color line was drawn in any part of the house, both white and colored occupying boxes.... Yet no calamity occurred because the colored citizens were not segregated in certain parts of the house as some of our theater managers think it necessary to do, despite laws forbidding discrimination [Southern 1978: 74–75].

This concert brought African American music from Harlem to an established classical music venue in Midtown Manhattan, placing it before new audiences and critics. Similar concerts in aid of the Music School were presented annually at Carnegie Hall until 1915 (Southern 1978: 71). Europe left the Clef Club to pursue his association with the dance team Vernon and Irene Castle, but others such as Will Marion Cook continued to present black music in the concert hall. Cook's Southern Syncopated Orchestra enjoyed great success on the Continent from 1919, implicitly presenting a lineage from plantation songs and spirituals via ragtime to improvised blues, the latter featuring Sidney Bechet (Parsonage 2005: 143). Contemporaneously in New York, W. C. Handy conducted his Memphis Blues Band of Clef Club musicians in a program of "Real Blues, Jazzy and Classics" at the Manhattan Casino (Charters and Kunstadt 1962: 75). In 1928 Handy staged a concert at Carnegie Hall that made the "evolution of Negro music" an explicit focus (Handy 1941: 212). The program ran from "The Birth of

Jazz," with "tomtoms and drums," through spirituals, blues, plantation songs, work songs, cakewalks, and contemporary popular and art songs, culminating in a "Jazz Finale" (Howland 2009: 89; *New York Times* 1928). As well as the roots of this concept in previous presentations of black music in the concert hall, Handy's concert was a direct response to Paul Whiteman, who presented the evolution of jazz beginning with the Original Dixieland Jazz Band in his "Experiment in Modern Music" concert at the Aeolian Hall on February 12, 1924. Whiteman repeated the "Experiment" concert in March and then at Carnegie Hall on April 21, 1924, prior to a national tour (Schiff 1997: 61).

Subsequent attempts to emulate Whiteman's "Experiment" concert by Vincent Lopez (November 1924 at the Metropolitan Opera House) and Harry Yerkes (December 1925 at the Aeolian Hall) drew on Handy's blues compositions as a basis for new works, anticipating Handy's own response in 1928 (Howland 2009: 87). The major work in Handy's concert was an orchestral arrangement of James P. Johnson's *Yamekraw* with Fats Waller as piano soloist, representing "a unique African American parallel—and musical response to—Gershwin's *Rhapsody in Blue*," the main feature of Whiteman's concert (47). However, whereas Handy used symphonic writing to glorify the blues, Whiteman used it to improve "primitive" jazz. Commensurately, the presentation of musical "evolution" in Handy's concert provides artistic and cultural roots for contemporary practices, but for Whiteman a justification and valorization of his improvements. In both cases, African American popular music was a basis for creating works and performances that could be considered aesthetically compatible with concert-hall surroundings. Subsequently, symphonic jazz works represent a significant trend in modern music. An apparent precursor to Goodman's concert was a "jazz concert" given at Carnegie Hall almost exactly a year earlier by Ferde Grofé, a composer and arranger who famously orchestrated *Rhapsody in Blue*. In fact this concert consisted mainly of orchestral performances of jazz-influenced works (and intriguingly included "Bennie Godman's [sic] 'Stompin' at the Savoy'" (*New York Times* 1937a)).

Further to the incorporation of jazz into art music composition and performance, "when the jazz concert finally did emerge as a viable institution in the 1930s, it was to come 'from below' as an outgrowth of the ordinary situations within which jazz was performed" (DeVeaux 1989: 8). Prior to 1938 the youthful audiences in these "ordinary situations" were becoming more like those of concert halls, namely often listening and not always dancing, demolishing the oft-cited simplistic alignment of dancing with swing and listening with bebop. The development of listening to jazz performances is well illustrated by Benny Goodman's career as a bandleader. In

1934 Goodman put together his first permanent band to play at Billy Rose's Music Hall. Rose was prepared to seize opportunities offered by the end of Prohibition, having already opened "a large theater restaurant" called the Casino de Paree. The Music Hall promised a "multimedia extravaganza" every evening, which included films, vaudeville acts and a nude tableau as well as two bands (Firestone 1993: 90–91). Goodman had a clear idea about the concept for his band, as he recalled in his 1939 autobiography:

> I was trying to get a band together that would play dance music in a free and musical style—in other words, in the way that most good musicians wanted to play, but weren't allowed to on the ordinary job [Goodman and Kolodin 1939: 142].

As a result, although Goodman's band had been engaged primarily to play for dancing at the Music Hall,

> some people who came in stood around the bandstand to listen, and while we thought that was fine Rose got the impression we weren't getting across because everybody wasn't dancing. However, we managed to survive that when somebody explained that the sort of music we played, with members of the band taking solos and so on, was something that some people just came to listen to, without dancing [Goodman and Kolodin 1939: 143].

Rose's reaction shows that equation of the positive reception of popular music with a physical response through dancing was clearly well established.

Although the Music Hall closed after only a few months, the engagement did begin to establish Goodman's profile not only for audiences that heard the band live but throughout New York through broadcasts on local station WMCA, and more widely, through recordings. Multimedia dissemination became a characteristic of swing, which "attracted a youthful audience through a complex media network of radio broadcasts, recordings, movies and cross-country tours" (Stowe 1994: 8). Radio, with its ability to disseminate live performance nationally in real time, was central in the development of the swing industry and to Goodman's success. The driving force behind creating these opportunities for jazz musicians was advertisers, who recognized the potential of radio to provide "direct access into the nation's homes" as a result of the affordability of sets (Erenberg 1998: 164). A place on a commercially sponsored program was considered the "swing era's greatest prize" for bands, because unlike broadcasts from hotels and clubs these programs provided a good fee in addition to national promotion (Stowe 1994: 109).

In December 1934 Goodman began broadcasting on *Let's Dance*, "the longest sponsored program that had been put up on the air at that time, fifty-three stations carrying the music for three hours from coast to coast," which brought him to national attention (Goodman and Kolodin 1939: 153). Since Goodman was engaged specifically to provide the "hot" band alongside Xavier Cugat's Latin group and Kel Murray's newly formed sweet orchestra, *Let's Dance* encouraged his stated musical intentions (Firestone 1993: 107). Prior to this, Goodman had only "twelve to fourteen special arrangements that we thought really represented an individual style," but supported by the program's budget for new arrangements this was quickly augmented and led to his defining relationship with Fletcher Henderson (Goodman and Kolodin 1939: 146). He recalled that

> we left most of the pop. tunes to Kel Murray's band…and played mostly standards like "Farewell Blues," "I Know That You Know," "Dear Old Southland," "Bugle Call Rag," and as many arrangements of that kind as the program would stand.

Goodman cited complex up-tempo arrangements by Jimmy Mundy, Fletcher Henderson and Spud Murphy with plenty of opportunities for solos (Goodman and Kolodin 1939: 165).

The importance of *Let's Dance* in developing a youthful audience of listeners for Goodman's style and material was confirmed by his notorious success at the Palomar Ballroom in Los Angeles on August 21, 1935. Goodman described the layout of the venue, which encouraged listening as well as dancing: "It has an enormous dance floor, to which there was an admission charge of forty or fifty cents. But there was also a big section with tables, where food and liquor were served" (Goodman and Kolodin 1939: 197). From the start, Goodman noticed that "some of the kids congregated in front of the band stand and seemed to know what to expect of the different musicians." But the reaction of the crowd was muted until he decided that he might "as well have a good time of it while we had the chance" and "called out some of our big Fletcher arrangements for the next set.…To our complete amazement, half the crowd stopped dancing and came surging around the stand" (198). Various explanations have been posited as to the cause of Goodman's defining success at the Palomar, but whether this was influenced by prior encounters with his music on the radio (*Let's Dance*), on record, or on radio broadcasts of records (*Make Believe Ballroom*), the Palomar crowd's response was influenced by and symptomatic of the desire to listen to the band.

Stowe proposes a tripartite typology of swing enthusiasts distinguished by their responses to the music as well as by race and class. "Jitterbugs" were so called after a dance of the same name, also known as the Lindy Hop, which was particularly developed by black dancers at Harlem's Savoy Ballroom (Stowe 1994: 33). In contrast to ballroom dances with set steps, these dancers improvised in response to the music, which required closer attention to musical details, blurring the distinction between dancing and listening. Jitterbugs were active participants in the performance, rather than passively adhering to the music, which in turn was no longer merely functional as a backdrop for dancing and so engendered mutual respect between musicians and dancers. Leon James recalled dancing to Dizzy Gillespie at the Savoy in 1937: "Every time he played a crazy lick, we cut a crazy step to go with it. And he dug us and blew even crazier stuff to see if we could dance to it, a kind of game, with the musicians and dancers challenging each other" (in Stearns and Stearns 1994: 325). Goodman asserted that he was "crazy about the chandelier-kicking type of jitterbug dancing. It's rhythmic mathematics, sometimes as gifted as the music that inspires it. It's even inspiring to the musicians, adds heat to their playing" (Goodman and Shane 1939: 60).

The "icky" was "a more publicized and despised variety" of jitterbug, "the white youth of high school and college age who alarmed moralists and generated disdain among more sophisticated enthusiasts" (Stowe 1994: 34). They did not dance but adopted self-conscious listening postures, vividly described by Goodman:

> The bugs, literally glued to the music, would shake like St. Vitus with the itch. Their eyes popped, their heads pecked, their feet tapped out of time, arms jerked to the rhythm. They joined in background choruses, ran temperatures up and down in unison with the heat and coolness of the music [Goodman and Shane 1939: 12].

Unlike the jitterbugs, whom they watched as part of the performance (since the Savoy permitted racial integration), the ickies remained external to the performance yet apparently totally absorbed by it (Erenberg 1998: 155). When the band wasn't playing, the ickies indulged in fetishist fan behavior, attempting to obtain not only autographs but also instruments and music stands from the stage (Goodman and Shane 1939: 12). Their behavior during the performance suggests an attempt to similarly capture the music itself, marked externally by unusual bodily reactions as a demonstration of the depth of their listening. Their more extreme sonic reactions (such as clapping out of time or so as to obscure the music, or shouting out) were symptomatic of their attempts to exert control over the music, and were particularly loathed by bandleaders.

Finally, there was the "okay" who would "stand transfixed in front of the bandstand, listening intently for deviations from the recorded versions he knew so well," absorbing and internalizing the music and, unlike the icky, demonstrating complete dedication to listening through a minimal physical response. Critic and producer John Hammond, who became influential on Goodman's career, was considered the archetypal okay (Stowe 1994: 35). These fans could afford to purchase records as permanent icons through which their idols could be remembered, whereas the younger and less affluent ickies were more reliant on jukeboxes and radio broadcasts of records, which may partially explain their desire to capture the ephemeral (and even the material) at performances. This attitude extended to radio broadcasts, and it is significant that a private recording of Goodman's first *Let's Dance* broadcast was "the first known instance of any off-the-air Goodman recording" (Connor 1988: 45). The subsequent prevalence of this practice among fans is reflected in the use of such recordings in research, including this book.

Fans could also purchase Goodman's studio recordings, which from April 1935 were released on the Victor label. The record industry had bottomed out in 1932 but then grew steadily until 1938, when it began to boom (Stowe 1994: 112). It is no coincidence that by the time the recovery of the industry meant Victor was able to offer Goodman a lucrative royalty deal, specialist magazines such as *DownBeat* had commenced publication and various Rhythm Clubs were about to be founded, providing opportunities for criticism of jazz records (Firestone 1993: 128). This echoed developments in Europe, where, necessarily more reliant on recordings as sources of jazz, similar publications and organisations had already been formed. Indeed, the development of Rhythm Clubs was influenced by those of the UK and the Hot Clubs of France, which were linked globally by the International Federation of Hot Clubs. The aim of the movement, as articulated by Secretary General of the Federation Marshall Stearns, was to ensure the progress of swing music, particularly by commissioning special hot records and reissuing old ones, but also through staging jazz concerts by "orchestras freely offered by the record companies" (Stowe 1994: 81). Implicit in this statement is a critique of the commercial motives of the record industry—ironic since many members of the Federation were primarily reliant on recordings for their experiences of jazz.

On Sunday, December 8, 1935, it was the Chicago Rhythm Club that presented Benny Goodman in the Urban Room of the Congress Hotel (Firestone 1993: 162). Although he had been resident there since November, it would have been unusual for the band to play on a Sunday afternoon. This format recalls the concerts in the UK, sponsored by *Melody Maker* magazine, by visiting artists such as Duke Ellington, Louis Armstrong and Benny Carter; Sunday afternoon was a time when bands were usually free from their obligations, and local musicians were similarly available to attend (Parsonage 2005). Goodman's performance was planned as a "regular concert" but billed as a "Tea Dance." This was "on the theory that more people would be interested in it from this angle," but presumably in the expectation that fans would see straight through the unlikely scenario of a Rhythm Club presenting a hot band playing sweet dance music and would know that they were expected to listen rather than dance (Goodman and Kolodin 1939: 208). According to Goodman, "There was tremendous enthusiasm all through the program (the few people that tried to dance were booed off the floor)," and a report in *Time* magazine confirms that "800 Chicago jazz academicians.., would no more have thought of dancing than they would of gavotting at a symphony concert" (Goodman and Kolodin 1939: 208; *Time* 1936). These concerts circumvented commercialism literally, as profits were given to charity, and to some extent aesthetically, by attracting fans who had come to listen to the band rather than using it to provide functional dance music. However, they essentially adhered to commercially established norms in terms of venue, ensemble and performance style (although subsequent Chicago Rhythm Club concerts, which I consider later, began to redefine the practice of racial segregation in jazz performance in particular).

The jam session, romanticized for jazz fans because only "a few outsiders gained admission to the inner circle," seemed to match the Rhythm Club's utopian desires by providing the opportunity for musicians to play free from commercial motives or restraints (Shaw 1983: 62). Trading on the "Hot Club" name, Milt Gabler launched a reissue label and began running free Sunday afternoon jam sessions in recording studios that were otherwise vacant (245). However, the popularity of these events ensured that they quickly developed as commercial ventures in clubs—much to the disgust of Rhythm Club advocates (DeVeaux 1989: 12). Nevertheless, as Gabler noted, "these jams were really the start of commercial jazz concerts in New York" as a result of the desire to listen and the lack of space for dancing (Shaw 1983: 248).

The growth of listening to jazz was also compatible with the fact that "a high proportion of swing performances took place not in ballrooms, where dancing was to be expected, but in theaters" (Stowe 1994: 42). Goodman returned to New York in October 1936 to play at the Madhattan Room in the Hotel Pennsylvania, which George T. Simon described as a basement room with "fine acoustics and its small size and low ceiling lent an aura of immediacy conducive to jazz listening" (Simon 1968: 208). In March 1937 the band took on an additional engagement at the Paramount, a movie theater, which meant playing an additional five shows per day from 10:30 A.M. (Goodman and Kolodin 1939: 220). Whereas the Hotel Pennsylvania performances attracted an audience of "well-heeled college kids" and "older, musically more conservative big spenders," the cheaper, daytime appearances of the band at the movie theater were accessible by younger, less wealthy fans (Firestone 1993: 193). The formal seating arrangements of a theater suggested listening rather than dancing, but the management chose to create publicity by deliberately precipitating a break in the expected mode of reception. Firestone points out that Paramount hired ringers to begin dancing in the aisles at Goodman's first show, and that as a result of the press coverage this became a standard response akin to the icky (Firestone 1993: 201). This was to become a source of frustration for Goodman, who wrote in 1939:

> That reception topped anything we had known up to that time, and because we felt it was spontaneous and genuine, we got a tremendous kick out of it. It's only in these latter days, when some of the youngsters just come to cut up that it gets in our way. After all, if a fellow like Jess Stacy or Ziggy Elman or Vernon Brown gets up to play a solo, he has a right to be heard—and the people in the audience who know what they're listening to feel the same way about it [Goodman and Kolodin 1939: 218].

Other events managed to create an atmosphere closer to a concert hall in a theater. A concert at New York's Imperial Theater on the evening of Sunday, May 24, 1936, was billed as "New York's first Swing Music concert." Several groups were included, ranging from the large Casa Loma Orchestra to the Carl Kress and Dick McDonough guitar duo, but most were closer in style and instrumentation to Dixieland jazz (Shaw 1983: 85). The billing and the timing of the concert, which was sponsored by the Onyx, a 52nd Street jazz club, suggests that this was a response to Goodman in Chicago, where he began to use "swing" in his publicity for the first time (Firestone 1993: 154). Despite the inclusion of some significant jazz musicians, notably Louis Armstrong and Tommy Dorsey, it was Artie Shaw's performance of his new composition "Interlude in B Flat," inspired by the clarinet quintets of Mozart and Brahms and scored for a string quartet and rhythm section, that was best received and encored (Shaw 1983: 86). As he began to play, Shaw heard 'people shushing all over the place. And in a few moments the theater had quieted down.' His encore (a repetition of the same piece) was heard 'in deathly silence' (Shaw 1992: 295, 297).

The influence of musical style on audience behavior at the Imperial Theater is similar to the effect that Goodman's performances had at the Music Hall and the Palomar Ballroom. However, the development of different physical responses when listening to swing, as seen at the Paramount and ballrooms throughout the country, meant that "if 'jazz concert' was to be more than an oxymoron, adjustments were necessary, either in the deportment of the musicians or the expectations of the audience" (DeVeaux 1989: 7). DeVeaux is referring here to the early concerts by African American musicians, but if "deportment" is broadened to "performance," in order to encompass content as well as style, the statement is equally applicable to the 1930s. Essentially "jazz concerts" had often been achieved, including by Artie Shaw in 1936, by "adjusting" jazz to fit within the expectations of a concert. Conversely, the Congress Hotel concerts and public jam sessions demonstrated that audience expectations could be managed so as to create concert-like conditions without musical sacrifices. At Carnegie Hall in January 1938, the solidity of Goodman's established performance style and the weighty symbolism of the Hall itself appeared to offer very little room for maneuver. This apparent incompatibility was the basis for promotion of the event, but there is also evidence of subtle adjustments to performances and audience expectations, often drawing on precedents, to avoid an outright clash.

PROMOTION

THE IDEA FOR Goodman's concert at Carnegie Hall is said to have originated with Wynn Nathanson, a publicist responsible for the *Camel Caravan* radio show, on which Goodman had appeared since 1936. In December 1937, Sol Hurok was approached and agreed to promote the concert. The music critic of the *New York Sun*, Irving Kolodin, recalled that the thinking behind the concert was that "The 'King of Jazz' in the previous decade (Paul Whiteman) had done it; why not the 'King of Swing' in the present (1930) one?" (Kolodin 1950: 9). This title had been bestowed on Goodman in 1936, who at the time "wanted to play that down and keep the expression 'king of swing' out of our publicity, because I didn't know how long this was going to last, and I didn't want to be tied down to something people might say was old-fashioned just because they got tired of the name, in a year or so. But there was no way of avoiding it, so we had to go along with what the public wanted to call us" (Goodman and Kolodin 1939: 209). At the time of Goodman's "coronation," "New York's first Swing Music concert" had taken place without him, although he was certainly aware of this event (216). Whereas the program for that concert demonstrated that "swing was still an enigmatic concept," the Carnegie Hall concert presented Goodman with an opportunity to define swing, embracing his status rather than shying away from it (Shaw 1983: 85).

The date chosen for Goodman's concert was a Sunday, well established as a day for such events, but the choice of January 16, 1938, is interesting. It was the day after the general release of the film *Hollywood Hotel*, in which Goodman and his band were featured, and the last performance at the Madhattan Room at the Hotel Pennsylvania from where they had broadcast six nights a week since October 11, 1937 (Connor 1988: 74). The band did not appear to have another long-term engagement organized, so the intention may have been to aim for maximum publicity at a time when any new opportunities could be taken up. Goodman was initially resistant to the idea of the concert at Carnegie Hall, asking Nathanson, "What the hell would we do there?" (Collier 1989a: 215), indicating that he couldn't see how his usual performances were compatible with the venue. He explained further in his autobiography:

> When the thing [the Carnegie Hall concert] was first put up to me, I was a little bit dubious about it, not knowing just what would be expected of us. But as soon as it was understood that we could handle the thing in our own way, and let people listen to it as they would any other kind of music, the proposition really began to mean something. Certainly, if the stuff is worth playing at all, it's worth playing in any hall that presents itself. I didn't have any idea of putting across a "message" or anything like that—I was just satisfied to have the kids in the band do what they always had done [Goodman and Kolodin 1939: 232].

Goodman was unwilling to make musical compromises, but plans were made to adjust the presentation of his performance. First, there was the idea of engaging Beatrice Lillie, a British comedienne, as a "commentator." Lillie had appeared with Goodman on a *Camel Caravan* broadcast on December 28, 1937, performing a novelty vocal with the band, and she was particularly known for her spontaneous interaction with her audiences (Connor 1988: 80; Morley 2004). Her involvement was firmly rejected by the promoter Hurok, who wrote in a letter to Goodman's manager, Willard Alexander, "I do not think that the idea of Miss Beatrice Lillie acting as commentator is a very good one and believe that it will bring about a certain amount of ridicule from the music critics—who are the very ones you should be seeking to impress" (Hurok 1938). Hurok was equally scathing about the plan "to have Mr. Goodman play against a background of black curtains, with special lighting effects, and with the musicians clad in theatrical costumes." Hurok, a self-made impresario, does not mention Goodman's concert in his autobiography, but he fulfilled an early dream of staging events at Carnegie Hall with a concert by the Russian violinist Efrem Zimbalist while still working in a hardware shop and subsequently presented numerous artists there during his career (Hurok and Goode 1947: 32). His funeral was even held in the hall in 1974. The "S. Hurok presents" brand was evidently one that could be trusted by the public, and Hurok was obviously keen to uphold his integrity.

Both of the ideas suggested for the presentation of Goodman's concert seem oddly incongruous with Carnegie Hall, as Hurok pointed out in his letter: "The point of this entire event is that it is a concert we are offering, subject to the tradition and decorum of such an event" (Hurok 1938). They are, however, both consistent with the precedent of Paul Whiteman's 1924 "Experiment in Modern Music" concert. John Howland explores at length how Whiteman's concert was "built on the contemporary variety entertainment model" (Howland 2009: 83). Whiteman's concert might have been considered a suitable model for Goodman's concert by those associated with *Camel Caravan*, which was in effect a contemporary version of the variety show for radio. In this context, Lillie could have functioned like a vaudeville or radio show host. When Whiteman took his concert on tour, he employed "theatrical effects" of the type proposed for Goodman:

> The audience saw a curtain of gold cloth with a silhouette of the Whiteman orchestra; this withdrew to reveal the orchestra dressed in its summer whites and seated in white bentwood chairs on tiers of dove gray trimmed with vermilion . . . behind them all was a glittering metallic curtain with huge vermilion floral designs. . . . To cap it all the

stage was lighted (as it had been at the Aeolian Hall) with shifting lights of green, yellow, pink, and blue [Schiff 1997: 61–62].

The plans for a "theatrical" presentation are not mentioned in the promotional flyer that notified Goodman's concert to the public, despite its effusive language:

> From Louisiana's swampland a trumpet blared and a clarinet screamed to trapdrum syncopation. Critics thought it vulgar, cacophonic, and scowlingly called it jazz. The infant idiom begged at the door of musical America. Refused admittance to the homes of pundits, it swirled clamorously into the life of the common man. Still yearning for acceptance by the tutored, it became "sweet" and "symphonic" in turn, a traitor to its origins. Losing finally its inferiority complex, it surged forward again, flying its own colors, but with a new name "swing". Despite the mysticists, swing is jazz grown mature and strong. Its orchestrations and polyrhythmic structure have earned the admiration of such musicians as Stravinsky and Stokowski. Said Olin Downes recently: "Real Jazz is an intensely creative thing. It is full of improvisations, of life bubbling up in music from musicians who feel it." Benny Goodman is a musician who "feels it". Foremost among swing musicians, the leading innovator in America today of swing, and himself one of the world's greatest virtuosi of the clarinet, Benny Goodman and his orchestra will give, under the pioneering auspices of S. Hurok, the first concert of swing music in the history of Carnegie Hall. He will render music which is the daily stimulus of fifty millions of Americans—music which centuries from now will be unquestioningly called American folk-music, compositions which are as indigenous to this life as a Bach passacaglia is to the eighteenth century ["S. Hurok Presents" 1938].

Although Goodman was apparently ambivalent about "putting across a message," it is clear that those around him were prepared to exploit the novelty of the first swing concert at Carnegie Hall to do just that. The flyer demonstrates a careful balance between the obvious tension of swing in the concert hall and reassurance that Goodman's music aspired to the qualities of high art through the presentation of an evolutionary historical narrative for swing that both references and emulates the history of art music. The historical dimension offered by precedents such as Whiteman's "Experiment" and Handy's 1928 concert was more than just philanthropy, as the process of educating audiences placed musicians in a position of authority through which cultural and material capital could be obtained and reinforced by self-alignment as the most advanced stage of the historical evolution. Similarly, the text of the flyer begins by identifying inadequacies in the *critical response* to early jazz rather than the music itself, which is excused for its weaknesses because it is not yet fully developed ("the infant idiom"). Later manifestations are criticized for being inauthentic to these origins, but swing is "real," "mature" and "strong." The historical contextualization of swing also had the potential to establish it as an autonomous art form ("creative," containing "improvisations" and "flying its own colors"), and its performers and composers as innovative artists. Having been cast as "Professor Goodman" educating students at his "Swing School" on the *Camel Caravan* show, Goodman is further established here as an authentic ("feels it") and "foremost" protagonist of swing. By demonstrating the permanence of swing, the concert also addressed Goodman's longevity, a concern that was manifest in his previously cited doubts about the King of Swing billing but that would also be of interest to his management. To create maximum publicity, the concert would have to attract coverage from the newspaper music critics, who were not jazz specialists, so the more unusual qualities of swing are tempered by references to aspects more readily associated with art music ("orchestrations," "polyrhythmic structures," "virtuosi," and "compositions") as well as the direct comparison with Bach. The passacaglia, which consists of variations over a ground (repeating) bass, is selected for its broad similarities to improvised jazz. The ongoing relationship between jazz and the critics is addressed directly as a counterpoint to the historical narrative, with the lack of critical acceptance of previous forms contrasting with swing, which is appreciated by well-known pillars of the art music establishment—a composer, a performer and a critic.

Gama Gilbert, author of the most extended preview, published on the day of the concert in the *New York Times Magazine*, argued that rather than legitimizing the presence of swing in the concert hall indicating inevitable success, the concert itself would be a crucial test of whether swing could attain the status of art while "being true to itself" (Gilbert 1938: 21). Gilbert develops themes similar to those of the flyer, but with the title "Swing It! And Even in a Temple of Music: Hottest of Rhythms Vibrates in a Sanctum" his article highlights tension from the outset, where the official publicity sought unity. Here Goodman's biography is seamlessly grafted onto a similar history of the music, but this extends to the concert itself, which will be "decisive in the history of swing" (21). Gilbert identifies a likely middle ground in the reception of the concert for the majority situated between those who are "unable and unwilling to see any merit in swing" and those who "exalt swing to supreme artistic heights":

> Swing does merit respect because it has deep, authentic feeling expressed in fullest measure by its own terms and in a balanced design. The authenticity of its emotion is amply testified by the universality of its appeal; indeed, it is hardly an exaggeration to say that swing is today the most widespread artistic medium of popular emotional expression. It is this very universality that forces itself upon the attention of those who, unable to accept swing as art, must regard it as a social phenomenon—and not a very happy one [Gilbert 1938: 21].

Gilbert dwells on negative interpretations of social argument for the importance of swing, writing "Spenglerites, no doubt, hail swing as a fitting danse macabre for a society tobogganing to its grave" (referring to the philosophy of Oswald Spengler epitomized in *The Decline of the West*). The flyer presents the opposite view: if potential audiences were not convinced by the musical arguments, they might respond to nationalist sociopolitical ones based on identifying swing as "American folk-music." Contemporary American music critics would, of course, be familiar with fusions between jazz and art music (epitomized by *Rhapsody in Blue*) as well as Copland's contemporaneous works, which drew on folk music to create a distinctively American classical style. Swing, however, is presented here as an indigenous American art form in itself, but crucially of and for the "common man," aligning it with positive aspects of contemporary political thought. Stowe argues that "swing was the preeminent musical expression of the New Deal: a cultural form of 'the people,' accessible, inclusive, distinctively democratic, and thus distinctively American" (Stowe 1994: 13). Presented in the flyer as the "the daily stimulus of fifty millions of Americans," swing is positioned as a complement to the economic measures being passed by Congress as a catalyst for social change.

The racial dimension of social equality, which might also be illustrated by swing, is only loosely implied by the flyer, perhaps because the argument for recognition of African Americans could not be made more fully when a white artist was being promoted. An announcement of the concert made in the *New York Times* as early as mid-December noted that Goodman's (integrated) Quartet would be taking part in the concert, but there might have been some reluctance to highlight this in the flyer (*New York Times* 1937b: 9). Gilbert, however, identifies the origins of swing as specifically black, albeit in romanticized, primitivist terms: "a rowdy, convulsive music…from the hot lips and agitated fingers of a handful of darkies who had started life as stevedores, cotton pickers or river rats." Similarly, Hampton's "primeval grunts" figure in Gilbert's description of an imagined Quartet performance of "I Got Rhythm," which would have the potential to represent swing as art at Carnegie Hall (Gilbert 1938: 21).

PROGRAM

THE MUSIC CRITIC Irving Kolodin was commissioned to produce program notes for the Carnegie Hall concert, balancing an initial consideration of the idiosyncratic aspects of swing with quasi-analytical descriptions of each piece in a style familiar to regular concert-goers. Specific aspects of these notes will be considered in Part Two, but it is notable that Kolodin makes no attempt to follow this format for the Trio and Quartet numbers or the "Jam Session," implicitly establishing these areas of the program as most different from art music. Indeed, against a backdrop of ongoing attempts to define swing, Kolodin's Foreword perceptively highlights the role of improvisation and hence the importance of performers and arrangers, rather than composers, in swing in unusually realist terms:

> Even the best swing players have moments and nights of stodginess when their ideas run to formal figures and clichés, lacking the improvisational flame which is the heart of "hot" jazz. Thus it is not reasonable to expect that all the performances in the space, say, of two hours, will be white hot with inventiveness and originality.
>
> Almost all swing playing reflects an effort to escape from the most confining element in present day jazz, the prison whose bars are the thirty-two measures of the average tune.... To aid the improvisation by the solo players, the arranger creates a framework on which the variations may be hung [Kolodin 1938b: 193–194].

Howland's comparison of the 11 sections of Whiteman's 1924 "Experiment in Modern Music" concert with the typical structure of a vaudeville program as described by producer George Gottlieb ("head booker for New York's famous Palace Theater") is compelling and relevant in broad terms to understanding the structure of Goodman's concert (Howland 2009: 83–87). The program was divided into 10 sections, each between 10 and 15 minutes in length, in accordance with variety practice. If the Trio and Quartet had been separated in the second half as in the first, the structure would have been identical to Whiteman's with five "acts" before the intermission and six afterward. Like Whiteman, Goodman places his most overtly comedic item ("Twenty Years of Jazz") second on the bill and, as Gottlieb suggests, introduces "big name" personalities in the act prior to the intermission (Lionel Hampton) and the second act of the second half (Ziggy Elman on "Swingtime in the Rockies" and "Bei Mir Bist Du Schön") (Howland 2009: 85). Goodman reserved his most spectacular act, "Sing, Sing, Sing," for the penultimate slot on the bill, where Whiteman placed *Rhapsody in Blue*. A crucial difference is in the final act of the evening, where Gottlieb recommends a "showy" closing act and Whiteman had his arrangement of Edward Elgar's *Pomp and Circumstance*. Instead, Goodman's concert concluded with the relatively sweet "If Dreams Come True" followed by an unusually restrained rendition of "Big John Special."

TRIO AND QUARTET   Erenberg argues that "as the predominant white employer of black musicians in the 1930s and early 1940s, Goodman was the most visible symbol of racial integration in the music business" (1998: 82–83). In the 1930s, the race relations situation in Northern cities was not as explosive as in some Southern states, but *de facto* segregation still meant it was generally impossible for racially mixed bands to perform live. However, "black and white musicians did occasionally perform together in recording studios, special concerts, special jam sessions, [and] a few nightclubs" (Lopes 2002: 128). Precedents for racial integration, then, were closely linked with those "ordinary situations" that led to the emergence of the jazz concert and can be similarly illustrated with reference to Goodman's career, in particular his Trio (Goodman, Teddy Wilson and Gene Krupa) and Quartet (with the addition of Lionel Hampton).

A vital impetus for integration, especially with respect to Goodman, was provided by John Hammond, a wealthy young man whose aspirations in the swing industry were inextricable from his political philosophy, both founded on his desire for racial equality (Hammond and Townsend 1977: 60). Hammond's involvement with Goodman extended back to 1933, when he organized recording sessions for the English Columbia Graphophone label that included a band under Goodman's leadership. Hammond's initial proposal was for Goodman to lead a jam session with a racially mixed group, reflecting emerging beliefs about "real" jazz—he had organized broadcast jam sessions by black musicians on the Jewish station WEVD in 1932 (Hammond and Townsend 1977: 75)—as well as his personal ideology. Although mixed bands had made records previously, as Goodman recalled this often involved a white band with "some outstanding [black] personality around whom the sessions revolved," such as Fats Waller with Ted Lewis's band (including Goodman) in 1931 (Goodman and Kolodin 1939: 129). Bubber Miley's inclusion in an otherwise white recording band including Goodman and Bix Beiderbecke in 1930 could be seen as an extension of this practice, since he was featured prominently in a solo with his distinctive mute and growl effects (110). Miley was working with Leo Reisman's white band at this time, performing not only in the studio but also on stage as a "special feature," sometimes in the role of a theater usher or even playing from behind a screen (Chilton 1999: 95; Dodge 1940: 455).

Goodman realized that the proposal for a *fully* integrated band had unprecedented implications. Even Hammond was unable to disagree with his reaction that "If it gets around that I recorded with colored guys I won't get another job in this town" (Hammond and Townsend 1977: 110). Richard Sudhalter observes that "as an element of popular culture, jazz inevitably reflected the prevailing system: if musicians themselves were relatively color-blind (and indeed they were), their managers, agents, customers, employers, audiences—and particularly critics—were not" (Sudhalter 1999: xvi). Hammond assembled an all-white band instead but later organized a racially mixed backing band, including Goodman on at least one number, "Gimme a Pigfoot," for what was to be Bessie Smith's last recording session in November 1933 (Connor 1988: 41). Goodman also led the band for Billie Holiday's recording debut in the same month, which included the black trumpeter Shirley Clay. With Hammond's encouragement, Goodman regularly included black musicians on his recordings, which began to redefine the previous limits of integration in the studio (Firestone 1993: 87). Though Hammond's motives were ideological, Goodman's were primarily musical. According to Teddy Wilson, "Benny's feeling was that music was more important than race" and would take any opportunity to employ the best musicians (Wilson et al. 2001: 46).

Goodman's objection to a recorded jam session, irrespective of the membership of the band, is revealing of a further distinction between private and public modes of jazz performance in the early 1930s. Whereas jam sessions mainly took place behind closed doors, Goodman probably did not want to leave his recorded performances, on which his reputation was reliant, to chance. It is maybe not surprising that although Goodman had already recorded with the black pianist Teddy Wilson in larger groups, it was the opportunity to jam informally (with an amateur drummer) at a party in 1935 that led to formation of the Goodman Trio

(Firestone 1993: 135). Hammond was instrumental in immediately arranging a recording session and maintaining the concept for the group: "John wanted just the same sound: no bass player—just Goodman and me and a drummer" (Wilson et al. 2001: 40). Hammond was already a great admirer of Wilson, whom he had identified as a key player in his aims for racial integration as "he had the bearing, demeanor, and attitude to life which would enable him to survive in a white society" (Hammond and Townsend 1977: 116).

Initially the Trio (with Gene Krupa at the drums) was convened as a one-off studio group, recording their first sides in July 1935, thus adhering to established precedents for integration while breaking new ground musically. Gunther Schuller writes:

> The instantaneous success of the Goodman Trio (soon to be expanded to a quartet) had two major consequences: (1) it reaffirmed the viability, both artistically and commercially, of a true chamber-jazz concept, fundamentally different from an orchestral one; and (2) it inaugurated the notion—tried only once before (by Ben's Bad Boys, drawn from the larger Ben Pollack band—of extracting a small group from a larger orchestra [Schuller 1989: 811].[2]

However, the musical success of the Trio should not be isolated from the social circumstances that brought it about. Restrictions on racial integration in live performance more or less dictated that Goodman's opportunity to play with Wilson would be in the context of an informal jam session, and this in turn established the Trio's musical characteristics. *De facto* segregation also meant that the group's activity would be mainly restricted to recording, and as a result dissemination of the jam session aesthetic on record. This coincided with the growing critical appreciation of jazz on record and recognition of the jam session as authentic jazz, supported by the specialist press and institutionalized by the Rhythm Clubs. Although the Trio recordings were reviewed positively and sold well, the "viability" of the group remained essentially limited (Firestone 1993: 139).

The Chicago Rhythm Club gave the Trio their first opportunity to play in public. Following Goodman's first concert at the Congress Hotel, the Club presented Fletcher Henderson's band in the Urban Room. When Krupa and Goodman sat in, this was "the first time, probably, that white and colored musicians had played together for a paying audience in America" (Goodman and Kolodin 1939: 210). Rhythm Club stalwart Helen Oakley persuaded Goodman to include the Trio in a further concert arranged for April 1936, and she even paid Wilson's fare to come to Chicago from New York (Firestone 1993: 164; Goodman and Kolodin 1939: 213). Oakley also conceived of a way in which a black musician could be included so as to limit the potential for causing offense: "Teddy played intermission piano (while the band was off the stand) and the trio was made part of the floor show, spotted separately" (Goodman and Kolodin 1939: 214). In this way, Wilson was presented as a "special feature" similarly to how black musicians had initially appeared with white bands on record (Goodman and Kolodin 1939: 213).

Despite the undoubted importance of the Congress concert in the development of racially integrated jazz performances, this arrangement actually served to highlight not only racial but also musical difference. In contrast with the full orchestra, the presentation of the Trio in a spotlight emphasized the intimacy among the three musicians and also with the audience, as the group was positioned on the same level rather than elevated and distanced by a stage. This gave the impression of Goodman and Krupa playing informally with a black musician, which was not only more socially acceptable but also commensurate with Rhythm Club members' romanticized notions of the jam session as authentic jazz performance. This pre-dated and anticipated the popularity of the public jam session, but the similarity between this type of jazz performance and Goodman's small groups was highlighted in Kolodin's program notes for the Carnegie Hall concert. (1938b: 201). Although the Trio was not technically a "band within a band" as Schuller suggests, it precipitated a trend for small groups drawn from big bands, which allowed more expansive demonstration of the jazz credentials of musicians, live and on record, which attracted different audiences (Firestone 1993: 139).

The intimacy of the Trio was also important to Goodman, who wrote in his autobiography:

What I got out of playing with Teddy was something, in a jazz way, like what I got from playing with the string quartet in the Mozart. It was something different than playing with the band, no matter how well it might be swinging, because here everything was close and intimate, with one fellow's ideas blending right in with the other's, and each of us getting a lift from what the other one was doing [Goodman and Kolodin 1939: 186].

Given this degree of musical satisfaction, the decision to add the vibraphonist Lionel Hampton to form a Quartet in August 1936 might seem strange. The Trio was already a non-standard combination of instruments (which Goodman had used once before in 1928; it is also represented on some Jelly Roll Morton recordings from around the same date), and addition of the vibraphone, which previously had been used mainly for occasional color in dance band arrangements, provided a further unusual feature. Hampton also brought an extrovert dimension to the group that was not particularly represented by Goodman, Wilson, or even Krupa's performances, which tended to be limited by the small-group format. But above all, a group numbering black and white musicians equally was an even more explicit demonstration of racial equality. The addition of Hampton was again influenced by Hammond who "discovered" him "leading an eight piece group at the Paradise Café, on Main Street, a crummy section of downtown Los Angeles" (Hammond and Townsend 1977: 175). As with the Trio, the informal setting of the jam session quickly brought about a recording, as Hampton recounted in his autobiography:

> [Goodman] got up on the bandstand with me, pulled his clarinet out of his case, and we started to jam. We jammed all night and into the morning.... The next night was even more exciting. I'm up onstage playing as usual, and I hear this clarinet player next to me, and I turn and there is Benny Goodman, playing right next to me. He had brought Gene Krupa and Teddy Wilson along, and the four of us got on the bandstand together, and man, we started wailing out. We played for two hours straight, and Benny liked the sound we made so well that he said, "Come on and join me at a recording session tomorrow at RCA Victor, out in Hollywood" [Hampton and Haskins 1989: 53].

The Quartet recorded "Moonglow" the following day and further numbers a few days later. Following the Congress Hotel concert in April, the Trio was incorporated into Goodman's usual performances there and at the band's return to the Palomar Ballroom (Connor 1988: 60). The Quartet began live performances once Hampton arrived in New York in November 1936, initially in the Madhattan Room but also at the Paramount Theater (Hampton and Haskins 1989: 58). Despite some opposition, the Trio and Quartet were also included on *Camel Caravan* broadcasts (Collier 1989a: 174). Hampton and Wilson traveled with the band in the South, although they could not stay in the same hotels, circumstances that Wilson recalled were "considered so normal in those days" (Wilson et al. 2001: 45). There were a few race-related incidents, but the response was far from the race riots that some predicted (Firestone 1993: 182–183). An important exception to the generally inclusive attitude toward the

Trio and Quartet was exhibited by the film industry. Goodman's band had been invited to appear in *The Big Broadcast of 1937*, which was shot in Hollywood in summer 1936, but Wilson was not involved since the film makers wanted to use his performance on the soundtrack with a white musician substituting on screen (Firestone 1993: 179). The following year, Wilson and Hampton were included in a Quartet performance in *Hollywood Hotel*, although presentation of the integrated Quartet is countered by the film's presentation of black stereotype in a scene depicting a film shoot on location at a plantation. By the time of the Carnegie Hall concert, racial integration was largely accepted in the recording studio and for "special features" in live performances.

Kolodin's program notes hinted at the socially progressive aspect of the Quartet: "it is an example of a band leader participating in a small ensemble on a footing of equality with the other members of his organization." Given the articulate discussion of swing in the Foreword to Kolodin's program notes, the statement that "the trio is unique in the realm of jazz for several reasons, not the least of which is the fact that none of its performances have been written down, though many of them have been recorded" seems oddly naïve, but it is offered as part of an excuse for not providing more detailed notes (Kolodin 1938b: 201). Although the program listing gave details of the numbers to be played by the small groups, this differed considerably from the pieces that were actually heard in the concert. In the first half, the Trio was scheduled to begin with "Tiger Rag," but this was omitted. The Trio and Quartet performances in the second half show more drastic alteration of the printed program. "Who" and "Dinah" were both omitted, and the set instead began with "China Boy"; "Stompin' at the Savoy" was retained but followed by "Dizzy Spells" instead of "I'm a Ding Dong Daddy." The changes were unannounced, and therefore the content of the printed program was often reflected in reviews.

These alterations would appear to relate to the balance of the program. "Who" and "Dinah" are specifically mentioned in Kolodin's notes as typical numbers for jam sessions (Kolodin 1938b: 200). "Tiger Rag" was long established as a standard up-tempo showpiece for soloists in a variety of contexts following the Original Dixieland Jazz Band's 1917 recording, and it is the second most recorded tune in Crawford and Magee's core repertory of early jazz based on a survey of recordings between 1900 and 1942 (1992). Omission of these numbers suggests that Goodman may have been trying to distinguish the small-group performances from the "Jam Session." Although all of the numbers played by the small groups had significant recorded histories, none was as dominated from the outset by a particular jazz performer as "I'm a Ding Dong Daddy" was by Louis Armstrong, which suggests it was dropped from the program to avoid any duplication of the "Twenty Years of Jazz" in which Armstrong was represented by a rendition of "Shine." Its replacement was "Dizzy Spells," an original composition, which meant that Goodman ended both small-group sets with numbers that the Quartet had not yet recorded. In this period, "I Got Rhythm" had been much less frequently recorded by jazz musicians than "Tiger Rag" or "Dinah" as it was relatively new. Its inclusion, together with "The Man I Love," may have been intended as a tribute to Gershwin, who died in July 1937. With the exception of "The Man I Love" and "Dizzy Spells," all of the tunes performed by the small groups at Carnegie Hall are included in Crawford and Magee's core repertory (1992).

THE "JAM SESSION" The decision to include a jam session in the concert undoubtedly drew on public interest, which had resulted in the phrase attaining "an esoteric vogue suggesting proceedings of almost a ritualistic flavor" (Kolodin 1938b: 199). Kolodin's program notes included an extensive explanation of a jam session, which despite asserting that this was "nothing more than a meeting of hot musicians for the pleasure of mutual improvisation" perpetuate the exoticism of a practice that at the time relatively few members of the public had experienced. Kolodin locates the jam session obliquely but precisely within a nightclub environment with references to "stale air, tobacco fumes and drinks within easy reach," stimuli said to be "indispensable" to the musicians. In contrast with "commercial jobs," which fail to provide an outlet for the "musical energy" of a jazz musician and result only in "routine playing," the jam session unequivocally produces the best music. In a jam session the musicians are transcendent, communicating "without perceptible sign" and "almost telepathic understanding." They are immersed in a performance in which individual "fancy" is not bound by the constraints of either melody or arrangement, since decisions are made by "mutual consent" within an invariable procedure, or ritual, that is collectively understood. Kolodin's notes emphasize the incongruity of the jam session, not only with the surroundings of Carnegie Hall but also with the usual concept of a concert because of its unpredictable length, which is dictated not by a composer's work but by "the reactions of the players to each other and to the audience" (Kolodin 1938b: 199–200). The program listing reinforced the informal spontaneity of the jam session, which was described as "Collective improvisation by a group of soloists to be announced. The length of the session is indeterminate, and may include one or more tunes." However, Goodman's autobiography indicates that "Honeysuckle Rose" had been selected in advance and also rehearsed *in situ* by the musicians who would take part:

> Actually that jam session was a real thrill—not the way it worked out in the concert, unfortunately, because it is always a difficult thing to know how such a set-up will turn out on any particular occasion, but when the boys first came together, just to try things out, a few days before [Goodman and Kolodin 1939: 231–232].

The Carnegie Hall jam session significantly stretched the contemporary limits of racial integration in live jazz performance. In one sense, as the participation of black guest musicians from the bands of Count Basie (Lester Young, Buck Clayton, Walter Page, Freddie Green and Basie himself) and Duke Ellington (Johnny Hodges, Harry Carney and Cootie Williams) was limited to the "special features" of the concert ("Twenty Years of Jazz" and the "Jam Session") this was therefore commensurate with established practice. But there is also evidence that the jam session convention was used to test the boundaries of integration in live performance. Although the activities of Goodman's small groups had been supported by *DownBeat* magazine, the possibility of an integrated big band remained more controversial (Erenberg 1998: 139). Such an ensemble was not completely unprecedented; Hammond had made plans for an all-star integrated band led by Goodman to perform in Europe, though this did not come to fruition (Goodman and Kolodin 1939: 148). Mezz Mezzrow's short-lived integrated Disciples of Swing had played at the Harlem Uproar House (in midtown Manhattan) and the Savoy Ballroom in 1937 (Mezzrow and Wolfe 1999: 286).[3] Given the strong ideologies of Hammond and Mezzrow, *DownBeat* was probably right to be concerned that "if social ideals took over, musicians could not relax and play their best" (Erenberg 1998: 140).

Hammond had helped Goodman "to get musicians from the Basie and Ellington bands to complete the cast" for the Carnegie Hall concert (Hammond and Townsend 1977: 200). He acted as a powerful advocate for Basie, securing him management and prestigious dates, and also initiated a previous jam session with Goodman and Basie in early 1937 (Hammond and Townsend 1977: 172). It is interesting that Hammond was the producer for sessions in which Fletcher Henderson (1932) and Basie (1937) recorded their versions of "Honeysuckle Rose," evidencing his continued interest in recording jam sessions and suggesting a possible influence on the choice of repertoire at Carnegie Hall, although this was, of course, usual jam session material. Other than Kolodin's acknowledgment of Hammond's input to the program notes, there is little evidence of any further involvement in the Carnegie Hall concert, but this is consistent with his unofficial though influential behind-the-scenes role in Goodman's overall career. The "Jam Session," which in fact presented an integrated big band consisting of four reeds, three brass and a complete rhythm section, with a racial split of four white and seven black musicians, strongly suggests his influence.

"TWENTY YEARS OF JAZZ"   "Twenty Years of Jazz" most obviously aligned Goodman's Carnegie Hall concert with its precedents. As discussed earlier, inclusion of historical and therefore educational content in jazz concerts allowed the artistic qualities of the music and musicians to be established. *Melody Maker* initially reported that Goodman's Carnegie Hall concert would include "an elaborate rendition of St. Louis Blues in the chronological styles of W.C. Handy, Dixieland, Louis Armstrong, Duke Ellington, and finishing with Goodman's own interpretation of the jazz classic" (Brackman 1938a).

The choice of repertoire stated here is particularly revealing, as Handy's "St. Louis Blues" was used as a basis for a symphony (entitled *Blue Destiny*) by Albert Chiaffarelli in Yerkes's 1925 concert and had featured heavily in Handy's own Carnegie Hall concert (Howland 2009: 87). However, it is notable that although Dixieland, Armstrong and Ellington were retained in the final selection for "Twenty Years of Jazz," the idea of W. C. Handy's composition as a basis for the historical presentation was not. Kolodin's notes for *The Famous 1938 Carnegie Hall Jazz Concert* album explain the approach that was adopted in the form of a confession: "The idea for the historical 'Twenty Years of Jazz' was, I am afraid, mine. I apologize for it because it probably caused more trouble in listening to old records and copying off arrangements than it was worth" (Kolodin 1938b: 12). "Twenty Years of Jazz" was based on jazz recordings that were made to function similarly to works of classical music; indeed, Kolodin indicates that the recordings were made into scores as part of the preparations for the concert. Presentation of performances based on specific recordings rather than generalized stylistic imitation of historical styles more firmly positioned the musicians within the history of jazz, since they were in effect providing the embodiment of the disembodied voices of the recordings.

The differences between the two approaches to "Twenty Years of Jazz" can usefully be explored through the concepts of intertexuality and hypertextuality, as developed by Serge Lacasse from Gérard Genette to address the relationships between popular music recordings (Lacasse 2000). Lacasse explains that intertextuality is "a relationship of copresence between two texts…the actual presence of one text within another" (36). Hypertextuality describes "any relationship uniting a text B [the 'hypertext'] to an earlier text A [the 'hypotext'], upon which it is grafted in a manner that is not a commentary" (37). As David Horn suggests, intertextual and hypertextual relationships often occur simultaneously in jazz, but

> the combination is rarely an even one. To put it another way, not all jazz performances that are predicated upon the presence of one text within another appear to want to transform that text in order to create a new one out of the encounter. Equally, not all jazz performances that arise out of a separate text have much interest in that text beyond the raw data it provides (which usually means chord progressions) [Horn 2000: 248].

In the original concept for "Twenty Years of Jazz," "St. Louis Blues" forms a basis for performance in a type of intertextual relationship common in jazz, but it also functions as a hypotext to be *transformed* stylistically into various hypertexts. This process would take place most obviously through pastiche, defined as "imitation of a particular style applied to a brand new text," but in a modified version since "St. Louis Blues" would also remain present as a basis for the resulting hypertexts (Lacasse 2000: 43). However, an added complication is the definition of style with reference to a particular person (such as Armstrong or Ellington), which diverts the subject of the performance so that it is no longer just "about" the "St. Louis Blues"—a characteristic of parody (41). On the other hand, in the "Twenty Years of Jazz" that was actually performed at Carnegie Hall, the "texts" in question were already performances and the nature of the relationship with the original *composition* was more distant and less relevant. In general terms, the focus at Carnegie Hall was not on creating a "brand new text" but on reproducing an existing one, a process simply described by Kolodin as "copying." Producing an exact copy of a text might be regarded as impossible or aesthetically worthless, but Lacasse argues that attempts to do so in popular music can be valued in terms of "the ability of a particular artist to re-perform as faithfully as possible what has already been performed" (45). Although there is evidence of close imitation of the recorded texts in "Twenty Years of Jazz," these texts are also *adapted*, similarly to "cover versions" in popular music, as a result of Goodman's performance practice and other factors associated with the function of these performances in the concert. "Covering" can denote copying, but Lacasse associates the practice specifically with an interpretation or reading, defining it as a "rendering of a previously recorded song that displays the usual stylistic configuration of the covering artist" (46). In fact each item within the "Twenty Years of Jazz" sets up subtly different relationships with the "source" recordings, which will be examined in more detail in Part Two.

The choice of repertoire for "Twenty Years of Jazz" reflects not only the emergence of the jazz canon on record but also Goodman's biography. The Original Dixieland Jazz Band, generally considered to have made the first jazz recordings in 1917, was an obvious starting point for Goodman, as it had been for Whiteman in 1924. The performance of the ODJB's "Sensation Rag" placed Goodman in the role of clarinetist Larry Shields, whom he later acknowledged as an influence (Collier 1989a: 19). It is notable that the interpolations into the initial outline of "Twenty Years of Jazz" as reported by Brackman in *Melody Maker* were based on recordings by Ted Lewis and Beiderbecke, musicians who both figured in Goodman's past. Goodman's imitation of the distinctive style of the clarinetist Ted Lewis had secured his first professional engagement at the age of 12. This was the result of formative experiences demonstrating the importance of recordings in dissemination and development of jazz:

> Somehow we had gotten hold of one of those old phonographs with a horn, and [Goodman's brother] Charlie used to bring home records. One of them was played by Ted Lewis, who we figured was a pretty hot clarinet player. Charlie used to play this thing by the hour, and after a while I got so that I could play the tune just the way Lewis did [Goodman and Kolodin 1939: 23].

Lewis was a contemporary of the Original Dixieland Jazz Band, with which he was in competition as a member of Earl Fuller's band before the First World War (Schuller 1986: 183). He continued to thrive on the light-hearted presentation of novelty jazz-influenced numbers and popular songs throughout his career, and his style was the source of a musical alter ego for Goodman when this was required for commercial recordings. This seems to have originated with Goodman's recording of "Shirt Tail Stomp" in 1928, which is also a possible source for the original "Twenty Years of Jazz" concept as it was based on "St. Louis Blues." Goodman had played with Beiderbecke on an excursion boat as a teenager in Chicago, and recorded with him in 1930, a year before his death. Recalling the Carnegie Hall concert in his autobiography, Goodman wrote,

"We were playing for 'Bix' and the fellows on the riverboats, in the honky tonks and ginmills that night," offering Beiderbecke as a tragic icon for all the musicians who had failed to attain the successes that the Carnegie Hall concert epitomized for him (Goodman and Kolodin 1939: 233).

Kolodin's program notes elucidate an evolution of jazz from "unsophisticated" Dixieland and "exaggeration and distortion" of Lewis that is dependent on a series of "great men": Beiderbecke, Armstrong, Ellington and Goodman. Allied to its aim to present jazz as art, the program contains criticism of Armstrong's then recent popular work, despite the fact that "Shine" was representative of this: "The best of Armstrong's talent is undoubtedly contained in his records of a decade ago. There one finds these devices rarely employed merely for the purpose of astonishing the laity, but only as the crisis of a series of remarkable variations or because no other expression will contain his marvellous fertility of thought." Similarly, Ellington's "Blue Reverie" is not "the Ellington of…wide popular appeal, but the Duke of…solid jazz" (Kolodin 1938b: 198). Unlike the other items in "Twenty Years of Jazz," Ellington's music was considered inimitable by musicians other than his own sidemen, and so the Carnegie Hall performance of "Blue Reverie" included Cootie Williams, Johnny Hodges and Harry Carney. Goodman recognized that "somebody else might have learned Johnny's runs on alto, but it didn't sound genuine until they got their *feeling* into it" (Goodman and Kolodin 1939: 248). The possibility of Ellington giving a concert at Carnegie Hall had been discussed as early as 1936, but his manager, Irving Mills, was reluctant and the idea came to nothing (Collier 1989b: 217). If, as Hammond indicated, he was responsible for securing Ellington's sidemen for the 1938 concert, it is not surprising that Ellington himself refused the offer since there had been personal differences between the two men since at least 1936 (196). Ellington may have wanted to appear first on the Carnegie Hall stage with his own band, rather than under the auspices of another musician. He eventually gave his own concert there in January 1943 and continued to do so annually until 1948.

Harry James's composition "Life Goes to a Party," performed by Goodman's full band, brought "Twenty Years of Jazz" up to date, as the number referred to the inclusion of the band in the popular magazine *Life*. The publication was instrumental in developing the technique of photojournalism in which stories were constructed primarily with images rather than text, a novel idea at the time of the magazine's launch in 1936. The "Life Goes to a Party" feature depicted social gatherings of all types. Parties visited in issues juxtaposing the one in which Goodman was featured were an opulent and mysterious "Veiled Prophet's

Ball" in St. Louis and a "corn husking bee" in rural Connecticut (*Life* 1937b: 123; 1937c: 122). In November 1937 the "Life Goes to a Party" story on Goodman's performances in the Madhattan Room served to confirm ideas that had already been established in the media. Goodman is described not only as a "schoolmaster," similarly to his role on the *Camel Caravan* show, but a "high priest of swing" reflecting the devotion of his worshipful audience. Goodman's fans are shown to be mainly college students who "spend more time listening than dancing." The photographs are indicative of the balance of styles still required of the band, illustrating orthodox "dancing to sweet music," but also modern lindy-hop dancing, which was supplied by a professional troupe, an addition no doubt inspired by uptown venues such as the Savoy Ballroom. The magazine also commented on the current situation regarding racial integration: "Because mixed bands are not the rule in New York, Wilson is not the regular pianist but steps up twice during each evening to play in a mixed quartet"; it emphasized that Wilson had "many a White admirer" (*Life* 1937a: 122).

THE ORCHESTRA   The successful development of Goodman's orchestra as represented at Carnegie Hall was as much a result of the persistence of racial segregation at the full band level as integration contributed to the small groups. Goodman's employment on *Let's Dance* in 1935, despite his inexperience, demonstrates the lack of suitable "hot" bands available, as opportunities of this sort were restricted to white bands at this time (Firestone 1993: 108). Under Hammond's guidance, Goodman looked to black bands and arrangers as the basis for the "hot" music that his position on *Let's Dance* demanded. At the age of 21, Hammond presented Fletcher Henderson's band in a variety theater he had taken over, and then he included the group in the sessions he organized for English Columbia (Hammond and Townsend 1977: 70, 88). Goodman obtained some of Henderson's existing arrangements to inject the necessary "hot" content into his performances, and he used them in particular "to wind up a set" (Goodman and Kolodin 1939: 161). However, this highlighted the fact that "the band didn't have the right material for the regular sequence of numbers," namely suitable arrangements of "the more melodious popular songs from Tin Pan Alley publishers, who saw Goodman's new job as a major opportunity to plug their latest products" (Magee 2005: 193). As Goodman recalled, "It was then that we made one of the most important discoveries of all—that Fletcher Henderson, in addition to writing big arrangements...could also do a wonderful job on melodic tunes" (Goodman and Kolodin 1939: 161).

Goodman realized that it was Henderson's approach to the mainstream popular music rather than his "big arrangements" (such as "King Porter Stomp" and "Down South Camp Meeting") that "really set the style of the band," as this consistently and decisively distinguished Goodman from his competitors playing similar material. The Henderson numbers performed at Carnegie Hall are all arrangements of older popular songs. Specifically, "Sometimes I'm Happy," "Blue Skies" and "Blue Room" were all published in 1926 or 1927, a formative period in Goodman's career when he worked mainly in Ben Pollack's band and thus became more widely aware of trends in popular music. Henderson was also responsible for the arrangement of "If Dreams Come True," the first encore of the concert, which is generally attributed to its composer, Edgar Sampson. With the addition of "Big John Special" by Fletcher's brother Horace, "Hendersonese" (Schuller's term for the Goodman band's "adopted language") dominated the Carnegie Hall program (Schuller 1989: 22).

Henderson's arrangements represented a significant departure from models established in the 1920s, as summarized succinctly by Magee: "Flow and cohesion had replaced variety and contrast" (Magee 2005: 195). Earlier arrangers attempted to supply interest within a particular number, often by exploiting the differences between the verse and the chorus of the original song; Henderson focussed on an evolving "sequence of variations" on the chorus alone, a concept closely allied to emergent practices in small group jazz (194). For Goodman,

> what Fletcher could really do so wonderfully was to take a tune like "Sometimes I'm Happy" and really improvise on it himself, with the exception of certain parts of the various choruses which would be marked solo trumpet or solo tenor or solo clarinet. Even here the background for the rest of the band would be in the same vein, so that the thing really hung together and sounded unified. Then, too, the arranger's choice of different key changes is very important, and the order in which the solos are placed, so that the arrangement works up to a climax [Goodman and Kolodin 1939: 162].

Hammond similarly delighted in arrangements culminating in "last choruses in which the Goodman style, rather than the tune, prevailed" as a revolt against the commercial dominance of the song publishers, but this also meant that Henderson's arrangements posed significant interpretive challenges (Hammond and Townsend 1977: 142). For Goodman,

It was one of the biggest kicks I've ever had in music to go through these scores [he cites "King Porter Stomp" and "Big John Special"] and dig the music out of them, even in rehearsal. We still didn't have the right band to play that kind of music, but it convinced me more than ever which way the band should head—and it was up to us to find the men who could really do a job on them [Goodman and Kolodin 1939: 157].

Hammond put it more bluntly: "The only trouble with Benny's band at the beginning of the *Let's Dance* broadcasts was that it did not swing" (Hammond and Townsend 1977: 143). Henderson's arrangements demanded rapid development of the band's performance style, which, as his statement suggests, Goodman achieved through appropriation (to define in practical terms the "way the band should head"), rehearsal (to "dig the music out") and personnel ("the men who could really do a job on them").

APPROPRIATION With Henderson's own band inconsistent and working only intermittently, there was a need for Goodman to find an alternative model for his performance style. After *Let's Dance* had been on the air for a couple of weeks, Willard Alexander arranged for Goodman's band to play for a few nights "informally and without publicity" at the Savoy Ballroom (Goodman and Kolodin 1939: 158). The Savoy had made its name as a place to dance from opening night in 1926, and the presentation of two bands was the basis for the famous band battles (Charters and Kunstadt 1962: 192–193). By the time Goodman visited the Savoy in 1934, Chick Webb had established a residency, which he held until his death in 1939, achieving success to which Edgar Sampson's compositions and arrangements were crucial (Schuller 1989: 295). In 1939 Goodman wrote that Webb's orchestra "has always played with tremendous drive; that gave us a wonderful opportunity to compare our playing with his, to try to match some of the guts he got into the music, without trying to copy him in any other way" (Goodman and Kolodin 1939: 158). The Carnegie Hall concert included three of Sampson's compositions, all recorded by Webb in 1934; "Stompin' at the Savoy," which Goodman had been using since his Music Hall days; "If Dreams Come True"; and "Don't Be That Way." When the two bands met at the Savoy in a "Battle of Jazz" in May 1937, Webb turned appropriation to his advantage:

[Goodman] picked up "Big John Special" right after Chick got through with it and offered his own magnificent interpretation of the number....The climax and thrill of the evening was provided by Chick Webb who in answer to requests, followed Benny with Benny's own hit number, "Jam Session," and blew the roof off the house with it [Oakley 1937].

Count Basie's "One O'Clock Jump," Claude Thornhill's "Loch Lomond," Louis Prima's "Sing, Sing, Sing" and Horace Henderson's "Big John Special" are further examples of Goodman's appropriation of music from other bands. The intertextual relationship between the source (frequently and demonstrably a recording) and Goodman's version varies from case to case; the aim was often not to reproduce the style of the original but to render the material in a style that was distinctively Goodman's own. This represents extension of the practice of adapting published "stock" orchestrations to present individualized versions of popular material, which was familiar to Goodman from earlier in his career and described in the final chapter of his autobiography, entitled "So You're Organizing a Band!": "You can change [the orchestrations] around so that what you play doesn't sound like every little band in town" (Goodman and Kolodin 1939: 259). In this chapter, Goodman offers hints for the aspiring bandleader that are based on his own experience. He is unequivocal on matters of style: "You'll have an idea of some band whose style you like, to model your own playing after. That's all right as far as a general style is concerned, but I wouldn't let it go too far" (Goodman and Kolodin 1939: 255). Advising young musicians to develop their own style, Goodman recommends encouraging "anyone in the band who can write things, even if they sound pretty corny and imitative in the beginning," as "a band that has a few things of its own, that expresses the style of the players themselves, always will attract more attention than a band that just plays what everybody else does" (Goodman and Kolodin 1939: 260). At Carnegie Hall, this is demonstrated by two original compositions: "Life Goes to a Party," by his trumpeter, Harry James; and "Dizzy Spells," by Lionel Hampton. These pieces are up-tempo "killer-dillers," definitively of their time.

Ziggy Elman's Jewish interpolation in Jimmy Mundy's arrangement of "Bei Mir Bist Du Schön" is a further example of individual expression that distinguished Goodman's version from other contemporary recordings by making explicit reference to its roots as a Yiddish song. Goodman avoided contemporary popular songs in the instrumental repertoire for Carnegie Hall, but the two vocal numbers were based on recent hits ("Bei Mir Bist Du Schön" for the Andrews Sisters and "Loch Lomond" for Maxine Sullivan). The obvious references to traditional Jewish and

Scottish music might have lent artistic justification for their inclusion in the program, but these songs also constituted a less inflammatory variation of "jazzing/swinging the classics," a growing, if not entirely novel, trend in appropriation that had yet to hit the headlines (Stowe 1994: 95). Collier notes around this date that "bandleaders, beset by the need for constantly finding something fresh to do, were somewhat desperately reaching out in various directions for novelties" and recording classical pieces, older standards and folk songs (Collier 1989a: 238). This material may also have been chosen to avoid potential accusations of song plugging for a particular publisher. Although "Bei Mir Bist Du Schön" was a recent composition, it was widely assumed to be a traditional song, and on that basis a new English lyric and the recording by the Andrews Sisters were made without permission of the copyright holders (Secunda 1982: 149).

REHEARSAL   Rehearsal was vital to development of the band around the time of *Let's Dance*: "We kept rehearsing all the time, trying to get a real blend in the saxes, smoothing out the other sections so they phrased together, and worked in with each other" (Goodman and Kolodin 1939: 166). Magee argues that "Goodman structured his rehearsals in a way which emphasized Henderson's strengths," but it seems more likely that Goodman's rehearsal methods evolved as a practical response to the demands of Henderson's arrangements (Magee 2005: 212). Goodman devotes a large proportion of the "Organizing a Band" chapter of his autobiography to a description of rehearsal methods. To tackle Henderson's "sequence of variations," Goodman emphasizes the importance of familiarizing the band with the overall shape of a new arrangement, even having slowed the tempo down "always aiming to play the arrangement through, from beginning to end without stops if possible." Henderson's sectional writing was matched with Goodman's recommendation of "section rehearsals," where "the reeds and the brass … go off separately … and work on things by themselves" (Goodman and Kolodin 1939: 258). Trumpeter Chris Griffin, who played in the 1938 concert, remembered Goodman using these techniques:

First we'd run the chart down as a group, then the brass and reed sections would rehearse separately. Finally the two sections would rehearse the number together, over and over, without the rhythm section. None of the other leaders I worked with rehearsed a band in this way—without the drums, bass, guitar and piano. We had to keep time and make the tune swing by ourselves. Benny's idea was that, in this way, the band would swing better and have a lighter feel. If you didn't depend on the rhythm section to swing, you would swing that much more when the rhythm section finally was brought in [Deffaa 1989: 45–46].

As a result of the repetitive nature of this process, Goodman's vocalist Helen Ward "knew the tune without looking at the music. I just needed the music for the words" (Firestone 1993: 115). Similarly, this meant the rhythm section would know the arrangement by the time they rejoined the rest of the band. This may explain why drum parts for the Carnegie Hall arrangements are frequently missing; they may have never existed or never been used. Further, the existent band parts do not reflect the level of detail of the Goodman band's performances. Interpretations of particular pieces varied considerably and were often reconceptualized, but there are very few pencil marks in the parts beyond alterations to the structure of the arrangement, such as when used in broadcasts. This is indicative of constant and rigorous rehearsals within which details of the interpretation were thoroughly internalized, enabling performances that were both superlative and consistent. Ward recalls Goodman saying in a rehearsal, "You don't need the arrangement. Don't *read* the notes; *play* 'em" (Firestone 1993: 115). Goodman stated in his autobiography: "My idea was to get good musicians, work on intonation, a blend of tone and uniform phrasing in rehearsals, then depend on them to take care of themselves pretty much on the stand" (Goodman and Kolodin 1939: 140). This explains why mistakes received the legendary Goodman "Ray," which trumpeter Chris Griffin described as 'a way he had of staring over the top of his glasses" (Vaché 2005: 46).

Beyond obtaining and rehearsing the arrangements, Goodman advised bandleaders that "it's just as important to get out and play as much as you can" (Goodman and Kolodin 1939: 261). On the basis of Helen Ward's recollections, Magee identifies "Road, Radio and Recording" as a "rite of passage" for the band's arrangements (2005: 206). The Carnegie Hall concert presents an interesting cross-section of numbers at different stages of this process, which is considered in detail in Part Two. Certainly, the coherence of the ensemble with consistent personnel who performed together nearly every day meant that with reference to as early as the time of the Palomar ballroom success, tenor saxophonist Art Rollini could state, "we seldom had to go over a chart more than twice [in rehearsal], even with Fletcher Henderson's difficult arrangements, which were always highly syncopated" (Rollini 1989: 47). Nevertheless, it was necessary for Goodman to rehearse for the concert *in situ*:

We'd rehearsed for it a couple of days in the Carnegie to get used to the acoustics, which is what you might call bringing the musicians in to hear the hall. We'd been playing in the Madhattan Room, where the sound was stuffy and dense, and to go into a place where it was so lively was very upsetting at first [Balliett 1978: 163].

PERSONNEL   A final important aspect of development of the band prior to the Carnegie Hall concert was its personnel. By the time of the concert, the band included three players who had been with Goodman prior to *Let's Dance*: his brother Harry on bass, Art Rollini on tenor and Hymie Shertzer, who took over on lead alto from mid-1935 before an extended tour. A couple of weeks after the broadcasts began, which would date contemporaneously with Goodman's visit to the Savoy Ballroom (suggesting the influence of Webb's drumming), Gene Krupa joined the band, making his first broadcast on December 22, 1934 (Connor 1988: 46). Goodman and Krupa were well acquainted, having worked together frequently since 1929. Hammond took the credit for securing Krupa for the band, and also the pianist Jess Stacy (Hammond and Townsend 1977: 144). With the addition of Allan Reuss on guitar, the Carnegie Hall rhythm section was complete by late summer 1935. The consistency in the personnel of this section would be especially important to create self-sufficiency since, as we have seen, Goodman's rehearsals were mainly focused on the reeds and brass. Although there were small changes to the band during 1937, when Vernon Brown (trombone) and Babe Russin (tenor) joined, once Harry James was in place in January 1937 to complete a formidable trumpet section the band that played at Carnegie Hall was ostensibly complete. Ultimately, this stability of personnel, which persisted until Krupa's departure in March 1938, was essential in allowing Goodman to achieve the standards to which he aspired.

A final, crucial, dimension in the preparations for the concert was Albert Marx's decision to record it using equipment that was already installed in Carnegie Hall. The exact technical specification—a matter for continued debate—certainly involved a wire feed from at least one microphone (which Ewing observed hanging over the stage) and probably also Martha Tilton's vocal microphone to Harry Smith's studio close to Times Square (Hancock 2008: 147, 149). The practice of off-air recording was by this time well established, not only for fans but also for bandleaders, for whom Smith provided a well-used service. Although Goodman stated in a recorded announcement accompanying the 1950 release that "we didn't know the concert was being recorded," he later recalled: "In those days, I had air checks of the band made the whole time—just to hear how new things sounded—and my hotel room was flooded with them. But when Marx told me he was going to record it and would I like a copy, I said sure" (Balliett 1978: 163). Marx's recollections are slightly different, but he certainly obtained permission from a disinterested Goodman before the concert, whose attitude suggested he was not expecting anything other than the band's usual performances. Indeed, almost all of the material performed in the concert was probably already represented on the discs (studio recordings and airchecks) littering Goodman's room. According to Marx, Goodman borrowed the acetates shortly after the concert and probably copied them, indicating that after the event he considered the performances worth keeping, in his own words, "as a sort of heirloom" (*DownBeat* 1956; Marx 1987).

PART TWO
Performance

IN PART TWO, I present analysis of compositions, arrangements, performance practice and improvisation in the 1938 Carnegie Hall concert, including comparisons of these performances with broadcasts and studio recordings of the same numbers by Goodman, and others where relevant. Rather than necessarily presenting a "bar-by-bar" account of each piece, the aim of the analysis is to develop contextual understanding of the Carnegie Hall performances and specifically to determine the extent to which they were consistent, divergent, definitive, or developmental. The items are grouped by ensemble in order of appearance, beginning with the full band numbers, then "Twenty Years of Jazz" and the "Jam Session," and finally the Trio and Quartet. Basic transcriptions (in concert pitch) are used to guide the reader toward particular features. As such, they do not necessarily indicate every nuance and cannot act as a substitute for the experience of hearing the performances. Where possible the text, and in particular the examples, should be read in conjunction with listening to the recording.

FIGURE 2.1   Benny Goodman and His Orchestra at Carnegie Hall, January 16, 1938. Courtesy Carnegie Hall Archives.

FIGURE 2.2   Benny Goodman and His Orchestra at Carnegie Hall, January 16, 1938, showing some of the audience seated on the stage. Courtesy Jon Hancock, Prancing Fish Ltd and Carnegie Hall Archives.

"DON'T BE THAT WAY" (EDGAR SAMPSON, PROBABLY ARRANGED BY SAMPSON)   Edgar Sampson wrote "Don't Be That Way" for Rex Stewart's band between 1933 and 1934 (Driggs, n.d.) but it was not recorded until he joined Chick Webb in 1934. Webb recorded the number again in 1936 and doubtless performed it live on many occasions. Sampson had filed an unpublished manuscript of his pianoforte composition "Don't Be That Way" with the copyright authorities on May 16, 1935 (Crawford 2004: 165), and a further version of the piece was copyrighted on February 26, 1938. In this instance, however, the "words" are attributed to Mitchell Parish and the melody jointly to Benny Goodman and Edgar Sampson (Library of Congress 1938: 233). The 1938 sheet music publication features photographs of Goodman on the cover, emphasizing the extent to which the number had become associated with him. By the time "Don't Be That Way" was published in 1938, Goodman was given a co-composer credit, as was the practice at the time for bandleaders who popularized particular pieces. The arrangement Goodman performed at Carnegie Hall is broadly similar in design to that recorded by Webb, consisting of four choruses beginning in D flat major. There are some similarities in the orchestration too, which means that superficially the two arrangements sound alike. Gunther Schuller uses recordings of "Don't Be That Way" (and "Stompin' at the Savoy," Sampson's other famous composition that came to Goodman via Webb) as a basis for comparing the two bands, arguing that:

> The gulf between Webb and Goodman was a wide one, the former delivering these pieces with a raw excitement, rhythmic drive (faster tempos, too), and heated sonority; the latter with a neatly packaged cooled-off sound, bouncing along in a safe inoffensive manner [Schuller 1989: 296].

A more detailed analysis of Goodman's appropriation of "Don't Be That Way" that goes beyond identifying the aforementioned differences in "feel" yields insight into how he drew on models of other bands and pre-existing material to establish and develop his own style.

Kolodin's program notes explained to the Carnegie Hall audience that "'Don't Be That Way' is a new arrangement and thus virtually a new work by Edgar Sampson" (Kolodin 1938b: 195). Certainly, the differences with the Webb version are numerous, suggesting that Goodman may have commissioned an entirely new arrangement that brought the piece into line with his overall style and performance practice. But further to this, Kolodin's description of the piece in the program notes is at odds with the version we hear the band perform in the Carnegie Hall concert. Specifically, he mentions solos for alto and piano in the third chorus, where tenor and trumpet are heard. An alto solo seems unlikely, since the alto saxophonists did not play solos in Goodman's band in this period, and it could be explained by a simple error of identification. However, it would not be so easy to mistake Harry James's trumpet for a piano solo. Goodman had played "Don't Be That Way" at least once in public prior to the Carnegie Hall concert, in a *Camel Caravan* broadcast on January 11, 1938, for which recordings are not available (Connor 1988: 80). It could be possible that Kolodin's notes reflect the earlier performances or rehearsals of "Don't Be That Way," especially in the absence of a studio recording that he could use as a guide.

Evidencing this hypothesis in relation to "Don't Be That Way" is somewhat problematic. Although band parts can contain some useful information about particular numbers, we know that Goodman's thorough rehearsals meant the music became internalized and notation had limited use. Trumpeter Chris Griffin recalled, "We never got the [sheet] music out, ever, except for the two or three arrangements we'd been given last. We sat on the books [the folders of music]" (Deffaa 1989: 40). Certainly the Goodman band parts are not usually extensively marked, other than for various cuts. The set of parts for "Don't Be That Way" in the Benny Goodman Papers in the Irving S. Gilmore Music Library of Yale University MSS 53 (box 7/17) reflects the arrangement as performed at Carnegie Hall and offers no clues as to its development. There is also no score or "Benny" part (a single-stave guide score with indications for Goodman's solos usually produced by his arrangers) in the Yale set that might yield details of the arrangement's authorship. The precise date of this set is uncertain, but study of Goodman's discography shows that a third trombone was added to the band in May 1939 and baritone saxophone in late 1940. As these additional parts are in a different hand, it seems likely that the majority of the set were originally produced before these instruments were in use in Goodman's band.

The polished Carnegie Hall performance of "Don't Be That Way" must have been the result of intense rehearsal, especially as early performances of many Goodman numbers tend to be rather methodical in the case of studio recordings and even scrappy on broadcasts. The overall performance of the number also remains consistent in subsequent recordings, indicating that the Carnegie Hall performance represents a mature interpretation, even though "Don't Be That Way" had been in the band's repertoire for significantly less time than the other large ensemble pieces in the concert. Notwithstanding that the band was now more experienced than at the time at which many of the first recordings of Carnegie Hall numbers were made, these circumstances suggest that Goodman could have had some sort of authorial role in formulating a plan for the rearrangement that either reflected the processes in the rehearsal room, with definitive parts made retrospectively, or allowed him to shortcut this process by stipulating an arrangement in accordance with how he wanted to perform the number, a style with which the band was familiar. Other numbers in the Carnegie Hall program, notably "Sing, Sing, Sing," are known to have been developed collectively in rehearsal.

The introduction to "Don't Be That Way" was completely rewritten for the new arrangement. Webb's introduction is built on a functional circle of fifths progression without a particularly distinctive melodic line. Goodman's version begins with a clearly audible chromatic pickup in the saxophones onto chord ii (E flat minor) and remains on this chord for more than half of the introduction, heightening the impact of its resolution. As the brass play a rising phrase in unison, the saxophones hammer home the cadence, which uses the distinctive augmented version of dominant chord heard throughout the piece. The metanarrative surrounding the concert often comments on the start of "Don't Be That Way" reflecting the reported apprehension of the musicians at the beginning of the concert, for example:

> Benny set the tempo for "Don't Be That Way" and gave the downbeat. Still feeling a bit pressured, the band started out tense and unsettled but then Gene Krupa took command with a forceful drum break that drew tremendous applause and put everyone in the right groove [Firestone 1993: 212].

The roots of this commentary appear to be George T. Simon's review in *Metronome*, in which he suggests that the "men were neither relaxed nor in any sort of a groove," but "the crowd cheered, yelled, howled" in response to Krupa's drum break: "Gene's hair fell into his eyes. The band fell into a groove" (Simon 1938b: 15). However, attempts to quantify precisely what was "tense and unsettled" in the performance quickly flounder. Hancock acknowledges, "One story that is often repeated about the concert is that Benny set the tempo too slow for the first number" (Hancock 2008: 85). Certainly, a "gear change" in the tempo can be detected during the first phrase of the first chorus, led by Krupa's hi-hat, but the tempo Goodman selects for the opening is consistent with his other available performances of this number from around this date.

The harmonic basis of "Don't Be That Way" is the "rhythm changes." Since its inclusion in Gershwin's show *Girl Crazy* in 1930 (for which, incidentally, Goodman played in the pit band), "I Got Rhythm" spawned innumerable interpretations by singers and jazz musicians, as well as a vast array of new compositions based on the song's harmonic framework. Richard Crawford notes that "Don't Be That Way" "seems to have had the most active independent life of all 'I Got Rhythm' contrafacts during the swing era," meaning that before 1942 it was the most consistently recorded song based on this progression (Crawford 2004: 165). In the A section of the first chorus, Sampson's melody is played by saxophones accompanied by brass stabs in both Webb's and Goodman's versions, but there are subtle differences between the two, as shown in Examples 2.1 and 2.2. As well as adding an upbeat figure to the start of the melody, Goodman's version also standardizes the small variation to the first note of bar 6 of the original melody to match bar 2. The variation can be heard clearly in both of Webb's recorded performances and turns the phrase more firmly (and arguably more predictably) toward the cadence. Goodman's version also varies the harmony by employing a tritone substitution (D^7) as an alternative to the augmented dominant in the fourth bar of each A section, resulting in clearer articulation of two four-bar subphrases. The brass stabs have a different rhythm from Webb's version, replicating a riff used in "One O'Clock Jump" and also demonstrating similarity with the melodic rhythm of "I Got Rhythm." This pattern enhances the melody more directly than just anticipating the changes of harmony. Sampson's A section melody is distinctive (although it has obvious similarities with "Stompin' at the Savoy"), but the B section follows the melodic line of "I Got Rhythm": Goodman's version employs the saxophones in antiphony with the brass at this point in the first chorus, where Webb has a chordal ensemble texture.

Goodman's version employs a four-bar modulating passage so that the second and third choruses, which are dominated by solos, are in F major whereas Webb's version remains in D flat. The first solo of the Carnegie Hall concert was taken by Goodman himself over the A sections of this second chorus; the B section is played without a solo by the saxophones answered by muted brass, in a reversal of the orchestration used in the corresponding section of the first chorus. Although Webb's 1934 version alternates two tenor players, his 1936 recording prophetically has a clarinet solo on the A sections in this chorus. As shown in

Example 2.3, Goodman bases the first part of his solo closely on the melody but avoids this completely in the following two phrases of this chorus, in which his lines are increasingly blues-inflected, with more pronounced vibrato, slides and even growling. This approach is consistent in his other performances of this number from early 1938, with the first eight bars of the solo being very similar across all these performances. Although Goodman's solo in the second phrase (bars 9–16) varies considerably across the available recordings from this period, he includes one figure around or ascending to f''' at some point in this phrase with remarkable consistency. Generally speaking, this note was the upper limit of Goodman's comfortable range in solos, and although he did occasionally play higher notes they tended to be in isolation rather than as part of fluid phrases. The juxtaposition of improvisation primarily conceived around melody and that which is based on the chord progression, incorporating blues inflexions, is relatively unusual in Goodman's solos and is, perhaps, a compromise commensurate with a melodic composition having a relatively familiar harmonic basis.

EXAMPLE 2.2 "Don't Be That Way," Benny Goodman version, first chorus, bars 1–7 (MSS 53, the Benny Goodman Papers in the Irving S. Gilmore Music Library of Yale University)

An interesting exception to Goodman's usual conception of this solo is an alternate take from the February 1938 studio recording. In this session, the third chorus (usually featuring trumpet and trombone) was omitted in order to fit the number within the time limit of the disc, and Harry James was given a solo on the B section of the second chorus backed by saxophones only. Having recorded a "conventional" version of the solo in the studio for the first take, on the second attempt Goodman ignores the melody almost completely and produces a more bluesy interpretation, culminating in pronounced growling. This solo anticipates his approach in a Quartet performance of "Don't Be That Way" broadcast in April 1938, suggesting that he came to conceive a solo on this piece based on the chord changes rather than the melody.

Webb's third chorus juxtaposes trombone and trumpet soloists, and similarly Goodman's third chorus features tenor and trumpet, Babe Russin with Harry James on the middle eight at Carnegie Hall. The melody is provided in the first tenor part for the solo over the A sections,

EXAMPLE 2.3 "Don't Be That Way," second chorus, Benny Goodman's solo (transcription)

but close position triads and chord symbols are given in the first trumpet part. Both Russin and James avoid the melody in their solos, although Russin's second eight bars are identical to the performance broadcast two days later, exemplifying the need for consistency from Goodman's performers (discussed in Part One). On both occasions, Russin is backed by Krupa's exuberant drumming: a snare drum roll ending in a powerful bass drum strike on the fourth beat of every other bar. This pattern serves as extended preparation for the final chorus, where these bass drum punctuations are heard in every bar.

Both arrangements modulate at the start of the final chorus, Goodman from F to A flat major and Webb from D flat to G flat major; both abandon the melody of the main theme entirely in favor of a brass-dominated passage, a loose development of the earlier backing figures. Both also feature the drums here; Webb is given an entire section of stop-time breaks in the middle eight, but Krupa is allotted only two bars in the first A section for his solo. In both of his recordings, Webb's solo is built around sextuplets on the snare drum, whereas at Carnegie Hall Krupa plays sixteenth notes punctuated by showy cymbal crashes. Krupa's drum break, which is followed by a rambunctious trombone solo backed by more cymbal crashes, could not offer a greater contrast to Goodman's restrained solo over the middle eight section that follows. The difference between Goodman and Krupa's performances as demonstrated here was not lost on contemporary critics; it anticipates the breakdown of the Goodman-Krupa partnership, which was one of the major repercussions of the concert and will be analyzed in detail in Part Three.

The coda to Goodman's version repeats the A section theme a total of six times, having modulated once again to the sharpest key yet (D major) but is actually only a semitone higher than the opening and thus able to employ identical orchestration without the need for adaptations to account for the limitations of instrumental ranges. The gradual decrease in dynamic over the first five repetitions of the main theme builds tension and anticipation, a feature Schuller suggests furnished a model for Glenn Miller's "In the Mood" (Schuller 1989: 296). Duke Ellington's version of Billy Strayhorn's "Take the 'A' Train" employs a similar device, but this was probably composed in late 1938 or early 1939 and the famous arrangement came even later, in 1941 (van de Leur 2002: 47). Another Krupa drum break, as extroverted as the first, heralds the final loud and emphatic repetition of the theme.

"SOMETIMES I'M HAPPY" (VINCENT YOUMANS, ARRANGED BY FLETCHER HENDERSON) The first Fletcher Henderson arrangement heard by the Carnegie Hall audience was the ballad "Sometimes I'm Happy," composed by Vincent Youmans. The song dates back to 1923, where under the title "Come on and Pet Me" and with lyrics by Oscar Hammerstein II and William Duncan it was included in the show *Mary Jane McKane* (Suskin 2000: 79). With new lyrics by Irving Caesar, in 1925 "Sometimes I'm Happy" was included in the American version of *A Night Out*, originally an English musical play (Bordman 1982: 82). Although the new production closed after its previews in Philadelphia (Suskin 2000: 79), Youman's music was praised and the critic of the Philadelphia *Public Ledger* devoted a paragraph to "Sometimes I'm Happy," concluding prophetically: "It is haunting, lulling, soothing and seems made to order for jazz bands and radio. Fortunately, they sing and play it a lot. That's the wisest thing they do" (Bordman 1982: 84). Finally, in 1927 the song became associated with a more successful venture, an adaptation of the play *Shore Leave* called *Hit the Deck* ("a nautical musical comedy"), which had a substantial run on Broadway and then transferred to the London Hippodrome later in the year. This musical was made into a film in 1930.

"Sometimes I'm Happy," in its 1927 published version, has a conventional structure with introduction, verse and a 32-bar refrain (16 bars plus 16 bars repeated with a different final phrase). The defining feature of the refrain, on which all subsequent recorded versions are mainly based, is the pervasive use of chromatic appoggiaturas, more specifically a blues third (G sharp, enharmonically A flat) in the melody, as shown in Example 2.4a. This underlines the bittersweet nature of the lyrics (for example, "Sometimes I love you, Sometimes I hate you, But when I hate you, It's 'cause I love you"). The expansive melody in bars 9–16 contrasts with the very restricted pitch range of the previous lines. At this point the harmony moves away from the tonic-dominant alternation of the first eight bars toward the subdominant, but reaching the chord of the subdominant minor in bar 12 (see Example 2.4b). Again, this passage is indicative of a blues-like ambivalence between major and minor.

There are differences between the lyrics and melody in the published version and a contemporary recording by members of the cast of *Hit the Deck* (the verses in particular are completely different), indicating that this number was subject to constant change and variation. Numerous recorded interpretations of the song that pre-date the Henderson/Goodman treatment, as well as several performances from the formative years of the Goodman band, show that such development was ongoing, especially in respect to tempo. Fortunately in this case, we may begin examining the recorded history of the song with a version

EXAMPLE 2.4A   "Sometimes I'm Happy," refrain, bars 1–2 (1927)

EXAMPLE 2.4B   "Sometimes I'm Happy," refrain, bars 9–12 (1927)

made in 1927 by members of the original cast of *Hit the Deck*, in which it was a duet for the leading lady and gentleman, Louise Groody and Charles King. The song is performed at a steady tempo (*moderato con moto* and then "slowly" for the refrain are indicated in the 1927 sheet music) with significant *rubato*. Numerous other more or less jazz-inclined groups sought to capitalize on the song's success, and in advertisements for recordings the song is normally designated "foxtrot." Hence, in 1927 Roger Wolfe Kahn and His Orchestra perform this number significantly faster than Groody and King and in strict tempo (to facilitate dancing). In addition to repetitions of the chorus, the second of which is designated for the vocal, Kahn's arrangement includes an instrumental verse (later jazz versions of popular songs were usually based solely on the chorus).

The cornetist and bandleader Red Nichols recorded "Sometimes I'm Happy" twice, coinciding (probably not by chance) with the opening of *Hit the Deck* on stage and later as a film. According to Richard Sudhalter, "Nichols's best records divide easily into two major groupings, 1925–28 and 1929–30, and constitute a valuable index to what happened to white jazz in New York in the five years they represent" (Sudhalter 1999: 144). Although neither the 1927 nor the 1930 version of "Sometimes I'm Happy" is among Nichols's best sides, these recordings are indicative of the changes in the jazz-influenced performance of this song following its appearance in print. Like many musicians at the time, Nichols recorded for different record labels under various pseudonyms; his 1927 version of "Sometimes I'm Happy" was issued on Banner under the band name The Six Hottentots. This recording does not best exemplify the skillful "hot chamber jazz" arrangements for which Nichols's groups are known, but it is indicative of a jazz approach to popular song at this time. Like Kahn's version, the recording by the Six Hottentots also contains an instrumental verse and one vocal chorus. The performance includes Dixieland-style collective improvisation by the front line of Nichols, Miff Mole (trombone) and Jimmy Dorsey (clarinet), particularly over the verse where it might have been felt less important to keep the melody distinct. There are also individual solos from Nichols and Dorsey, for which the latter changes to alto saxophone. Within the standard three-minute time span, Nichols's version delivers considerable variety: a "commercial" vocal, short bursts of New Orleans jazz, stride piano (by this time both well-established styles) and a more modern concept of a jazz soloist.

This version is only slightly slower than Kahn's, but Nichols's 1930 recording is even slower than Groody and King's, redefining "Sometimes I'm Happy" as a ballad. This change in the conception of the piece might be linked at least in part to contemporaneous definition of the foxtrot as a slower dance, in contrast with the quickstep, which had developed as the up-tempo dance by the end of the 1920s (Norton, n.d.). Nichols's 1930 arrangement is relatively simple, consisting of an initial *tutti* chorus, then two choruses of solos (shared among bass saxophone, clarinet, tenor saxophone and trumpet) and finishing as it began, hence omitting the verse. This recording group included Babe Russin and Gene Krupa, who would play the number as members of Goodman's band at Carnegie Hall. Adrian Rollini, brother of Art who played at Carnegie Hall, is also featured on bass saxophone. Further, use of muted brass in the first chorus prefigures Fletcher Henderson's distinctive application of the same timbre in his arrangement for Goodman.

The earliest evidence of Goodman playing "Sometimes I'm Happy" is a recording from a remarkable session that took place in New York on June 6, 1935. The band spent all day in the studio, recording 51 sides as electrical transcriptions to be distributed on a lease basis by the National Broadcasting Company to subscribing radio stations. The series included a wide range of music and several swing bands, which were all credited as "The Rhythm Makers" (Connor 1988: 51). Art Rollini recalled the session in his autobiography: "We ran through almost our entire library, just one time, with different men filling in the vocal parts with solos. . . . We received a grand total of fifty-one dollars—one dollar per tune" (Rollini 1989: 40).

Although there is no evidence of Goodman playing "Sometimes I'm Happy" prior to this date, Rollini's statement suggests that the number would have been familiar to the musicians through its inclusion in previous live gigs. Yet it was relatively rare for Goodman to commit to record numbers he had not already broadcast, and it was probably the extraordinary circumstances of this session that led him to include "Sometimes I'm Happy." Unusually, Goodman recorded the number again (on July 1, 1935), and then broadcast it at least five times before the Carnegie Hall concert, three of which are now available on commercial recordings. Therefore, it is likely that the June 1935 recording represents a performance at an earlier stage of gestation than most other Goodman recordings.

In general, the overall tempo of Goodman's performances of this number decreases over the period leading up to Carnegie Hall, with a remarkable difference between the two 1935 recordings, which took place within a month of each other. Krupa's drums are much in evidence on the June 6, 1935, recording, but they are increasingly relegated to the background on the later versions, which is symptomatic of the arrangement becoming more specifically defined as a ballad through adaptations in tempo and performance style. Goodman alluded to the rapprochement of the extremes of sweet and swing, which was the basis of his musical style and a key to his popularity, in his broadcast introduction to "Sometimes I'm Happy" on August 24, 1937:

Some of our students have been arguing about sweet and hot music. Tonight we're going to prove that swing music can be either sweet or hot. From [sic] our first lesson we'll take "Sometimes I'm Happy" and swing it sweet. All right boys, from the heart.

Jeffrey Magee discusses Henderson's arrangement extensively in his book *The Uncrowned King of Swing: Fletcher Henderson and Big Band Jazz* as "a model of ballad arranging in the swing era and beyond" (Magee 2005: 221). Like Nichols's 1930 version, Henderson's arrangement for Goodman uses a succession of choruses, omitting the verse altogether. The six bar introduction begins with the final phrase of the chorus over a sustained string bass note, which can be heard very faintly on the 1935 recordings. This is an example of one of Henderson's introductions without a regular pulse being provided by the rhythm section, which can be found on other arrangements for Goodman such as "Sandman" (Magee 2005: 213). Following this, Henderson establishes the two sonorities that will feature in the first chorus, saxophones and cup-muted brass. In the first chorus, the muted brass play the melody in close harmony while Henderson uses "the melody's gaps for subtle saxophone punctuations" that suggest call and response (Magee 2005: 217). Magee notes that "in ballads, the brass provide color instead of power, and Henderson exploits a variety of coloristic possibilities by specifying passages for hat mutes and cup mutes, and for 'open' (unmuted) brass" (Magee 2005: 217). The expectation would be for cup-muted brass to be playing backings and lending "color" in a ballad rather than necessarily carrying the tune. Initially in the introduction, the brass "answer" the saxophones, conforming to this idea, but Henderson then subverts this by using muted brass for the melody in the first chorus. Example 2.5 shows a reduction of the brass parts together with the bass line and chords Henderson provides. This part of the arrangement can sound deceptively simple, but even Henderson's initial treatment of the tune shows how his work goes beyond an arrangement in the conventional sense and into the realm of recomposition.

Henderson has restricted use of the all-pervasive chromatic "blue" appoggiatura by altering the original melody in bars 3 and 6. The harmony is more complex than in the original song, and it gives a clearer sense of shape to four-bar phrases. Though each two-bar subphrase played by the brass is subtly different in its part writing—notice how the second (lowest) trombone begins doubling the melody but then pursues a unique line—Example 2.6 shows the saxophones' "answer," which remains exactly the same until the end of bar 8, where a change in register and harmony heralds the contrasting expansive melodic

EXAMPLE 2.5   "Sometimes I'm Happy," first chorus, bars 1–8, brass and rhythm (MSS 53, the Benny Goodman Papers in the Irving S. Gilmore Music Library of Yale University)

Saxophones

Bars 2-3, 4-5, 6-7   Bars 8-9

phrase that the saxophones then punctuate every four bars rather than every two.

The available performances of Henderson's arrangement of "Sometimes I'm Happy" prior to Carnegie Hall show more decorative than merely functional "comping" from the piano and guitar during this first chorus. However, the impression from the Carnegie Hall recording is that the brass and reeds form a backdrop to a piano solo. This could be blamed on the inability of the brass players to project when muted, and therefore the inadequacies of the recording equipment to pick up the subtle sound. However, the brass and saxophones are louder at the start of the number and appear to make a deliberate diminuendo toward the end of the introduction. Further, comparing "Sometimes I'm Happy" with "If Dreams Come True" (with which it has many similarities that I explore later) also shows that it was possible for the muted brass to project more strongly. Above all, Jess Stacy is definitely projecting in a soloistic way in "Sometimes I'm Happy," using the upper end of the keyboard, rather than "comping," an approach that can be heard on the 1937 broadcasts and also on a recording from a similar date of "If Dreams Come True."

A four-bar link passage into the second chorus has the lead initially scored for muted trumpet solo and is played as such, with straight eighth notes, on both 1935 recordings, but was taken over by Goodman from 1937. He plays the passage swung on the 1937 broadcasts, and he elaborates on it a little at Carnegie Hall. The second chorus has space for solos from trumpet and tenor saxophone, indicated by the notation of the melody on the second trumpet and second tenor parts, but as is consistent with Goodman's propensity to take a solo away and give it to another player at will, indications of "solo" and "play" also appear on the first tenor and third trumpet parts. As was the convention in the 1930s, chord symbols are not given on the parts, although they have been added onto the second tenor part in a different hand. The solos on the 1935 recordings are noticeably restricted to the phrasing and shape of the melody. The trumpet solo was performed by various players (Pee Wee

Erwin on June 6, 1935, and Bunny Berigan on July 1, 1935), and the tenor solo by Art Rollini is practically identical on both 1935 recordings. By 1937, Harry James and Rollini are moving decisively away from the phrasing of the melody and playing confidently over the changes, reflecting their development as musicians over this period as well as their familiarity with the chart.

In addition to the instrumental soloists, Goodman defined Henderson's arrangements, and particularly "Sometimes I'm Happy," as a form of improvisation (Goodman and Kolodin 1939: 162). The saxophones and brass are featured separately in the third chorus. At the time, Fletcher Henderson was "doing about three arrangements a week, and many of them had to be produced at the last minute" (Firestone 1993: 116). Having completed the saxophone half-chorus, Fletcher apparently prevailed on his brother Horace to complete the chorus with 16 bars for the brass. Magee points out that in the passage for saxophones "Henderson constructs most of the passage in four bar units, with a two-bar phrase as the model for a repetition or slight variation to complete the four-bar unit" (Magee 2005: 218). But in addition, a macrocosmic view of the section in Example 2.7 shows that Henderson alternates four-bar sections that are subtly syncopated (A) with those in which the syncopation is more rigorous (B). This rhythmic contrast is made explicit in early recorded versions. In both 1935 recordings, the rhythm section accompanies the A phrases sensitively with a two-beat feel and the guitar filling in with triplets that echo the saxophone line. Krupa's snare or rim shot pickup drives into phrase B, where the bass plays four beats in the bar, and in the first B phrase Stacy contributes a high, rolling blues-like piano riff. Although no longer made so explicit by the rhythm section from 1937, mainly because they were playing more consistently in a four-beat feel throughout, this approach clearly informs that of the saxophone section to this passage at Carnegie Hall. Incidentally, there is no indication of these changes of feel in any of the existent parts for the piece, testifying to the importance of rehearsal in working out, developing and changing these significant details.

Undoubtedly, Horace Henderson's brass passage, which Magee compares to a Louis Armstrong solo, has a different character from the saxophone phrases that precede it (Magee 2005: 220). Krupa accompanies on hi-hat and the bass plays with a four-beat feel. In the earliest recording, the brass are still muted for this section, but this was abandoned for the second recording a few weeks later. By 1937 the brass sound is developing toward the sustained power evident on the Carnegie Hall recording, and as a result there is greater contrast be-

EXAMPLE 2.7 "Sometimes I'm Happy," third chorus, bars 1–16, first alto saxophone (MSS 53, the Benny Goodman Papers in the Irving S. Gilmore Music Library of Yale University)

tween the saxophone and the brass half-choruses. This is indicative in part of the consistency of personnel that Goodman had achieved and then cultivated, but also of the evolution of the performance practice of swing between 1935 and 1938, which is demonstrated most clearly in the final chorus of this particular chart. In the 1935 performances, the eighth notes are performed quite *staccato*, and their rhythm is near dotted eighth plus sixteenth. In 1937, the section is performed *legato* and with longer notes sustained more fully, but the eighth notes are nearly straight. At Carnegie Hall, the band plays with a now-conventional *legato* triplet swing feel, and the fuller sound of the brass in the preceding section is clearly commensurate with the approach to swing here. Originally this final *tutti* included a bell-tone note for trombone, similar to that found at the start of the link passage before the solos, but this is not heard on any extant performance.

All the parts and score of "Sometimes I'm Happy" available at Yale (MSS 53, box 25, folder 8) show a final complete chorus, that is, 16 bars repeated, but the first time bar has been crossed out by the musicians in all instances. The score, in Henderson's hand, probably dates from 1939–40 since it contains a third trombone part (probably also copied by Henderson), but not fourth trumpet or baritone saxophone. Consistent with other arrangements in the Goodman collection, the score is likely to have been made for the purpose of adding the extra part as well as facilitating recopying of lost or damaged parts, and therefore it is unlikely the arrangement would have been changed significantly from the original.

Inclusion of the cut portion suggests that no concessions were made, in the recopying, for the usual alterations adopted in Goodman's performances and that therefore this set probably reflects the parts the musicians had on their stands at Carnegie Hall. The alteration to the final chorus is indicative of the decrease in speed in Goodman's performances, which necessitated a cut to avoid the number becoming too long for a record side or even a dance.

"Sometimes I'm Happy" illustrates Goodman's involvement in developing popular song arrangement and performance in the period immediately prior to the Carnegie Hall concert. Rather than the constant contrasts within the arrangement that can be heard in Kahn and Nichols's versions as well as Goodman's earlier interpretations, the overall sound and approach become much more unified and the number more clearly identified as a ballad. Goodman's Carnegie Hall performance is the slowest available on record, demonstrating the culmination of this development. There is also a clearer shape to Henderson's arrangement of the entire number, a trajectory that builds from a two-beat ballad, through solos, the saxophone ensemble passage, the brass ensemble in full swing, to the final *tutti*. Subsequent performances in 1938 are faster, but the overall interpretation remains similar. This suggests that Goodman was able to employ a slower tempo at the Carnegie Hall concert, where there were no time restrictions of the sort imposed by recording and broadcasts.

"ONE O'CLOCK JUMP" (COUNT BASIE, ARRANGER UNKNOWN)   "One O'Clock Jump" is a composition based on a 12-bar blues progression, foregrounding a succession of soloists over riff backings, the most distinctive of which is a tuneful saxophone fragment shown in Example 2.8. According to Schuller, this riff was derived from a 1929 Chocolate Dandies recording of a number called "Six or Seven Times" that was then worked into a head arrangement by Count Basie and his band while they were still in Kansas (Schuller 1989: 237). "One O'Clock Jump" was first recorded by Basie in July 1937, and Goodman broadcast the number several times in the latter part of the same year. Harry James included it on

EXAMPLE 2.8   "One O'Clock Jump," saxophone melody (MSS 53, the Benny Goodman Papers in the Irving S. Gilmore Music Library of Yale University)

Saxophones

his second recording date as a bandleader on January 5, 1938 (when he was still working with Goodman), but aside from this the first year of "One O'Clock Jump" on record was completely dominated by Goodman and Basie.

The basic shape of "One O'Clock Jump" is consistent on all recorded performances pre-dating the Carnegie Hall concert. The piece begins in F major with an introduction for rhythm section and then a piano solo. Following a rather abrupt key change to D flat major, there is a series of solos including tenor saxophone, trombone and trumpet in that order. Most of the solos are accompanied by riffs, played by saxophones or muted trumpets. The final part of the piece builds to a climactic ending with sections of the band playing different riffs. In this multiriff section, the trumpets and trombones play the same idea throughout, but the saxophones vary their material. The precise order and combination of the particular elements in this final section varies even among Basie's own recordings, but the saxophones play a new riff in each new chorus in both of his 1937 performances available on record. Undoubtedly the circumstances of the performance, such as the limits of a recorded disc, the time pressure of a radio broadcast, or the expectations of a live audience, influenced the differences between the recorded versions of "One O'Clock Jump." Comparison of the two 1937 Basie recordings offers a good illustration of this. On the studio recording from July 1937, the soloist and the accompanying riff change for every chorus with the exception of the opening piano solo, and the final multiriff section is restricted to three choruses. However, on a radio broadcast in November 1937 each soloist plays two or three choruses, which allows the accompanying riffs to be developed, and the final section is four choruses long.

Goodman's Carnegie Hall performance retains the essence of the form of "One O'Clock Jump" as presented in Basie's contemporary recordings, but with some alterations that once again illustrate Goodman's practices of appropriation and adaptation. First, Basie's introduction for rhythm section over a standard harmonic loop is replaced with a rather incongruous four-bar phrase for the full band that bears no relationship to any of the material heard elsewhere in the piece. Second, at the point in the center of the piece where Basie features the rhythm section, even laying out himself for an entire chorus to feature bass and guitar, a sustained saxophone accompaniment is introduced, and this section becomes another piano solo. Goodman's version also changes the order so that the trumpet solo, rather than the rhythm section, leads into the final part of the piece. These alterations serve the purpose of deflecting attention from the rhythm section at points where Basie deliberately places it in the spotlight. In addition, in Goodman's version the saxophone theme (shown in Example 2.8) is extracted from the multiriff section and presented in its own right, after the trumpet solo, with answering fills from Harry James. This emphasis on melodic material is commensurate with the style of the Goodman band. Finally, Goodman creates a solo spot for himself by taking over the second tenor saxophone slot of Basie's version and a chorus is added to the multiriff section on which Goodman wails high above the band, predominantly on the flattened third, clearly positioning himself as the ultimate soloist. This idea can be heard in embryonic form on the late 1937 broadcasts.

Though these fundamental alterations are consistent in all of Goodman's performances leading up to the Carnegie Hall concert, "One O'Clock Jump," like "Sing, Sing, Sing," is relatively unusual in his repertoire in allowing Goodman some freedom to structure the performance in the moment, working with the large ensemble as if with a small group. The first available recording of the band playing this number, on a broadcast from the Madhattan Room on October 20, 1937, demonstrates that this chart was ideal for when the band needed to be flexible. Possibly because he was alerted to the need for an announcement to be made, Goodman takes the place of the expected trombone solo, causing some confusion in the saxophonists, who begin and then stop playing the accompanying riff. In the event, Goodman finishes his solo and the announcement is made over the trombone solo anyway. The cue for the ending of the number also seems to be unclear in this performance, with the band nearly coming to a halt one chorus too soon. Perhaps mindful of this previous confusion, Krupa clearly cues each new section with his cowbell at Carnegie Hall.

Goodman is heard encouraging Jess Stacy to "take one more" chorus in his solo in the middle of the piece in the October 1937 performance. On the subsequent broadcast of the number in November 1937, Goodman allows several of the soloists to take two choruses, and he plays three himself. The arrangement is expanded further at Carnegie Hall, with Goodman taking six choruses and Stacy four choruses in the opening section, although the other soloists are restricted to two choruses each (counting James's answering fills as his second chorus). The opportunity for Stacy to extend his solo in the introduction appears to be unexpected, as he clearly prepares to play the modulation at the end of his second chorus. The piano part for "One O'Clock Jump" contains a transcription of the first chorus of Basie's distinctive solo from his July 1937 recording, from which Stacy quotes the first few bars on the first available performance of the number by the

Goodman band. Stacy is clearly also aware of Basie's recording as he repeatedly references the cadential formula Basie uses at the end of each solo chorus, and this is not notated in the part. The piano part gives only the vague direction "modulate to D flat" over two completely empty bars, and Stacy also uses Basie's figure for the modulation. Stacy's playing in this solo and elsewhere at Carnegie Hall uses predominantly octaves and octave rolls in the right hand, although there is a characteristic syncopated emphasis in the eighth notes (3+3+2) at the start of the third chorus, which suggests the influence of earlier piano styles. This solo gives a glimpse into the variation in Stacy's performances typified by his work outside the Goodman band.

In comparison with other numbers in the concert, there is less consistency between the solos of the Goodman sidemen at Carnegie Hall and previous performances of "One O'Clock Jump," as might be expected from solos over familiar blues changes. Goodman's six choruses, using blue notes and growling, lack the clear trajectory that would be supplied by an original melody or harmonic interest. His noticeable drop in dynamic in his third chorus initiates a sympathetic response from the rhythm section and Stacy's counterpoint to his final chorus anticipates what he offers in Goodman's solo on "Sing, Sing, Sing" toward the end of the concert.

Goodman did not record "One O'Clock Jump" in the studio until after the Carnegie Hall concert, in February 1938. On this recording and its alternate take, his solo takes the place of the first tenor solo and later in the arrangement, instead of another piano solo, there is a bass solo, which was unusual for the period (see my later discussion of Walter Page's solo in the "Jam Session"). Maybe Goodman was persuaded to include this, having experienced Page's playing at Carnegie Hall or at the following "battle" between Webb and Basie at the Savoy Ballroom (see Part Three). In May 1938 Goodman broadcast "One O'Clock Jump" from the Madhattan Room, reverting to the order of solos used at Carnegie Hall but introducing a distinctive new riff, shown in Example 2.9, in the final section. This also featured in Harry James's "Two O'Clock Jump," which he recorded in 1939. These descending chromatic triplets in canon between clarinet and the trumpet section recall the canonical treatment of a descending triplet figure in "Sing, Sing, Sing" (following the tenor solo) shown in Example 2.10. The substantive changes in later performances of "One O'Clock Jump" demonstrate that Goodman's arrangement was not only flexible in accordance with particular performance situations but still subject to development at the time of Carnegie Hall.

EXAMPLE 2.9   "One O'Clock Jump," triplet figure in later recordings (transcription)

Trumpets/Clarinet

EXAMPLE 2.10   "Sing, Sing, Sing," triplet figure (transcription)

Trumpets/Clarinet

"LIFE GOES TO A PARTY" (HARRY JAMES)   The Carnegie Hall concert program clearly shows that "Life Goes to a Party" is part of the "Twenty Years of Jazz" sequence. However, I consider it in detail at this point owing to the full-band orchestration. "Life Goes to a Party" was an appropriate choice to bring the concert proceedings back up to date as it had been named, and possibly written, in response to Goodman's band being featured in *Life* magazine in November 1937. Goodman wrote to the magazine to thank the editors for a "lovely spread," saying that "In appreciation Harry James and I have written a song called 'Life Goes to a Party'" (Goodman 1937: 6). This letter, along with a page of handwritten piano music (the first 17 bars of the number), was printed in the magazine on November 15, 1937, by which time Goodman had already recorded the number and broadcast it twice. It is a piece very much of its time; though Goodman performed it several times in the months prior to the Carnegie Hall concert, he played it infrequently after that date.

Clearly Goodman needed some music that was not already known to the public in order to dedicate it to the magazine in this way, and so he probably approached Harry James for some suitable material. James's "Peckin'" was already in the Goodman book, and at this time James could have been preparing the music for his first studio session as a bandleader, arranged by John Hammond. This took place on December 1, 1937, and included "Life Goes to a Party" as the only instrumental alongside three vocals for Helen Humes. James's recording band on this occasion, a nonet of three brass, three saxes and three rhythm, consisted almost entirely of Count Basie's musicians, with Jess Stacy from Goodman's band on piano. This version of "Life Goes to a Party" is a basic head arrangement with solos for piano, tenor and two choruses for trumpet, all with riff backings. It ends with an engineered fade-out, whereas the version for Goodman's band culminates in a rhythmically complex coda, which will be discussed further below.[4] Goodman's version also includes solo choruses, one for Goodman himself and one (two at Carnegie Hall) for James, but the tenor and piano solos are on the bridge only. Apart from James, Stacy is the only musician who plays in both versions of "Life Goes to a Party." His improvisation over the bridge at Carnegie Hall and on other up-tempo performances of this number with Goodman barely gives Stacy any time at all to develop a solo. In all these performances he consistently plays octaves, possibly in an attempt to project over the substantial saxophone backing. Stacy's solo on James's version is not only more convincing but even humorous. Example 2.11 shows Stacy's quotation of a repeated note figure often used by Goodman in his solo on this piece (including at Carnegie Hall; see Example 2.15), ending the figure with a mordent, also used by Goodman, but on a discord.

The concentrated performance history of "Life Goes to a Party" encompasses only versions by Goodman and James, which are chronologically intertwined. Goodman's initial broadcast of the number on November 4, 1937, is at a safe tempo. The performance on a further broadcast two days later has more abandon, to the extent that there is some confusion in the trumpet section in the rhythmically challenging ending, which is held together by Krupa. It is the spirit of this performance that Goodman evidently attempted to carry through into the recording studio less than a week later, where the performance is faster still. James's version of "Life Goes to a Party" discussed above was recorded the day before Goodman returned to the studio to record the number again on December 2, 1937. The similar, slower, tempo of these two studio versions is striking, and probably adopted in an attempt to secure an accurate performance. Goodman seems to have made the deliberate decision to tone down the performance; in contrast to previous versions the bass has a distinctive two-beat feel until the beginning of Goodman's solo, where a more driving four-beat feel begins. Stacy's solo was also cut from this recording, and James's solo, usually a vehicle for extrovert display, is surprisingly played with a mute, suggestive of Goodman's ability to control the performances of his sidemen, which

EXAMPLE 2.11 "Life Goes to a Party," extract from Jess Stacy's solo on Harry James's recording, December 1, 1937 (transcription)

would resultantly enhance his own solo. Goodman broadcast the number again on December 22, 1937, reverting to a faster speed, reinstating the chorus containing Stacy's solo and allowing James to play with more freedom.

Many of the parts for Goodman's version of "Life Goes to a Party" held at Yale (MSS 53, box 16, folder 33) indicate James as the composer and are stamped with his American Federation of Musicians details, suggesting he was also responsible for their preparation. The handwriting is not that of a professional copyist, and the neater parts are almost certainly later recopies; for example, the "Benny" part reflects alterations to the arrangement such as the two choruses for James's solo. On publication, the copyright of "Life Goes to a Party" was (in accordance with the standard practice at the time) assigned to James and Goodman (Library of Congress 1938: 374) but was also consistent with Goodman's claim of authorship in his letter to *Life* magazine. Although James's own recording and Goodman's performances are undoubtedly of the same basic piece, there are significant differences in the detail that suggest Goodman's influence on the arrangement. As with "Don't Be That Way," the question arises as to Goodman's role in formulating the version of the work he performed.

Example 2.12 shows an outline "head," including the elements common to all versions of "Life Goes to a Party." The piece is built on repetitions of this 32-bar AABA chorus where the A sections are based around tonic harmony with occasional use of the dominant, and the B section uses the circle of fifths drawn from rhythm changes. The two initial A sections together have the feel of a 16-bar blues, albeit without reference to the subdominant, as a result of the repetitive blues-inflected melodic material structured in clear four-bar phrases (XX'XY). All recorded performances of this head and the melody of the second chorus consistently incorporate scoops up to the written pitch on long notes, although this is not marked in the parts.

The most notable difference between the versions of the head is the melody of the B section (bars 17–24), shown in Example 2.13. Although only one bar can be seen on the piano sketch in *Life* magazine, this appears to be similar to James's recorded version, namely an arpeggiated pattern repeated, slightly altered in accordance with the underlying harmony. Although the melody in Goodman's version begins with similar pitches, these are displaced, syncopated and developed into two four-bar phrases, each encompassing a change of harmony. Density of syncopation is an important feature of Goodman's version, but not of James's own. It is the simpler version of the bridge melody, consistent with

EXAMPLE 2.12 "Life Goes to a Party," composite head

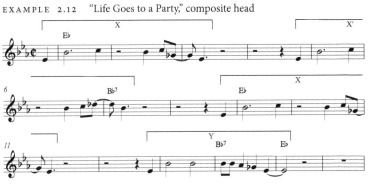

EXAMPLE 2.13 "Life Goes to a Party," B section melodies in Harry James's and Benny Goodman's versions (transcription; MSS 53, the Benny Goodman Papers in the Irving S. Gilmore Music Library of Yale University)

James's recording, that is penciled onto Goodman's tenor and trombone parts as a guide for solos, but this is never actually heard in his performances.

Goodman's version uses a considerably richer harmonic palette; after Krupa's initial four-bar solo the band enters on an augmented chord, a sonority that is heard elsewhere in the piece. But more significantly, as Schuller has noted, "Harmonically the piece is rather curious … it sounds at times simultaneously both major and minor." Symptomatically perhaps, Schuller hears the piece in E flat minor, whereas the parts give the key signature of E flat major and James's own recorded version is also unequivocally major (Schuller 1989: 24). The parts of Goodman's version of "Life Goes to a Party" furnish evidence of the deliberate harmonic ambiguity, aspects of which can be heard on the Carnegie Hall recording. The arrangement uses varying proportions of tonic major and minor as the basis for the A sections (the circle of fifths harmony of the bridge remains consistent throughout). These keys, presented separately at first, are increasingly mixed within A sections as the piece progresses. The first chorus, containing the head as discussed above, is heard over tonic major harmony; but the second chorus uses tonic minor harmony together with a melody that emphasizes the flattened third, as in Example 2.14.

The rhythm section is directed to repeat the harmony of the second chorus for the following two choruses; therefore the A sections remain ostensibly in the tonic minor. However, the beginning of the third chorus as performed at Carnegie Hall sounds particularly ambiguous. Example 2.15, a transcription of Goodman's solo at this point together with the saxophone backing as written in the parts, reveals the reasons for this. First, consider the saxophone parts. The first alto and second tenor (highest and lowest parts) have G flats, meaning the majority of the tonic chords in the backing part are minor, consistent with the chord provided in the guitar and piano parts; but the first tenor has persistent G naturals, creating a tonic major chord within this figure. This can be heard on all the available performances of this number. There are no signs of any corrective markings on the part, and bearing in mind Goodman's thorough

EXAMPLE 2.14 "Life Goes to a Party," second chorus melody (MSS 53, the Benny Goodman Papers in the Irving S. Gilmore Music Library of Yale University)

EXAMPLE 2.15 "Life Goes to a Party," third chorus, bars 1–16 and 25–32, Benny Goodman's solo (transcription) and saxophone backing (MSS 53, the Benny Goodman Papers in the Irving S. Gilmore Music Library of Yale University)

rehearsal process, at which the composer was of course present, it can only be assumed that this is what James intended. Second, against this predominantly minor backing, Goodman's Carnegie Hall solo begins in the major and works toward the minor. The first eight bars use G natural consistently, he incorporates G natural and G flat together in the second eight and in the final eight bars of the chorus he uses G flat. Goodman is more often bluesy in earlier performances, and the repeated note figure (imitated by Stacy on the James recording) that can be heard leading into the B section of his Carnegie Hall solo is the legacy of earlier performances (November 4 and 6, 1937, broadcasts) where this idea was heard throughout the middle eight. However, on the last available recorded performance of this number prior to Carnegie Hall, a broadcast from December 22, 1937, Goodman can be heard using the major mode extensively. This solo may have been in an attempt to play in a more melodic style and contrast, rather than compete, with James.

In the fourth chorus, the A sections are scored for brass and saxes in antiphony, again over the tonic minor harmony. The melody is now extended to the first five notes of the tonic minor scale, having been restricted to the first three notes in the second chorus (as shown in Example 2.14). The fifth and sixth choruses are designated as James's solo. The sixth chorus was evidently added to the arrangement after it had been copied, as the parts contain the instruction to play the fifth chorus twice. Here the predominant form of the tonic is major, but the minor version occurs in the seventh bar of each A section phrase. This is written into the chords provided for the rhythm section as well as within the saxophone backings.

Example 2.16 shows the first part of James's solo at Carnegie Hall. A notable feature of his solos on all the recorded performances of this piece is his use of a repeated note at the start. This is frequently b flat'', but played an octave lower than normal at Carnegie Hall. James's solo, as Schuller points out, uses a mixture of G flats and G naturals indiscriminately in the first sixteen bars (Schuller 1989: 25). However, the result is an overall blues-inflected solo rather than an uncomfortable clash between major and minor as heard at the start of Goodman's solo. Kolodin's program notes suggest he was aware of the potential for such effects to cause confusion for the uninitiated, writing "the freest and most involved elaborations of the theme are maintained against the background of the accompanying instruments without harmonic distortion or conflict" (Kolodin 1938b: 199).

In the final chorus of the arrangement, tonic major and minor reach equilibrium. This section is a development of the fourth chorus, with

EXAMPLE 2.16 "Life Goes to a Party," fifth chorus, bars 1–16, Harry James's solo (transcription) and saxophone backing (MSS 53, the Benny Goodman Papers in the Irving S. Gilmore Music Library of Yale University)

the trumpets playing a descending phrase using the tonic minor and the saxophones playing a rising phrase on the tonic major, as shown in Example 2.17. However, the Carnegie Hall recording gives the effect of trumpets in antiphony with drums, so this ultimate juxtaposition of major and minor cannot be clearly heard. The B section of this chorus pits Goodman against the whole band. Goodman approaches this in various ways in different performances, but perhaps wary of his insecurities above f''' (on the December 2, 1937, recording, his attempt at a break including a''' is the main weakness of the performance) he plays half-notes on a'' as notated in the "Benny" part at Carnegie Hall. The triplet introduced in the final chorus is the basis of the three-beat motive used in the 12-bar extended A section that forms the coda. Example 2.18 shows how this motive is displaced across the four-beat bar and punctuated by the saxophones and trombones, creating rhythmic intensity.

EXAMPLE 2.17   "Life Goes to a Party," final chorus, bars 1–2, trumpets and saxophones (MSS 53, the Benny Goodman Papers in the Irving S. Gilmore Music Library of Yale University)

EXAMPLE 2.18   "Life Goes to a Party," final chorus, bars 29–33, trumpets and saxophones (MSS 53, the Benny Goodman Papers in the Irving S. Gilmore Music Library of Yale University)

Examining the trumpet parts for "Life Goes to a Party," composed and almost certainly copied by James, reveals how this section of the band was organized. As James stated in an interview a few months after the Carnegie Hall concert, the three players (Harry James, Ziggy Elman and Chris Griffin) split the responsibility of playing the lead (highest) part:

> I'm just one of the lead trumpeters in the band. There's no definite rule about dividing the first book, either—nothing like Chris taking all the pretty tunes and Ziggy and I dividing all the ride numbers between us. We just get the first parts in rotation. If an arrangement comes in and it's Ziggy's turn to get the lead, he takes it; if it's Chris's turn, he takes it, and if it's my turn, it's handed to me [Simon 1968: 210].

The parts for "Life Goes to a Party," rather than showing the normal designation of first, second and third from highest to lowest in pitch, are inscribed "Harry," "Ziggy" and "Crisp." The order of pitch of these three parts changes throughout the piece, and the level of detail indicates that this was thought out carefully (see Table 2.1). James plays lead for the first three choruses, dropping to second for the chorus prior to his solo and then third following this in the final chorus. However, the final bar is scored differently, with James again on lead to blast out the concluding two notes of the number.

The arrangement of "Life Goes to a Party" on James's recording conforms to the Basie model, which was familiar to the musicians playing on the session; it may have been an attempt to align himself with this style as a bandleader. However, the arrangement for Goodman, with more *tutti* passages, harmonic richness and density of syncopation, is consistent

TABLE 2.1 Trumpet parts in "Life Goes to a Party"

	Highest		Lowest
Introduction	H	Z	C
Chorus 1	H	C	Z
Chorus 2	H	Z	C
Chorus 3	H	Z	C
Chorus 4	Z	H	C
Chorus 5 and 6	H solo, others *tacet*		
Chorus 7	Z	C	H
Last bar	H	Z	C

with the overall style of the band, again affirming the bandleader's influence on his arrangers.

Irving Berlin's song "Blue Skies" was interpolated in the Rodgers and Hart musical *Betsy*, starring Belle Baker, in December 1926, but the show was otherwise a flop (Suskin 2000: 49). The song was published in 1927 and featured in that same year in the first talkie, *The Jazz Singer*, sung by Al Jolson. Unsurprisingly, numerous bandleaders incorporated the song into their repertoires at this time, including several bands recording in Berlin. Discographies indicate that the song was largely ignored by jazz musicians from early 1928. Although the other popular songs of the 1920s included at Carnegie Hall fell into relative obscurity, Magee argues that "Goodman's performance of Henderson's arrangement launched the tune's life as a jazz standard" (Magee 2000: 196). Following Goodman's first broadcasts and recording of "Blue Skies" in 1935, it was subsequently recorded by many musicians and forms part of Crawford and Magee's core repertory of jazz standards (Crawford and Magee 1992).

The remarkable history of the song is analyzed in detail by Magee, who notes the similarities between "Blue Skies" and Henderson's own composition "Can You Take It?" recorded in 1933:

> The leaps [in the melody of "Can You Take It?"], tracing a perfect fifth…the underlying harmony consists of a descending chromatic chord progression that takes the music from the relative minor to major tonic in eight bars. In other words, it's a contrafact of Irving Berlin's "Blue Skies," which Henderson would arrange for Goodman two years later [Magee 2000: 179].

The introduction and first chorus of "Can You Take It?" also features virtuosic writing for clarinet ensemble, all the more remarkable considering that the key of the arrangement, A major, means on account of the transposition the clarinets are playing in B major, necessitating intense cross-fingering. Magee notes that only Coleman Hawkins takes a solo on the chromatic chord changes in this difficult key (which is also B major for tenor saxophone) (Magee 2000: 179). The other solos take place over a simpler blues progression. Similarly, Henderson selected a "sharp" key, D major, in which to begin his arrangement of "Blue Skies" but then modulates to G major and ultimately to E flat major for the final chorus. His use of clarinets on "Can You Take It?" may well have paved the way for their brief inclusion in the introduction of "Blue Skies," alongside flutter-tongued brass in the introduction. Although the clarinets are quite indistinct on the Carnegie Hall recording, they are definitely present. In September 1938 Goodman included "Blue Skies" on his *Camel Caravan* broadcast and invited Henderson onto the program to explain, in Goodman's words, "how an arrangement comes to be." The band demonstrates the brass and saxophone parts from the beginning of the second chorus of "Blue Skies" separately and then together, to which the rhythm section is subsequently added. This procedure is representative of Goodman's rehearsal process in microcosm, and it gives an excellent illustration of the synergy between arranger and bandleader discussed in Part One. Following the sectional demonstrations, Goodman then begins to play the whole arrangement, but he stops at the end of the introduction to ask Henderson, "Where did that introduction come from? What's that got to do with Blue Skies?". Henderson replies, "That's the storm—it's Blue Skies from now on."

"Blue Skies" was among the first arrangements Henderson made specifically for Goodman. There are a few of the original parts in Henderson's hand in existence at Yale, but no score has survived. These are supplemented by recopied parts to make a complete set (albeit without a drum part); only the first trumpet part is duplicated (MSS 53, box 4, folders 2 and 4). The performances represented on recordings prior to Carnegie Hall can be divided into three groups. The three available 1935 recordings show the band becoming more familiar with the arrangement, working at a relatively consistent tempo (around quarter note = 160). By the time of the studio recording in June 1935, the band plays the arrangement more convincingly than in the earlier broadcasts. In January 1936 Goodman included "Blue Skies" in a broadcast from the Congress Hotel in Chicago. This is the slowest performance among those available and stands alone as representative of a second, developmental phase indicative of Goodman refining his interpretation by making the most substantive alterations to both the arrangement itself and the band's execution of it. However, by the time of the broadcast from the Madhattan Room in November 1937, the number had been redefined as up-tempo swing, and it would be performed in this way at Carnegie Hall as well as on the aforementioned September 1938 broadcast. The consistencies among these three later recordings suggest that Goodman had reached a preferred interpretation at the time of the concert.

Henderson's arrangement of "Blue Skies" has four choruses based on the refrain of Berlin's song, a 32-bar AABA form. Henderson varies the presentation of each statement of the A and B melodies and shows that he could, as Goodman said, "really improvise on [the melody] himself" (Goodman and Kolodin 1939: 162). Henderson also marks each half-chorus (AA and BA) with a new orchestration. The first one is an embellished version of the melody for the whole band in rhythmic unison. In the Carnegie Hall performance, each note is articulated with considerable accentuation and then sustained more quietly and with vibrato for the notated length. This is a synthesis of earlier approaches to this passage; in the early broadcasts the notes are sustained but without as much attack, and the reverse in the June 1935 recording. The *staccato* articulation and dotted swing feel is commensurate with other Goodman recordings from around this date. The second half of the first chorus is dominated by the saxophones, with a short snatch of melody as a trombone solo.

The second chorus initially contrasts muted, detached brass with more mellifluous saxophones. The demonstration of this passage without the rhythm section on the September 1938 broadcast illustrates the unanimity of ensemble that the band had achieved by this time, even though there were some changes in personnel from the Carnegie Hall concert earlier in the year. Conversely, the trumpet sections on the earliest broadcasts of "Blue Skies" are particularly weak at this point in the arrangement. Although this does improve in subsequent performances, the first time the "Carnegie Hall section" of James, Griffin and Elman is heard playing this arrangement, at the Madhattan Room in November 1937, is notable. The tenor saxophone solo in the B section of this second chorus is played by Art Rollini on all the recorded performances. Example 2.19 shows that fragments of Rollini's Carnegie Hall solo are already present in the 1935 broadcasts. The second half of the solo is fully formed by the time of the June 1935 recording and replicated thereafter with only small differences, while the first half continues to vary, albeit remaining close to the original melody, in successive performances. Rollini's solos on the three recordings in the final group are virtually identical, attaining consistency at the same time as the overall interpretation reached maturity.

Chris Griffin is represented only in the latter group of recordings, but his trumpet solos on the third chorus are the most convincing of the pre-Carnegie Hall performances. The first two solos on record are probably by Pee Wee Erwin; the third, by Bunny Berigan, starts off strongly, but he appears to mispitch and end up on the wrong harmonic. The chords of the A section are chromatic, encompassing a modulation to the relative major. Griffin's solo, transcribed in Example 2.20, draws on the melody

but also achieves overall shape and coherence through initially emphasizing the flattened fifth (B flat) in the tonic minor, which becomes a flattened third in the relative major, but then predominantly opting for B naturals in the second half.

The fourth chorus contrasts two four-bar clarinet solos with *tutti* passages. Goodman's solos are different on every available recording, initially remaining close to the original melody, but from the 1935 studio recording onward (including at Carnegie Hall) Goodman disregards the melodic basis of these short sections entirely, as shown in Example 2.21.

Goodman's recorded performances of "Blue Skies" show how both ensemble and solo performances evolve toward a mature interpretation that was heard at Carnegie Hall.

"LOCH LOMOND" (TRADITIONAL, ARRANGED BY JIMMY MUNDY) "Loch Lomond" is a Scottish folk ballad of uncertain authorship. The first known publication was in 1841 under the title "Bonnie Loch Loman," as part of the *New Melodies of Scotland* series of songs with piano accompaniment. In this publication, it is said to be "Written by a Lady, arranged by Finlay Dun." The precise origins and meaning of the song are unclear, although there have been suggestions that it might be associated with a follower of Bonnie Prince Charlie singing goodbye to his sweetheart (the "low road" meaning death), or simply popularized by Lady John Douglas Scott, the composer of "Annie Laurie," another popular Scottish folk song (Fuld 2000: 336). The presence of Scottish folk music in Goodman's Carnegie Hall concert might seem at first consideration rather incongruous, but songs like "Loch Lomond"

had entered the popular song repertoire in America by the early 20th century, and it appears in widely used song books such as *The Golden Book of Favorite Songs* (Aitch 1915) and *The One Hundred and One Best Songs* (1919).

An important stylistic precursor for "Loch Lomond" was "Riffin' the Scotch," recorded by Goodman in 1933 in an arrangement by Dean Kincaide that features similar Scottish effects in the opening. The first generally acknowledged jazz recording of "Loch Lomond" was made by Maxine Sullivan on August 6, 1937. Sullivan performed "Annie Laurie" at the same session and went on to record many more folk songs in her career. Goodman was able to capitalize on the growing media interest in the concept of swinging folk songs, which culminated shortly after the concert when the manager of radio station WJR in Detroit "cut off his station when Tommy Dorsey started swinging *Loch Lomond* over the network and [the manager] proclaimed, with great heat, that such swinging of the old ballads was blasphemy," prompting nationwide debates (Archetti 1938b: 477). Sullivan's recording used an arrangement by Claude Thornhill for a septet of four front-line (including Babe Russin on tenor) and three rhythm (including Thornhill on piano and John Kirby, who was to become Sullivan's husband, on bass). Thornhill was already developing his own influential arranging style. Compared with the contemporary big-band sound, his writing for a small group demonstrated lightness of texture, notably his own tendency to play decorative lines rather than chordal comping behind Sullivan. In previous charts with a larger ensemble for Sullivan (recorded in June 1937), Thornhill made use of the more unusual timbres of vibraphone and flute, and he often favored the pictorial and pastoral. At this time his small-group arrangements made extensive use of the clarinet, which probably would have appealed to Goodman.

According to Collier's sources via personal correspondence, Goodman commissioned Thornhill to transcribe his arrangement of "Loch Lomond" for big band (Collier 1989a: 238); however, the score in the Yale archive is clearly stamped with "James R. Mundy" and dated 1937. Mundy, who joined Goodman as a full-time arranger from Earl Hines in 1936, was responsible for transcribing Thornhill's arrangement and adapting it for Goodman's full band (Firestone 1993: 160). The verse and chorus of "Loch Lomond" use very similar music; the 1841 source has no differences between the two sections other than to incorporate any extra syllables in the lyric. A distinctive feature of Thornhill's arrangement, adopted by Mundy, is to set the chorus at double the speed of the verses, thus distinguishing these sections. As a result, the verses and choruses are 16 and 8 bars long respectively. The notation of the vocal line on the score replicates many of the idiosyncratic details of Sullivan's 1937 performance, suggesting that Mundy was working primarily from her recording. Structurally, the two arrangements are identical on paper, but Goodman consistently omits the section containing a tenor saxophone solo (which comes after the trumpet solo) in his performances. However, like many of the arrangements Goodman appropriated from others, Mundy's version sounds superficially similar to Thornhill's while differing considerably in the detail. Goodman broadcast "Loch Lomond" several times in the latter part of 1937 and recorded it in November of the same year.

The arrangement begins with a characteristic drone fifth in imitation of the bagpipes. This device serves as a clear marker of exoticism and "Scottishness," and it frames the arrangement, reappearing as a brief interlude at its center as well as in the coda. Although this seems like a subtle allusion in Thornhill's version, it is made altogether more vivid in Goodman's performances, which is due in part to the use of muted brass in Mundy's arrangement. The drone continues under Martha Tilton's first vocal entry, the chorus of the song. The first verse, set in a more conventional swing style, provides a complete contrast to the opening section. Here Thornhill's instrumental accompaniment consists mainly of simple sustained chords, often scored with the majority of parts around or above the tessitura of the voice. Mundy writes more rhythmically active backing parts for saxophones, which follow the shape of the melody, but he too scores them in their upper registers toward the end of this section. Mundy extends Thornhill's instrumental fills halfway through this verse, in order to link the two phrases of the vocal line, and at the end of the verse, where he also replaces Thornhill's "classical" 4-3 suspension over the dominant on the approach to the cadence with a typical jazz ii-V-I.

Both versions use ad lib clarinet behind the voice in the chorus following the first verse, although this is only just audible on the Carnegie Hall recording. There is a simple modulation down a tone at the start of the trumpet solo, which was probably performed by James at Carnegie Hall. Earlier performances of this solo incorporated "Scotch snaps," but at Carnegie Hall this is notable as being more strongly blues-influenced than any other section of the piece. The vocal resumes after two bars of drone. Here Mundy takes up Thornhill's reharmonization with a piquant augmented chord on the tonic to coincide with "'Twas there that we *parted*" in the lyric and a major version of the submediant chord on "purple *hue*." These chromatic chords particularly stand out since the harmony of "Loch Lomond" is otherwise diatonic. Sullivan and Tilton both make alterations to the basic shape of the melody in the second verse, either in a quest for variety or because of the range of the melody, which is now lower thanks to the modulation. Thornhill's arrangement was pitched a tone lower than Mundy's, meaning that in the new key the original melody would have descended to f (below middle c'). (For ease of comparison, both parts are shown in Tilton's key in Example 2.22, and the chords supplied by Mundy have been adapted to indicate the full harmony of the saxophone accompaniment.) At Carnegie Hall, Tilton remains closer to the original melody than Sullivan in verse 2, although Mundy provides a basic version of Sullivan's performance in the score. In previous performances, Tilton stays true to the melody in bar 4 but at Carnegie Hall avoids descending to g (below middle c'). She follows Sullivan in extending the upper range of the melody, introducing the high tonic, which is particularly effective on "*sun* coming out."

The final chorus begins with the requirement for a male voice to sing the first line. Perhaps in anticipation of Goodman's reluctance to do this, Mundy writes this line for the whole band to sing. On Sullivan's recording, an unknown male voice reverses the lyrics for comic effect ("You'll take the low road and we'll take the high road"), and it is this version that is included in Mundy's score and parts. Although Goodman always performed the lyric "correctly," he simplifies the melody consistently, singing the tonic in two octaves. From the fifth bar of this final chorus, the melody is heard at half-speed and the lyric "on the bonnie banks" is repeated three times, stretching this chorus to 16 bars in total, as in Thornhill's arrangement. The vocal line in the coda has a final repetition of the song title over two bars of drone, and a final bluesy tag ending for the whole ensemble.

George T. Simon, reviewing the 1938 concert for *Metronome* magazine, mentioned that Tilton "appeared to do Loch Lomond *sans* a mike" (Simon 1938b: 18). At a party to celebrate the 30th anniversary of the concert, Tilton recalled that her microphone "went dead" in "Loch Lomond" (Wilson 1968). The resulting need to project her vocal unaided may account for Tilton's somewhat strained delivery. The Carnegie Hall performance is significantly slower than the previous performances and as a result sounds more similar to the Thornhill/Sullivan version. "Loch Lomond" was the only complete piece from the 1938 event included in the 40th anniversary concert, again sung by Tilton, but on that occasion a new and considerably different arrangement was used.

EXAMPLE 2.22 "Loch Lomond," verse 2, Martha Tilton and Maxine Sullivan (transcriptions)

"The Blue Room" was written by Rodgers and Hart for their second hit musical *The Girl Friend*, which opened in New York in March 1926. It was a romantic ballad for the show's leading couple, played in the original production by husband and wife Sam White and Eva Puck (Suskin 2000: 90). The song has the usual format of verses and refrains, with the latter based on scalar ascents and descents, over simple and mainly diatonic harmony in AABA 32-bar song form. Following the success of the show and of this particular song, it was recorded by a number of leading bands; there are early versions by the New York-based California Ramblers in 1926 and violinist Joe Venuti's Blue Four in 1928. The latter is notable for constant elaboration of the melody, especially by Venuti and in Rube Bloom's vocal chorus, which incorporates scat at a time when this technique was becoming more widespread. Several large ensembles recorded "The Blue Room" during the 1930s, among them the Dorsey Brothers Orchestra, Isham Jones and His Orchestra and Glen Gray's Casa Loma Orchestra. It was probably in the books of many other bands too; for example, we know that Bill Challis's arrangement was played by Jean Goldkette and Paul Whiteman before the Dorsey Brothers recorded it (Sudhalter 1999: 306, 314). These arrangements were indebted to the "symphonic syncopation" style, often employing significant orchestral forces to generate interest through changes of instrumental color, but also incorporating jazz solos.

Bennie Moten offered the most significant reconceptualization of the song as a vehicle for large jazz ensemble as a precursor to Henderson. "Blue Room" was one of 10 numbers recorded by Moten's band, which included Count Basie, in a session in December 1932, following a disastrous tour. Unlike the recordings mentioned above, the verse is completely omitted from Moten's version. The arrangement starts directly with an elaborate paraphrase of the refrain melody for the saxophones, and then it progresses through a series of solos with increasingly rhythmic ensemble backing to two final riff-based choruses in which the original melody has almost entirely disappeared. The first available recording of Goodman performing Fletcher Henderson's arrangement of "Blue Room" (which lost its prefix on the parts and many subsequent listings) is the Carnegie Hall concert. We know that Goodman included the number in his *Camel Caravan* broadcast on January 11, 1938, alongside another new number, "Don't Be That Way" (Jessup 2010: 300). Following Carnegie Hall, Goodman included "Blue Room" in several broadcasts and then recorded it in the studio on March 9, 1938.

Although no score of Henderson's arrangement is extant, there is a full set of parts in the Yale collection, probably dating from 1938 (MSS 53, box

3, folder 27). Prefaced by a four-bar introduction, the arrangement then consists of three choruses, in different keys, interspersed with two four-bar modulatory interludes and concluding with a four-bar coda. This is half the number of choruses in Moten's recording, indicative of the completely different tempo and feel intended by Henderson and Goodman. The Carnegie Hall performance has a significantly slower tempo than all of the previous versions discussed above. The recording that Goodman made a couple of months later is slower still, but an alternate take from the same session is almost exactly halfway between the tempo of the first take and that of Carnegie Hall. This session is also interesting as it was the first time the band had gone into the studio following the departure of Gene Krupa, who was replaced temporarily by Lionel Hampton. George Koenig and Allan Reuss had also left by this point, and Art Rollini and Harry Goodman missed the session. Dave Matthews joined the band on alto sax, and on this occasion Goodman borrowed Lester Young, Freddie Green and Walter Page from Basie's band to fill in.

Example 2.23 shows how, in the first chorus of his arrangement of "Blue Room," Henderson breaks up the diatonic melody and tonic-dominant-based harmony in the first two A sections through introducing a chromatic passing note in the melody on the last eighth note of the bar (which is similar to Venuti's 1926 rendition), accompanied by a passing diminished chord and reflected in the bass part. This first chorus achieves a balance between brass and saxophones; in the opening statements of the A section, the lead is passed from the brass to the saxophones for bars 5–8. A rhythmic subtlety in these sections is the emphasis on the second half of the second beat, from the saxes' backing figure in bars 1–3, brass and saxes together in bar 4, and the brass stab in bar 6. The first two bars of the B section are scored for full ensemble; then the saxophones drop out, leaving the brass to continue. The saxophones then take the lead for the final A section, and under this more complex version of the melody

EXAMPLE 2.23 "Blue Room," first chorus, bars 1–2, brass (MSS 53, the Benny Goodman Papers in the Irving S. Gilmore Music Library of Yale University)

Trumpets

Trombones

Bass

the rhythm section reverts to the tonic-dominant alternation of the original, albeit enriched. On both takes of the March 1938 recording, Goodman doubles the lead line at this point, playing in the low chalumeau register, but it is unclear whether this occurred at Carnegie Hall.

At Carnegie Hall (still in the early stages of the arrangement's "life" with the Goodman band) Henderson's elaborations and improvisations on Rodgers's material are far more adventurous than anything achieved by the soloists. The second chorus is scored for clarinet solo in the new key of E flat major, accompanied in the main by saxophones with occasional brass interjections—notably by the trombones, rarely heard without the trumpets in the Carnegie Hall repertoire, at the start of the B section. Goodman's solo diverges only a little from the melody in the repeats of the A section. His solos on both takes of the March 1938 recording are a little more adventurous, and on the released version Goodman departs from his mellifluous sound to growl his way through the final section of the chorus, a hint of which can be heard at Carnegie Hall. A curious transition passage leading into the final chorus has Goodman trilling on f''' to a drum accompaniment, alluding to the sound of a marching band. On the first take on March 1938, Goodman plays more rhythmically through this passage rather than, as at Carnegie Hall, trusting the drummer to keep time and give a clear lead into the next section. Goodman's failed attempt at the trill, at the limit of his comfortable improvising range, on the alternate take was probably one reason for its rejection.

The A sections of the final chorus are scored for full ensemble. The rehearsal process evidently led to omitting some notes, alterations that were uniformly indicated in the parts, which makes it slightly less relentless to play. The B section of the final chorus was originally intended to be another solo for Goodman, as indicated in the clarinet part, but there are no recordings of Goodman playing at this point. The solo was passed to the trumpet section and performed by Griffin at Carnegie Hall (Simon 1938b: 44). There is a consistent approach to this brief solo in all the 1938 recordings, consisting of a paraphrase of the melody for the first four bars of the solo, then ascending to c''' in a more freely improvised second four bars. The first trumpet part bears the indication "Doctor the first," suggesting that it could be rewritten to include the new solo, although there is no evidence that such a part was ever made. Confusingly, the solo line is notated in pencil onto the second trumpet part marked "Harry," so Griffin may not have always played this solo. Other annotations on the parts furnish definite evidence of a role that James had in the Goodman band. The first trombone part is marked "James beat," and several of the parts are annotated with the word "nose," although this has been crossed out in some cases. "Nose" was probably a nickname for James; in other sets of music a drawing of a nose denotes James's part. He observed:

> One thing Benny could never do was read lines [of a radio script] and beat off tempos at the same time...he'd finish an introduction for a band number and then there'd be dead air while he just stood there getting set to beat off the tempo, so finally they had me beat off all the tunes [Levinson 1999: 56–57].

In addition, the word "me" appears on the first trumpet part, possibly to remind James of his directorial role on the first broadcast of "Blue Room."

Like the other recent addition to Goodman's repertoire performed at Carnegie Hall ("Don't Be That Way"), the interpretation of "Blue Room" was formulated rapidly in the days prior to the concert and maintained in subsequent performances. A postscript to consideration of "Blue Room" is Chick Webb's recording of the number early in 1939 (he also broadcast it around the same time). Like the Henderson/Goodman version, Webb's version has three choruses, the second of which is a clarinet solo with trumpet on the B section, recalling Goodman and James. Webb's unison introductory figure is similar to that of the Casa Loma arrangement. This does not discount the possibility of Webb's arrangement pre-dating Henderson's, but it might suggest that the appropriation between Webb and Goodman was more reciprocal than is often implied, as evidenced by the famous Savoy "battle" between the bands in May 1937 discussed earlier.

"SWINGTIME IN THE ROCKIES" (JIMMY MUNDY, ARRANGED BY MUNDY)   Goodman recorded "Swingtime in the Rockies" in June 1936, shortly after its composer, Jimmy Mundy, joined his organization as a prolific staff arranger: "Benny estimated he [Mundy] produced some four hundred charts during the three years he remained with the band, more than forty of which were recorded" (Firestone 1993: 60). Although, as with Henderson, the bulk of Mundy's work for Goodman was writing arrangements of pop tunes, he also contributed some of Goodman's earliest up-tempo killer-dillers, among them "Madhouse" and "Swingtime in the Rockies," which had already been recorded by Earl Hines, the latter under the title "Take It Easy" in 1933. The new title was likely a play on the popular song "When It's Springtime in the Rockies," by Robert

Sauer with lyrics by Mary Hale Woolsey, published in 1929. The title was then adopted for a 1937 film starring Gene Autry, "the singing cowboy," who also recorded a version of the song later in the same year (Russell and Pinson 2004: 83). It may have been no coincidence that Goodman returned to "Swingtime in the Rockies," at this point, broadcasting it more than once between April 1937 and October 1939 as well as performing it at Carnegie Hall. However, Mundy's "Swingtime" is musically completely different from the waltz-ballad "Springtime."

"Swingtime in the Rockies," an arrangement virtually identical to the recording of "Take It Easy," is a virtuosic ensemble showpiece where the saxophone, trumpet and trombone sections are each given a chance to shine. There is a middle eight for tenor and full choruses for Goodman and Elman, to which Krupa inevitably also contributes. "Swingtime in the Rockies," as performed at Carnegie Hall and notated in the available score and parts (an undated set is archived in the New York Public Library for the Performing Arts; microfilm ZB-3524, roll 10, f. 211 and 212), consists of five 32-bar choruses in AABA form with no additional passages of introduction, transition, or conclusion ("Take It Easy" has a four-bar piano introduction and two-note tag ending). The piece is built primarily from riffs over harmony which is essentially based around I, ii and V, with some chromatic complexity that is discussed below. However, Mundy's arrangement creates a clear sense of overarching shape across this basic structure through variation in orchestration, register, dynamics and harmony, which is particularly well articulated in Goodman's Carnegie Hall performance.

Tension is generated and maintained throughout the initial section, shown in Example 2.24, not only through the syncopated riff—which incorporates extra notes to create a smoother oscillating line compared to "Take It Easy"—but also through the harmony. Although the progression in bars 1–6 seems conventional, the tonic chord is in first inversion and the dominant chord is elaborated by addition of the sixth, prominently in the melody. From bar 6^2 to 8^1, the harmony oscillates several times between A^9, introducing the chromatic chord that will feature heavily in the middle eight, and the dominant (A flat), before finally resolving onto the tonic with a weak cadence (onto an anticipation of beat 2) at the end of the phrase. The harmony of the A sections is varied later in the piece, but that of the B sections remains consistent throughout, using two chords, A^9 and D flat major, that are linked by a common tone (C sharp/D flat). Mundy scores the saxophones mostly in their lower octave for the A sections of the first chorus but contrasts this with a higher tessitura and wider pitch range for the bridge, where he also adds

EXAMPLE 2.24 "Swingtime in the Rockies," first chorus, bars 1–8, saxophones and rhythm (Benny Goodman Collection, New York Public Library for the Performing Arts)

sustained brass. In the second chorus, which uses very similar harmony to the first, the two groups are treated antiphonally in the initial two A sections. Mundy features the brass on the bridge, in the only section of the piece not based on a repeated riff. The final section of the second chorus presents a simplified sustained version of the initial melody accompanied by saxophone tremolos, ending this time with a strong cadence. The performance of these opening choruses is consistent across all available recordings, but the tempo increases leading up to Carnegie Hall, which is the fastest on record; subsequent performances are significantly slower.

The conclusiveness of the second chorus and subsequent introduction of new features marks the third chorus as the beginning of a new phase in the piece. Here the trombones are in the spotlight, answered by stop-time figures from the rest of the band. This chorus also includes the first solo, designated for tenor saxophone, on the B section. Goodman's 1936 recording suggests that this unusual harmony might have caused some problems for the players, since he takes the solo on this bridge and that of the final chorus himself. Both Vido Musso in 1937 and Jerry Jerome in 1939 do not sound at ease in this section, although Russin at Carnegie Hall and Bud Freeman in June 1938 are more convincing.

The harmony of the A sections is varied more substantially in the fourth chorus, Goodman's solo, and now comprises repetitions of A^7-$Ab^{\varnothing7}$-Db^6. In this context, A^7 functions as a tritone substitution for chord ii^7. Goodman's solos on available performances of "Swingtime in the Rockies" are not identical, but they have many features in common. Example 2.25 shows a transcription of Goodman's Carnegie Hall solo; on the lower stave is the solo "guide" as provided in the score and parts. His approach to the A sections is consistently based on playing breaks over the bars of tonic harmony in answer to the ensemble phrases. At Carnegie Hall, Goodman smoothes the transition to the B section by using a four-bar phrase over the start of the new section, using the idea that he plays at the same point in the structure of "Life Goes to a Party" earlier in the concert. In 1936 and October 1937 he used a repeated note to the same effect. The two principal ideas in Goodman's Carnegie Hall solo from which most of the material is derived (lick A, lick B and sustained d flat''') can also be heard in all available previous performances of this piece.

The final, climactic chorus begins with a trumpet solo backed by the full band for the first 24 bars, and in the final 12-bar section the whole band plays a version of the original theme. In Hines's recording of "Take It Easy," the trumpet solo is based around d flat''', and this is clearly emu-

EXAMPLE 2.25   "Swingtime in the Rockies," fourth chorus, Benny Goodman's solo (transcription) and "Benny" guide (Benny Goodman Collection, New York Public Library for the Performing Arts)

lated by the soloist on Goodman's 1936 recording. The trumpet solos on Goodman's performances of "Swingtime in the Rockies" are consistent with each other and the existent score and parts. The one played by Ziggy Elman at Carnegie Hall is most similar to, although not exactly the same as, the notation. The concert is the only available recorded performance at which the written trumpet part for the B section of this final chorus was played; Goodman even plays a solo in this section on the 1936 recording and a broadcast of March 1939. Because no date is given on the parts or the score and it is impossible to date any of them precisely, it is unclear whether the trumpet solo was pre-composed or notated in response to previous performances.

"BEI MIR BIST DU SCHÖN" (SHOLOM SECUNDA AND JACOB JACOBS, ARRANGED BY JIMMY MUNDY)   "Bei Mir Bistu Shein," as it was spelled alongside the Yiddish on the cover of the first published edition, was written by Sholom Secunda, with Yiddish lyrics by Jacob Jacobs, for a new show called *I Would If I Could* at the Rolland Theater in Brooklyn (*Life* 1938: 39). Despite the objections of the show's leading man, Aaron Lebedeff, who suggested alterations to the composition, the song was acclaimed at the first performance (Secunda 1982: 129–130). "Bei Mir Bistu Shein" became popular in the Jewish community, but it did not make Secunda a rich man. In 1937 he signed over copyright to the song to the publisher Kammen for $30, to be split between himself and Jacobs (Secunda 1982: 144). Just months later, Sammy Cahn and Saul Chaplin penned the English lyrics to the song, which the Andrews Sisters recorded in November of the same year: "In the first month, 75,000 copies of the record were sold, and by the end of January, 1938, a quarter of a million records, as well as 200,000 copies of the sheet music" (Secunda 1982: 149). The success of this version, now with the title of "Bei Mir Bist Du Schön" (sometimes "Schoen"), propelled Secunda into the spotlight. Although the publishers did later agree to give Secunda and Jacobs a share of the royalties, at this time 'the press had a field day chronicling the million-dollar song that slipped through [Secunda's] fingers' (Secunda 1982: 153), including a full-page photo story in *Life* magazine (1938: 39).

In the aftermath of the Andrews Sisters' hit and the ensuing media storm, it is unsurprising that a large number of artists made their own recordings of the song. According to Edward Gardner, who has compiled data from various sources to create "the charts that would have been" in the period 1900–1949, the song ranks at number one by the time of the Carnegie Hall concert (Gardner 2000: 222). Goodman, ever the astute businessman, responded to the popularity of the song and broadcast Jimmy Mundy's arrangement from the Madhattan Room on December 18, 1937. The radio announcer described the song tellingly as "a little foreign importation which is catching on like wildfire." Of course the song had actually been written in New York, but this comment may be indicative of the German-sounding title. This broadcast is Goodman's only other full-band performance extant from this period, as he made his contribution to the growing body of recorded versions of the song with the Quartet instead. It may seem strange that Goodman never recorded this popular number with his full band, but according to Michael Levin he

> had to record ["Bei Mir Bist Du Schön"] with the quartet with [Ziggy] Elman added because, if memory serves me right, Guy Lombardo had already recorded it on Victor [on December 15, 1937] and wouldn't hold still for a recording by Goodman's band [Levin 1951: 14].

The chorus of the song, on which Goodman's versions are based, is in standard AABA form, so all that was needed to give the song potential for achieving mainstream success was replacement of (most of) the Yiddish lyrics with English ones. However, the new lyrics are not just a simple translation of the original love song. In this new context, the Yiddish expression "Bei Mir Bist Du Schön" is positioned alongside American "grand," Italian "bella" and German "wunderbar" as ways for the song's protagonist to try to articulate her feelings toward her lover ("each language only helps me tell you how grand you are"). The new lyrics therefore develop the song into a reflection of contemporary cosmopolitanism.

Despite this attempt to broaden the appeal of the song, early recorded versions incorporate explicit musical signifiers of Jewishness, or general features of exoticism that might be read as such, albeit carefully balanced with the expectations of the mainstream audience. The Andrews Sisters use exaggerated *portamento* and ornamentation in their vocal delivery of the bridge; similar features are evident in the instrumental parts, all of which are heard over a heavy beat. However, the effect is moderated by the final section of the vocal, which transitions to the relative major for an upbeat coda, unrelated to the material or mood of the song. In her December 1937 recording, Ella Fitzgerald incorporates only a few elements of ornamentation into her vocal, which might be derived from Jewish music, but the ethnic origins of the song are clearly signified in

EXAMPLE 2.26   "Georgia Jubilee," lick (transcription from 1934 recording)

the accompaniment, especially the klezmer-style clarinet featured prominently throughout the arrangement.

By contrast, the first part of Mundy's arrangement of "Bei Mir Bist Du Schön" as broadcast in December 1937 seems conventional within the swing style, and Goodman's clarinet solo makes no obvious reference to klezmer. Quite unusually, the parts and score all lack a final double bar, suggesting that there were always plans for addition of a further section. A few days after the broadcast, Goodman went into the studio and recorded two takes of a four-chorus version of the song with his Quartet and Martha Tilton, which bears little relation to Mundy's big-band arrangement. As Loren Schoenberg points out, Goodman uses a lick from his 1934 recording of "Georgia Jubilee" (see Example 2.26) to provide introduction, interludes and codas in the Quartet arrangement (Schoenberg 1997). The arrangement fades out inconclusively on the same lick.

In addition to its structural function, this lick influences the harmony of the head in the small-group performance of "Bei Mir Bist Du Schön," which oscillates between the minor tonic and a major form of the subdominant, rather than tonic and (major) dominant as in Mundy's big-band arrangement. The former harmonic scheme seems to cause some problems for Goodman and Hampton when improvising. The same group, with the addition of Ziggy Elman, returned to the studio just over a week later and recorded part 2 (subsequently take 1 of part 1 and part 2 were issued as two sides of a 78 rpm disc, Victor 25751). Part 1 is in A minor, with a modulation to D minor for the vocal, but part 2 begins in C minor (in which context Hampton seems more comfortable). After a brief drum passage, Elman interpolates an explicitly Jewish solo section. The arrangement simply reverts to A minor for this and Tilton's subsequent reappearance (beginning at the B section) without any harmonic transition.

Goodman's experiences in the studio clearly influenced developments in the big-band version of "Bei Mir Bist Du Schön," which took place before January 1938. In the concert, after playing Mundy's notated arrangement Elman and Krupa proceed with the same interpolated material they had recorded with the Quartet; an excerpt from this is shown in

Example 2.27. This well-known Jewish melody is in the form of a *bulgar*, a klezmer dance form, in the misheberach mode on A. This mode includes a distinctive sharpened fourth degree creating an augmented second between the third and fourth degrees (C and D sharp). Elman includes characteristic mordent-like ornamentation of the melody throughout, and the solo ends with a cadential gesture typical of the genre. This section was not included in the initial broadcast of the big-band version and is not notated in the score or parts beyond scant indications of the band backing parts, a *dal segno* penciled in by the players, and the rather more descriptive "Drum vamp to Ziggie Frailach" (an older type of klezmer dance music) on the first tenor part. The band backing in this section is notable since it incorporates the minor tonic–major subdominant progression that was so pervasive in the Quartet versions. As in the studio recording, Tilton resumes her vocal at the B section, and the arrangement concludes with Mundy's final notated phrase.

Jewish influence should not necessarily be seen as located exclusively within the interpolated section. In fact, Mundy's arrangement subtly embodies the characteristics of Yiddish popular song as they would have been understood by audiences at the time. First, unlike Goodman's Quartet versions, Mundy modulates to the dominant minor (E minor) for the vocal. Magee notes that "E minor had been a particularly common key for Yiddish song, to the extent that it came to function as a stereotyped signifier of Jewishness" (Magee 2000: 547). However, this higher key meant that it was more difficult for Tilton to sing the main part of the vocal with the rich "chest voice" tone that can be heard in the Quartet versions (D minor) and in her reappearance in the coda (in A minor) at Carnegie Hall. Indeed, Tilton pulls out of singing the repeated highest

EXAMPLE 2.27   "Bei Mir Bist Du Schön," Ziggy Elman's solo, bars 1–16
(transcription, written-out ornaments)

Trumpet

note of the melody at the end of the B section ("how grand you are") in the December broadcast. Second, Mundy's arrangement begins with a prominent augmented second between the third and flattened fifth degree (enharmonically the sharpened fourth) of the A minor tonic scale, and subsequently E flat (enharmonically D sharp) is emphasized throughout the introduction, as shown in Example 2.28. The sharpened fourth degree is also a "blue" note in jazz, and it would be no surprise to find this to be generally inherent in Mundy's writing. However, it has been argued that the melodic augmented second within the context of a minor key melody was enough to signify Jewishness for New York audiences at this time, and it is possible that the emphasis here could have had this effect (Werb, n.d.). Similarly, although Goodman does not resort to klezmer clarinet clichés, he emphasizes the sharpened fourth/flattened fifth in his solo (which returns to the original key of A minor), and this note also appears in the trombone backing at this point (see Example 2.29).

"Bei Mir Bist Du Schön" demonstrates how Goodman drew on numerous sources, including his own previous performances and work with small groups, as well as the talents of particular musicians and arrangers,

EXAMPLE 2.28 "Bei Mir Bist Du Schön," introduction, first trumpet part (MSS 53, the Benny Goodman Papers in the Irving S. Gilmore Music Library of Yale University)

EXAMPLE 2.29 "Bei Mir Bist Du Schön," Goodman solo bars 8-16 (transcription; MSS 53, the Benny Goodman Papers in the Irving S. Gilmore Music Library of Yale University)

to produce a unique version of what was an extremely popular song in 1938.

"SING, SING, SING" (LOUIS PRIMA, ARRANGED BY JIMMY MUNDY) "The first performance extant" of Goodman's version of "Sing, Sing, Sing" is a broadcast from the Congress Hotel in Chicago on March 18, 1936, only a matter of weeks after Louis Prima's own recording of his composition (Connor 1988: 57). Don Tyler suggests that Prima was inspired by the phrase "Sing, Bing, Sing," which was the title of a 1933 short film featuring Bing Crosby (2007: 239). Goodman did not record "Sing, Sing, Sing" until July 1937, by which time the number had developed into an ensemble showpiece that encompassed both sides of a 78 rpm disc (Victor 36205). The original parts and score of Jimmy Mundy's arrangement no longer exist; the parts held at Yale (MSS 53, box 24, folders 14 and 15) were copied in Hollywood, possibly in 1955 for *The Benny Goodman Story*, a film that culminated in a reconstruction of the Carnegie Hall concert (discussed in detail in Part Three). This set represents a transcription of the July 1937 recording, including solos, with provision for the extra instruments of an enlarged band.

The musical material of the original song is straightforward; the chorus begins with a minor key melody using only four pitches over tonic and dominant harmony. The middle eight, in the relative major, begins with an apparent quotation from the popular song "Yankee Doodle." The simplicity of the melody and lyrics further encourages participation as suggested by the triple imperative of the title and lyrics ("you've got to swing in this man's town"). Prima's band join in singing more of each successive chorus, beginning with the nonverbal sounds ("la la; oh oh") and culminating in an ensemble vocal for the final section of the performance. Perhaps it was these compulsive and hypnotic elements ("the music goes round and round") of the original song that inspired Mundy to feature the beat of the tom-tom so prominently in his arrangement. The tom-tom had exotic associations, originally being imported to the United States from China. Although manufactured in America as part of the standard drum kit after the First World War, the tom-tom remained a signifier of exotic primitivism, as in Ellington's "jungle" music and the minor key setting of "Sing, Sing, Sing." In general terms, a piece that featured the drums so extensively was in itself still unusual at this time. Jazz drumming authority T. Dennis Brown writes: "There are few early recorded examples of lengthy drum solos, though drummers occasionally took short solo breaks. The main impetus for change came in the 1930s as a result of Krupa's drum feature on 'Sing, Sing, Sing'" (Brown n.d.).

Recordings show that the basic shape of what became the first side or part of "Sing, Sing, Sing" was established from the outset and maintained consistently from 1936 (there are three takes of each side from the July 1937 session available for comparison). Prima's original material plays a minor role in the Mundy/Goodman version, as the head is presented once near the start but has little direct influence on the rest of the arrangement. In fact, the performance of the number included in the 1937 film *Hollywood Hotel* and two later broadcast versions (August 1937 and November 1938) completely omit Prima's material. The arrangement consists of a series of combinations of riff-like phrases in the manner of "One O'Clock Jump," interspersed with the aforementioned tom-tom solos. The phrases used in "Sing, Sing, Sing" tend to be longer than the one- or two-bar riffs used in Basie's famous work, frequently stretching to four- or even eight-bar phrases. On the first broadcast of the number, the audience's astonished reaction to the interpolation of material from Fletcher Henderson's "Christopher Columbus," now in a minor key, is audible. This suggests that this was part of the original arrangement rather than a later addition, as Firestone implies (1993: 161).

Part 2 of "Sing, Sing, Sing" consists of solos with relatively simple backing figures that were developed collectively in summer 1936. Goodman's vocalist, Helen Ward, recalled:

> One night [at the Palomar Ballroom] Gene just refused to stop drumming when he got to the end of the third chorus, where the tune was supposed to end, so Benny blithely picked up the clarinet and noodled along with him. Then someone else stood up and took it, and it went on from there [Firestone 1993: 161].

Chris Griffin also describes this process, which can be dated fairly accurately to between May (when Griffin joined) and August 1936 (when Nate Kazebier left):

> We ran [the arrangement] down a couple of times, and then Benny said, "Let's give this a little free ride. Let's ad lib." So the saxophones played one chorus of the melody, and then began to riff around it, working up a "head arrangement," followed by the trombones and then the trumpets, a section consisting at the time of Pee Wee Erwin, Nate Kazebier, and me. When our turn came, Pee Wee played some original ideas, then Nate added a few, and I gave forth with something

I had in mind. And as time went on it continued to evolve, becoming more and more a freelance composition and growing longer, sometimes up to eighteen minutes. We didn't give it any thought, other than a fun thing that allowed some individual expression, but a couple of arrangers told us that the results were very involved and up-to-date [Vaché 2005: 45].

Around the time of the July 1937 recording, performances by Goodman's band were shot for inclusion in the film *Hollywood Hotel*, which was not released in New York until a few days before the Carnegie Hall concert. A recurrent device in the film is a shot of the hotel switchboard, where calls are put through to various rooms. In one scene the operator answers a call, saying, "Mr. Goodman? He's rehearsing in the Orchid Room [the function room in the eponymous Hollywood Hotel] and can't be disturbed." The film then immediately cuts to Goodman's band in action playing "Sing, Sing, Sing," beginning with the camera focused on Krupa's floor tom. The only obvious denotation of "rehearsal" is the band's relatively casual (yet matching) attire; and Goodman's comment at the end of the scene: "All right, boys, that's all, and don't forget, let's be on time tonight." However, the choice of this number for a rehearsal context seems appropriate as it was developed, at least in part, in undocumented rehearsals and performances in the lead-up to the recordings in Hollywood. From a practical point of view, it would be suitable for the film, since it had clearly differentiated sections based for the most part on the same chord, which would be relatively easy to edit to the required length. The inclusion of the number in *Hollywood Hotel* may have influenced the decision to omit the vocal from the number, which had been performed by Helen Ward in the March, July and September 1936 broadcasts (recordings of the last two instances are not commercially available). A band vocalist was superfluous in *Hollywood Hotel* as the main characters were required to sing diegetically and knowingly as part of the narrative, as well as non-diegetically, in a style typical of musical films, when characters are apparently not aware that they are singing. Part of the plot hinges on the ethics of stars miming their on-screen vocal performances. The irony of this is that Goodman was asked to mime to a pre-recorded soundtrack but refused: "We could never do that with 'Sing, Sing, Sing' because we would always improvise and we never knew exactly what we did" (Firestone 1993: 205).

Although part 2 may well have originated as a jam, a stable structure for this section was established prior to or at the July 1937 recording session. The extended version of "Sing, Sing, Sing" had to be organized into two equal portions to correspond to the sides of a record. Mundy's arrangement was retained for part 1, and a structure was developed for part 2 with ensemble sections and solos designated for tenor saxophone, trumpet and clarinet, ending with the same 16-bar coda as part 1. The resulting format was used as a basis for live performances, including Carnegie Hall. However, as with "One O'Clock Jump," the circumstances of the concert, unfettered by the time constraints of broadcasting and recording and the demands of dancers, allowed Goodman the potential freedom to stretch and adapt the form of the number. In fact, the structure and proportions of part 1 are maintained at Carnegie Hall, which has a tempo similar to that of the released take from the July 1937 session (the first take was slower and the final take faster). The main difference between the studio recording and the Carnegie Hall performance of part 1 is that two of Krupa's drum solos are shorter. Although Goodman's solo in part 1 is different in all available performances prior to Carnegie Hall (including the three studio versions), they all begin with the same figure and hit the bluesy flattened fifth at the halfway point. Indeed, the phrase that Goodman plays in the second half of the solo at Carnegie Hall is exactly the same as on the first take of the recording session, exposing this as an established archetype.

Within part 2, the ensemble sections are also consistent in length and performance in all extant recordings prior to Carnegie Hall. Following the tenor solo, Goodman introduces a triplet figure that is taken up in canon by a trumpet and complimented by riffs from growling trumpets and wailing trombones. However, the solos in part 2 show more variation in terms of length and content, in comparison to previous performances, than in any other big-band piece on the Carnegie Hall program. Goodman allows the tenor soloist to stretch out for three times longer than the usual eight bars before introducing the backing riff. Harry James's solo is similarly extended in the concert, allowing him to showcase his virtuosity, as shown in Example 2.30. This phrase is reminiscent of trumpet showpieces such as "Carnival of Venice" that were in his repertoire and with which he became famous after he left Goodman.

Although the solos are innovative, there are also consistencies that may permit insight into how a stable structure was established for part 2. James's solo always begins in B flat minor, a semitone higher than the key of the rest of the piece, and so he employs the sequential modulating phrase shown in Example 2.31 in order to return to the original key for an ensemble section. This phrase is exactly the same as the one James uses on the released take from the 1937 session. After the *tutti* passage, the trumpet solo resumes with another consistent phrase (Example 2.32).

EXAMPLE 2.30 "Sing, Sing, Sing," Harry James's solo (transcription)

EXAMPLE 2.31 "Sing, Sing, Sing," Harry James's sequential transition (transcription)

EXAMPLE 2.32 "Sing, Sing, Sing," continuation of Harry James's solo (transcription)

At Carnegie Hall, but not in the 1937 recording session, the rest of the trumpet section continues to sustain the last note of the ensemble passage and joins James on the last, punctuating note of the phrase. This demonstrates the possibility of ensemble parts being inspired and generated through improvisation.

Following this, James builds steadily toward a c''', recalling the climaxes of Louis Armstrong's solos, and then introduces a dramatic E flat augmented seventh chord for the ensemble that leads to a concluding cadence (Example 2.33). This serves as a transition between James and Goodman, since Goodman's solo consistently begins by echoing the end of the ensemble phrase. At Carnegie Hall, Krupa adds a heavy emphasis to the familiar drum pattern for Goodman's solo. Although this

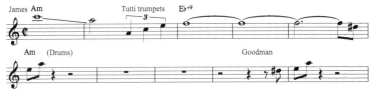

is unprecedented, Krupa had previously demonstrated an experimental approach to this part of the piece on the rejected first take from the 1937 session, substituting a regular beat with sporadic bursts of sound and large amounts of silence. Goodman's usual approach to the solo was to create contrast to the exuberance of James and Krupa, particularly by beginning and ending by playing quietly in the depths of the lowest chalumeau register of the clarinet. However, at Carnegie Hall, Goodman uses a similar idea as the conclusion of the trumpet solo, building chromatically toward a high a''', but unlike James, Goodman maintains a quiet dynamic. Goodman had incorporated this idea in a broadcast in August 1937 while maintaining quiet chalumeau playing at the beginning and end as before. As discussed previously, a''' was beyond the limits of Goodman's normal comfortable range for solos, but necessary in order to achieve a harmonically congruent climax. This is followed by a high c'''', which lies on the same harmonic. This may have been deliberate, but also tiredness may have played its part; the a''' sustained at such a quiet dynamic could have easily split into a c'''' with a small amount of tightness in the embouchure. An alternative reading of this note as deliberate is Goodman's definitive answer to James, playing a solo climaxing not only an octave higher but also pianissimo, demonstrating ultimate control of his instrument, the band and the audience.

A notable addition to the established form of this number at Carnegie Hall was, of course, Jess Stacy's piano solo. Again, this was not totally unprecedented, since Otis Ferguson among others offers a description of the way Stacy used to

> eat up the choruses on "Sing, Sing, Sing," getting higher with each one and beyond himself, truly wonderful piano.... The first time I heard it was at the New York Paramount, and when I began cheering afterward backstage, all Jess would say was: "Oh, you mean that old A-minor-chord thing; it's all right, that chord" [Ferguson 1937: 91].

As previously noted, Goodman extended Stacy's solo introduction to "One O'Clock Jump" in the first half of the concert, but his decision to feature his pianist on "Sing, Sing, Sing" may have been influenced more immediately by the interactions during his solo. Stacy was usually active in backing the tenor and trumpet soloists, but Goodman's solo was normally accompanied only by Krupa's drums. Stacy's contribution to Goodman's solo is technically straightforward, consisting mostly of primary chords voiced in the high register of the piano, but in effect this choice influences how the solo develops. Stacy follows Goodman's line and creates cadences with subdominant and dominant chords, but he also plays lower phrases to create free counterpoint. A descending phrase from Stacy in the middle of the solo initiates a similar response from Goodman, at which point Krupa resumes the usual groove. However, he seems to be influenced by Stacy's continuation of an understated backing, allowing Goodman to exploit the acoustics of Carnegie Hall.

I noted earlier that beyond the initial statement, Prima's original theme has little influence on the rest of the piece. However, Stacy clearly took the basis of the theme as presented by Mundy, an outline transcription of which is shown in Example 2.34, as a starting point for his impromptu solo at Carnegie Hall, in particular the distinctive conjunct motion in the bass that Mundy developed from Prima's original. Extracts from Stacy's solo are shown in Example 2.35. After two initial blues-influenced phrases over tonic harmony, Stacy uses the melody and tonic-dominant harmony of the theme as a basis for an eight-bar stride elaboration (A). For the remainder of the solo, Stacy elaborates the formula iv-V^7-i; he frequently

EXAMPLE 2.34 "Sing, Sing, Sing," outline head, bars 1–8 (transcription)

uses ivb-ic-V⁷-i, a common classical formula similar to the pattern of inversions implied by Mundy's bass line. Stacy draws particularly on triplets, established, in canon, as the main ensemble section of part 2, in his solo (B and C). He also references James's interpolated virtuoso figure (D; compare Example 2.30). Stacy's approach to "Sing, Sing, Sing" is completely different from many of the other solos in the concert, being reflective not only in mood but in content, with its retrospective take on the number. Krupa and James use the piece as a vehicle for projecting their jazz personas, but Goodman and Stacy's improvisations instead draw the audience in and encourage them to listen.

"IF DREAMS COME TRUE" (EDGAR SAMPSON, ARRANGED BY FLETCHER HENDERSON) "If Dreams Come True" was the first encore of the concert; it did not appear in the printed program and is not mentioned in Kolodin's notes. This arrangement, which presented a direct contrast to "Sing, Sing, Sing," is usually attributed to Edgar Sampson, who composed the original song. Sampson copyrighted his unpublished composition (apparently with lyrics) in December 1933 (Library of Congress 1935: 34), and it was published without lyrics the following year (Library of Congress 1934: 1055). It must be assumed that it was written for either Chick Webb or Rex Stewart as material intended specifically for jazz performance rather than musical theater. The copyright was reassigned on February 2, 1938, with a revision of the melody by Goodman and lyrics added by Irving Mills, both of whom are credited in the sheet music published that year (Library of Congress 1938: 361).

However, the cup-muted brass answered by reeds recalls "Sometimes I'm Happy;" further Henderson traits include the detail of the saxophone backing figures behind the solos and the entire saxophone section beginning the number on clarinets. This was not the only time the saxophone section played clarinets in Carnegie Hall, since they were needed for the start of "Blue Skies" (see examples 2.19 to 2.22). A score in Henderson's hand confusingly entitled "When Dreams Come True" in the Yale collection (MSS 53, box 30, folder 30), which Magee states has had "no documented performances" (Magee 2005: 269), in fact contains the arrangement of "If Dreams Come True" that was performed at Carnegie Hall and elsewhere by Goodman. This confirms the suspicion that Henderson, not Sampson, was the arranger. There is a set of parts in the New York Public Library that is probably more recent but exactly matches the Yale score (microfilm ZB-3524, roll 23, f.389). Each part in this set is labeled "When Dreams Come True," but the title of the conductor's lead sheet has been amended to "If." It seems that Henderson consistently mistitled the song; he recorded it with his own group as "When Dreams Come True" as late as 1940. It may be that he was confusing it with the title of a song by Irving Berlin, "When My Dreams Come True" (1929).

Goodman's first available performance of "If Dreams Come True" was a recording made on December 3, 1937. He then broadcast the number at least three times prior to the Carnegie Hall concert. Aside from a change from trumpet to trombone soloist in the second chorus, Goodman made no alterations to Henderson's arrangement as it appears in the Yale score. As with "Blue Room," the interpretation of "If Dreams Come True" is reasonably consistent across all the performances, with the exception of the tempo. Magee notes that Henderson provided tempo indications such as "Not Too Fast" for charts of more than two choruses intended as ballads (Magee 2005: 216). Henderson's score for his three-chorus version of "If Dreams Come True" gives the instruction "Medium Swing—Not Too Fast," which is somewhat ambiguous. Goodman's 1937 recordings are the slowest at around 130 and 125 bpm respectively. The first broadcast later in the month is the fastest at around 160 bpm, and the Carnegie Hall performance is around 156 bpm. In a reversal of the process observed with "Sometimes I'm Happy," "If Dreams Come True" became an up-tempo number yet still retained qualities of a ballad through the orchestration (muted brass and clarinets). In these latter performances, then, Goodman seems to have found a convincing realization of Henderson's "Medium Swing—Not Too Fast."

The 32-bar choruses in Sampson's composition consist of two similar 16-bar phrases, and his fairly straightforward five-chorus arrangement as recorded by Webb in 1934 clearly constitutes a basis for Henderson's three-chorus version. Both Henderson and Sampson used muted trumpets in harmony for the melody in the first chorus. Sampson's arrangement leaves the pianist to fill in the gaps in the melody, and Jess Stacy can be heard in a similar vein on many of Goodman's performances, if not at Carnegie Hall. However, Henderson writes a more sustained version of the melody for the brass. This is answered by the clarinets in unison, with only two brief moments of harmony when they divert from the regular riff toward the end of the first 16-bar section. At Carnegie Hall, Krupa adds some delicate touches to the performance of this chorus on the bell of the cymbal.

Henderson's second chorus begins with a clarinet solo over saxophones, recalling Sampson's use of the saxophones as backing in his 1934 arrangement; but whereas Sampson simply repeats the same sustained harmonization of the melody, Henderson develops a more elaborate harmonized paraphrase. Comparison of three performances in Example 2.36 shows that Goodman also consistently employs the technique of melodic paraphrase in his solo on "If Dreams Come True," with few obvious licks or blue notes, but he produces a different solo each time. Most of the pitches of the tune are present within each solo, and the first notes of the four-bar phrases (bars 2, 5, 9 and 13) are a set of linchpins. Goodman's Carnegie Hall solo is the least complex of those on record, with more sustained notes, and it draws strongly on previously established material, particularly in the latter half. Henderson's score indicates that the 16 bars following the clarinet solo should be a trumpet solo, but on all available Goodman recordings this is taken by a trombone soloist, Vernon Brown. Example 2.37 compares the trombone solos on the same three recordings as seen in Example 2.36. Like Goodman, Brown uses

EXAMPLE 2.36   "If Dreams Come True," second chorus, bars 1–16, Benny Goodman's solos (transcriptions)

EXAMPLE 2.37 "If Dreams Come True," second chorus, bars 17–32, Vernon Brown solos (transcriptions)

the melody to construct a broad outline for solos that are similarly varied. At Carnegie Hall, he reserves the top of his range for the final phrase. This solo also shows elimination of the flattened third that was particularly prominent in bar 15.

The final chorus uses a distinctive antiphonal texture, beginning with Goodman accompanied by the saxophones answering the phrases played by the whole band, but reversing this pattern after eight bars, where the ensemble closely replicates Goodman's phrasing and articulation. The eight-bar tenor saxophone solo is similar on all the recorded versions and is accompanied by a rhythmic phrase in the brass, based on a rhythmic pattern in the final chorus of Sampson's arrangement, where it was performed with plunger mutes.

Webb's two subsequent recordings of "If Dreams Come True" in 1936 and 1937 featured vocalists Charles Linton and Ella Fitzgerald respectively. The former uses a similar arrangement as in 1934, with the addition of Linton's high tenor, and is notable for the extremely short articulation of the muted melody by the brass section. However, the 1937 arrangement, recorded just weeks after Goodman, is completely different in style, demonstrating the influence of the smoother conception of the piece. The muted brass are now *legato* and accompanied by a mellifluous saxophone and clarinet line that has similarities with Henderson's clarinet fill. Aside from one unissued Quartet version from the 1960s, the last documented Goodman performance of "If Dreams Come True" is a *Camel Caravan* broadcast on February 8, 1938 (for which a recording not available). By this time, Billie Holiday had recorded the number with Teddy Wilson, and in the following months a number of other jazz musicians, including Bobby Hackett and Duke Ellington, began to use it as a vocal number featuring Lola Bard and Ivie Anderson respectively, coinciding with publication of the sheet music. Ellington's early version in particular appears to draw on Henderson's arrangement in the saxophone backings and use of antiphony in the final chorus.

"BIG JOHN SPECIAL" (HORACE HENDERSON) "Big John Special," one of the first numbers Fletcher Henderson gave to Goodman (Goodman and Kolodin 1939: 157), was an original composition by his brother Horace. It may have been named after Big John, proprietor of a café in Harlem (the number is also known, incorrectly, as "Big John's Special," probably the result of the release of Henderson's recording under this title in 1934). Although Goodman would have received the chart by the start of 1935, there is no evidence of his performing it until the following year. Goodman broadcast "Big John Special" several times in 1937, but it was not recorded in the studio until after the Carnegie Hall concert. Like "Life Goes to a Party" and "Swingtime in the Rockies," "Big John Special" features a riff-like repetitive melody over a simple looping harmonic progression. Such numbers were usually played at a fast tempo, supplying a basis for virtuosic solo displays over sustained harmonies or simple riffs. Although the arrangement Goodman and his band performed at Carnegie Hall is virtually identical to Horace Henderson's 1934 recording with his brother's band, the performance style is significantly different.

"Big John Special" is based on the eight-bar phrase in Example 2.38. Each 32-bar chorus is made up of four repetitions of this phrase, with the third one transposed to the subdominant to function as a B section. The whole arrangement consists of four choruses, with the only addition to this structure being a curious six-bar modulatory passage (into A flat major) before the last chorus, incorporating block chord harmonization of a whole tone scale. At the center of the arrangement, a unison brass passage, culminating in a conclusive two-bar tag that is also used at the end of the piece, produces a false ending. The arrangement begins, without introduction, with the saxophones playing the melody in block harmonies, colored by the brass. As with many of the numbers performed at Carnegie Hall, Goodman employs a more *legato* swing feel in the performance of the main theme, whereas Henderson's saxophones played in a much more articulated fashion four years earlier.

The second chorus of "Big John Special" features a trumpet solo interspersed with Goodman's clarinet, replacing the alto solo in Henderson's recorded version, on the bridge. The solos differ on the recorded performances prior to Carnegie Hall. It can be no coincidence that Goodman selected "Big John Special" ("a parting gesture," as the announcer put it) for the last night of his Madhattan Room engagement on April 29, 1937, because it featured his most recent acquisition, Harry James. This is the

EXAMPLE 2.38   "Big John Special," theme (Benny Goodman Collection, New York Public Library for the Performing Arts)

first available recording of the number since January 1936. On this occasion, James plays the first eight bars of Red Allen's solo from Henderson's 1934 recording before offering his own second eight. In contrast to this extrovert display of knowledge and virtuosity, James's solo is relatively restrained at Carnegie Hall, featuring the technique of half-valving to produce subtle timbral variations. The solo is punctuated throughout by Krupa, demonstrating the close musical relationship between the two players. At Carnegie Hall, the final phrase of James's solo on this chorus (Example 2.39) alludes to "Stompin' at the Savoy."

Stacy also demonstrates familiarity with Henderson's recording, as all of his solos on "Big John Special" available on record end with a distinctive ascending glissando inspired by Horace Henderson's solo. But at Carnegie Hall, Stacy also plays this final glissando after only 16 bars. Certainly, this third chorus was subject to alteration in Goodman's hands. Henderson's original version included a saxophone soli passage in the B section of this chorus, which Goodman included only on his first performance of the number in 1936, thereafter allowing Stacy to continue his solo instead. Stacy might also have been confused by a cut made in this chorus for a radio broadcast in November 1937, which reduced his solo to eight bars.

Goodman's interpretation of the start of the final chorus offers further evidence of the influence of Henderson's recording. Henderson simply brought back his trumpet soloist for a further climactic 16 bars, but Goodman opted to take this solo himself in his first performance of the number in 1936, rather similar to his role in the closing stages of "One O'Clock Jump." He then turned this over to James from at least April 1937. Both Goodman and James follow Allen's solo in playing repeated A flats at this point. However, at Carnegie Hall, the three-man trumpet section plays chords, harmonizing this repeated note and bringing aspects of Allen's solo permanently into the arrangement. This effect was first introduced in time for the November 1937 broadcast and eventually annotated onto all the brass parts, although only the trumpet section plays this pattern audibly at Carnegie Hall. The B section of the final chorus introduces antiphony between saxes

EXAMPLE 2.39   "Big John Special," second chorus, bars 25–28, Harry James's solo (transcription)

and brass. In the eight-bar coda, saxophones state the theme once again, this time over plunger-muted brass, the mute indications added to the parts by the musicians. The final bars repeat the false ending from the third chorus. In some performances (including Carnegie Hall), this final chromatic ascent can be heard with the addition of a line in contrary motion, although this is not indicated in the notation.

"Big John Special" was the second encore and the last piece the band played in Carnegie Hall, so Goodman was once again using this piece for a parting gesture, as he had done in the Madhattan Room nearly two years earlier. Yet the Carnegie Hall performance of "Big John Special" is quite unique among Goodman's recorded versions of this piece. In all but his first performance, Goodman's tempi approach or exceed Henderson's; the Carnegie Hall version is significantly slower, although not lacking in energy. In contrast with the other performances, the overall dynamic level is significantly reduced; the performance is also marked by sudden accentuations, particularly by Krupa. Considered against the other more extrovert versions of "Big John Special," the overall impression is of a performance in which the bandleader is in complete control. Goodman's interpretive choices could be read in several ways. It may be indicative of his assertion of power as a bandleader over the two most ebullient soloists from within his group—Krupa and James—who in turn rebel as far as they are able to. But in reconfiguring "Big John Special" in this way, Goodman demonstrates that he could also force the audience to listen, which was essential to the success of the Carnegie Hall concert.

"TWENTY YEARS OF JAZZ"

The Original Dixieland Jazz Band is still widely considered to have made the first jazz recordings, and so it is a convenient linchpin for the construction of jazz history. Almost inevitably, "Twenty Years of Jazz" began with an ODJB number, "Sensation Rag," just as Whiteman's "Experiment in Modern Music" concert had begun with the ODJB's "Livery Stable Blues." Whiteman paired numbers in his concert to contrast old and new, and this particular ODJB side was probably deliberately selected for its outdated barnyard effects, whereas "Sensation Rag" might be considered somewhat more refined. Nevertheless, Kolodin's program note emphasizes the "simple patterns, the unvarying rhythmic scheme, the generally unsophisticated formula of breaks, the lack of modulation" of early jazz, which laid a foundation for the later development of "higher skill and closer integration of hot jazz" (Kolodin 1938b: 196).

The ODJB recorded "Sensation Rag" twice, in New York in March 1918 and in London in May of the following year. It is clear that Goodman took the 1918 recording as a model for the Carnegie Hall performance. Structurally, it is a typical ragtime number with three 16-bar "strains" in related keys: an introductory section in B flat major (A), the main section in E flat major (B) and a "trio" in A flat major (C). Both ODJB recordings use the form AABBCCBABCB, but Goodman cuts the number of sections by half, resulting in a structure of ABBCB. Although Goodman's version is very similar to the ODJB's recording, close comparison reveals that the musicians are not simply playing a note-for-note transcription. For example, Goodman and trombonist Vernon Brown vary their parts on the repeats of the B section, following jazz performance practice rather than the exact notes of the original. Krupa's interpretation of the drum part is interesting: rather than copying the woodblock, cowbell and cymbal crashes of the original recording, he bases his performance on the snare drum, mostly without employing the snare. Just as the ODJB's Tony Sbarbaro contrasts his playing on adjacent B sections by playing the first mainly on woodblock and the second on snare drum, so Krupa uses mainly the rim or side of the drum the first time, playing on the drum itself on the repeat, and turning on the snare for the final section, conventionally the loudest part of a New Orleans jazz number.

The processes of early recording had a profound influence on the music that was widely disseminated in the early years of jazz, which ranged from racial discrimination privileging white groups such as the ODJB to modification of instrumental technique to produce good results on record, particularly in relation to the drums. The Carnegie Hall performance of "Sensation Rag" presents an implicit critique of the ability of recordings to represent jazz performance through reintroducing elements associated with live performance of this music. The performance is considerably shorter than standard length for jazz performances based on the capacity of the recorded disc. The musicians introduce variation through improvisation, which was arguably better represented in live performance and by other groups contemporary with the ODJB that did not necessarily appear on early recordings. Finally, the performance includes styles of drumming that would not have been so compatible with early recording techniques.

"I'm Comin' Virginia" was written by Donald Heywood and Will Marion Cook and popularized in a recording by Ethel Waters in 1926 with the "Singing Orchestra," consisting of violin, cello, trumpet and piano and a small vocal group directed by Cook. By this time, Cook was enjoying a successful career as a composer and music director of many significant black music theater productions and of the Southern Syncopated Orchestra. Cook acted as a mentor to other black musicians and composers, including Duke Ellington, and he may have helped Heywood, a member of his orchestra, in this way (Brooks 2004: 298). Waters's recording bears the hallmarks of music theater, where her subtly blues-influenced delivery accompanied by improvisational trumpet and stride piano is balanced stylistically by "classical" strings and eventual culmination of the number in a choral finale (not to mention a quotation from Edvard Grieg's "In the Hall of the Mountain King" from *Peer Gynt*). "I'm Coming Virginia" was recorded by Paul Whiteman, Fletcher Henderson and Frankie Trumbauer (with personnel from the Jean Goldkette Orchestra), who anticipated the song's success in Waters's hit show *Africana* in July 1927 (Peterson 1993: 8). These early versions all feature the trumpet prominently, to produce the "hot" jazz content in Whiteman's version, carry the melody for the first two choruses of Henderson's arrangement, and, in Beiderbecke's hands, bring Trumbauer's performance to a close. "I'm Comin' Virginia" was subsequently adopted as a trumpet feature by Bunny Berigan and Harry James in the period prior to Carnegie Hall.

Goodman included only Beiderbecke's two solo choruses from Frankie Trumbauer's May 1927 recording in the Carnegie Hall concert. Similarly to the shape of Waters's performance, the first half of Trumbauer's version is relatively subdued, especially the minor key verse that immediately precedes the trumpet solo. Beiderbecke's solo, together with introduction of Chauncey Moorhouse's hi-hat, then provides a more optimistic mood. Eddie Lang's guitar plays a fundamental role in the original arrangement, but other than Allan Reuss using Lang's break in the coda, the role of the guitar is comprehensively diminished in Goodman's version. Goodman's performance adds his own and Stacy's extemporization instead, which complicates the texture from the outset, meaning that the second chorus, where the other instrumentalists join to provide contrapuntal texture, amounts to less of a contrast. Whereas Moorhouse's hi-hat improvisation contributes subtle drive in the original, Krupa plays a regular pattern with brushes and bass drum throughout. Although the basic musical material is the same, these details, within a slower tempo, result in Goodman's version sounding less uplifting than the original;

this suggests a reading of the performance as a tribute to Beiderbecke, who died in 1931.

No doubt Beiderbecke's untimely death established him as an archetypal tragic great jazz musician, leaving a void that Bobby Hackett was equipped to fill: "Bix was only a few years gone when Hackett came to wide notice, and those who heard and cherished the ill-fated Iowan longed to find him again in the newcomer from New England" (Sudhalter 1999: 625). Hackett's recording career had begun less than a year prior to Carnegie Hall in the backing bands of Dick Robertson and the Andrews Sisters, but the Carnegie Hall program already describes him as having "modeled his entire style on the precepts of his great predecessor and perfected to a remarkable degree the intonations and phrasings of Beiderbecke" (Kolodin 1938b: 197). Having been previously unknown on his own terms, Hackett was an ideal choice to re-embody Beiderbecke at Carnegie Hall. Although Hackett performs a nearly exact transcription of Beiderbecke's solo, which might be regarded as an aesthetically worthless copy, in this context the performance retains its authenticity through the signifying of an absent other; the subject of the performance is Beiderbecke, not Hackett. This idea is part of what Allan Moore terms "third person authenticity": "when a performer succeeds in conveying the impression of accurately representing the ideas of another, embedded within a tradition of performance" (Moore 2002: 218).

Ted Lewis included "When My Baby Smiles at Me" when he appeared in the Greenwich Village Follies of 1919 (Tyler 2007: 113). Gardner's calculations position Lewis's subsequent recording as number one by May 1920 (Gardner 2000: 186). "When My Baby Smiles at Me" became Lewis's theme song, and he re-recorded it several times in increasingly "symphonic" arrangements. Although he became widely known for his speech-song vocal delivery, Lewis's clarinet style is similarly distinctive, with almost continuous scoops and bends and frequent flutter tonguing. Like the ODJB, Lewis's inclusion in "Twenty Years of Jazz" is justified in the program as representative of the aesthetic of a bygone age, in this case the eccentricity of the 1920s, after which, the program explains, "as a group of talented white players grew up who modeled themselves on the great Negro musicians, the popularity of spurious hot players steadily diminished" (Kolodin 1938b: 197).

"When My Baby Smiles at Me" is the only item in "Twenty Years of Jazz" for which score and parts are extant (New York Public Library microfilm ZB-3524, roll 8, f.160 and 161), and these exactly match the single instrumental chorus played at Carnegie Hall. The fact that no other parts for the "Twenty Years of Jazz" segment exist (but see Figure 2.3 and the discussion of "Blue Reverie") may suggest that some of the pieces were played from stock orchestrations or even from memory. A set list penciled on the trumpet part of "When My Baby Smiles at Me" corresponds to a reprise of "Twenty Years of Jazz" in February 1938, and therefore this arrangement was almost certainly commissioned for the concert rather than transcribed from the recording post-1950. The NYPL files give Joe Lippman as the arranger, but he was more likely to have produced a previous full-band arrangement that included a vocal from saxophonist Toots Mondello. Lippman was working for Goodman in 1935 when this arrangement was included on a *Let's Dance* broadcast.

The Dixieland style and instrumentation of the arrangement performed at Carnegie Hall clearly reference the final chorus of Lewis's first recording of "When My Baby Smiles at Me," as by his 1926 re-recording Lewis had enlarged his band considerably and the style of the arrangement changed accordingly. However, the Carnegie Hall arrangement does not match any part of this source: in the first chorus Lewis plays the melody on alto saxophone, the second chorus was the vocal and in the final chorus the trumpet carries the melody in typical Dixieland style. In the rearrangement for Carnegie Hall, Goodman plays the melody, incorporating Lewis's trademark glissando effects exactly as indicated in the notation, whereas the players of the muted trumpet and trombone perform the arrangement slightly more freely. The drum part is inaudible on Lewis's recording, and Krupa's contribution is played mainly on the rim or side of the snare drum. Goodman's imitation of Lewis was obviously well honed, having been in his repertoire since childhood, and he replicates Lewis's already exaggerated clarinet style. However, physical gesture also seems to have played an important role in the performance, as Annemarie Ewing reported in *DownBeat*: "The way that Benny Goodman took off Ted Lewis, even to the angle of the clarinet, with a nuance that said, louder than words, that he was playing a caricature" (Ewing 1938: 5). Conversely to Hackett's careful re-creation of Beiderbecke's solo in "I'm Comin' Virginia," Goodman's "When My Baby Smiles at Me" is an entirely new performance text in the manner of pastiche. It was also clear to Ewing (and others) that the performance is a parody; the subject of the performance is Goodman's temporary transformation into Lewis. In this way, Goodman references and satirizes his own past association with Lewis, which highlights a further measure of his development as an artist as demonstrated by the other numbers in the program.

"That's Why They Call Me Shine," by Ford Dabney and Cecil Mack, was published in 1910 when performances by Aida Overton Walker in a black musical theater production called *His Honor: the Barber* brought it to wider attention, but it may have been presented as early as 1907 by the double act of Bert Williams and George Walker (Aida's husband). The song may have been inspired by a person called "Shine," a friend of George Walker's who also features in James Weldon Johnson's 1912 *Autobiography of an Ex-Colored Man* (Brooks 2004: 397). The title of the song was shortened and the lyric revised in collaboration with Lew Brown in 1923. Following republication, "Shine" was recorded by many jazz musicians, including Louis Armstrong in 1931, who also performed it in the short film *Rhapsody in Black and Blue* the following year. Although Armstrong mugs through "Shine" and "You Rascal You" in the film, dressed in a leopard skin, Giddins argues that he

> transcends the racist trappings by his indifference to every sling and arrow. The director/writer is trying to tell the audience one thing. Armstrong is telling it something entirely different—he's doing it not only with the magnificence of his music, but with his physical muscularity, his carriage, his boding sexuality, the look in his eye (Giddins 2001: 9).

One argument is that even though Armstrong's vocal performance seems to embody the stereotype of the lyrics, transcendence occurs "when he puts his trumpet to his lips, [and] he becomes a different man" (Gabbard 1996: 211). Edwards, however, argues that "all these elements…*coexist* in the performance" and that "there is no transcendence here" (Edwards 2002: 647).

Armstrong prefaces his vocal performance of the famous chorus of "Shine" on record and film with the phrase "Oh Chocolate Drop that's me," a reference to the verse that describes the ongoing racial prejudice suffered by the protagonist. It was increasingly common practice to omit song verses in jazz performances of popular songs, and so the meaning of the chorus of "Shine" ("Just because my hair is curly/Just because my teeth are pearly") became an apparent celebration of stereotype rather than a defiant statement of racial pride. However, when Armstrong's allusion to the verse of "Shine" is taken into account, his performance of the chorus can be read as ironic, deliberately and knowingly playing up to the stereotype in the vocal, only to demolish perceptions with his trumpet solo, which becomes the ultimate retort. This double identity reflects the aesthetic of early-20th-century black musical theater, from which "Shine" originated. David Krasner explains this:

> Amidst deteriorating race relations between 1895 and 1910, African American musical theatre found itself caught between two competing forces: the demands to conform to white notions of black inferiority and the desire to resist these demands by undermining and destabilizing entrenched stereotypes of blacks onstage [Krasner 1997: 1].

The experience of encountering jazz through records frames *Rhapsody in Black and Blue*. Armstrong's performance of "Shine" is part of the dream of a jazz lover whose wife has knocked him out with her mop in exasperation with his obsession with the music; the film ends as he regains consciousness to find that the Armstrong record he was listening to has ended. Here, the jazz fan can only dream of seeing Armstrong in the flesh. Indeed, Armstrong's early appearances on film were instrumental in disseminating the *embodiment* of the persona that could be heard on his records, and they must have had a significant impact on contemporary audiences. As a result, it is hardly surprising that a number performed on film was selected as representative of Armstrong for the 1938 concert.

The Carnegie Hall performance of "Shine," featuring Harry James, consisted of a single chorus of trumpet solo prefaced by a cadenza and omitting the vocal (and even a clear statement of the song's melody). Without any clear musical or narrative contextualization, James's performance becomes primarily a display of virtuosity, and a safe one at that. On both of his 1930s performances, following a build-up on the dominant (b flat″) that creates tension and expectation, Armstrong only just makes the top e flat‴ at the end of the piece. However, James's version is pitched a minor third lower than Armstrong's, ultimately easily reaching a mere c‴, which was within standard trumpet range and never seems in doubt.

Example 2.40 shows a transcription of James's solo. James begins his performance with a statement reminiscent of the second phrase of Armstrong's opening cadenza from the June 28, 1928 recording of 'West End Blues' with his Hot Five. James does not replicate Armstrong's 1931 'Shine' solo exactly, although he borrows many of Armstrong's figures methodically in order to make up his single chorus. He begins similarly to Armstrong, repeating the dominant, a glissando between octaves still on the dominant, and an arpeggio of chord iii. At the halfway point, James begins borrowing from the lead-in of Armstrong's second chorus—a long glissando to the dominant in the upper octave—and concludes by playing the end of Armstrong's solo.

EXAMPLE 2.40   "Shine," Harry James's solo (transcription)

When James was asked why he didn't play like Armstrong more often, he replied: "The way I play is my way and when people hear me they say, 'Oh, that's Harry James.' They don't say, 'Oh, that's the guy that copies Louis.'" (Levinson 1999: 51). James's performance is pastiche; he makes no attempt to satirize, revere, or embody Armstrong, as with previous numbers focused on white musicians in "Twenty Years of Jazz;" nor does he produce a solo in his own style. The interest here is the spectacle of hearing James playing *like* Armstrong, a compromise that says little about either musician.

In the final piece in this section of the concert, not even pastiche was attempted but instead the originating musicians were included in the performing ensemble. For "Blue Reverie," a 12-bar blues in F, Goodman called on Johnny Hodges, Harry Carney and Cootie Williams from Ellington's band. Under the auspices of Cootie Williams and His Rug Cutters, these musicians, with the trombonist "Tricky Sam" Nanton and Ellington's rhythm section, recorded this number in March 1937. Vernon Brown and the rhythm section from Goodman's band stood in for the absent musicians at Carnegie Hall. Goodman also plays in the introduction and coda, as suggested by a photograph of a rehearsal printed in *Metronome* (Figure 2.3) and confirmed by photographs taken at the concert (Hancock 2008: 97).

FIGURE 2.3   Rehearsal for "Blue Reverie" at Carnegie Hall. From left to right: Jess Stacy, Benny Goodman, Vernon Brown, Cootie Williams and Johnny Hodges (Getty Images).

Jess Stacy is clearly familiar with Ellington's recorded piano solo, but he appears to get lost in the changes and plays for only nine bars, jumping to the final three bars of Ellington's (12-bar) solo in his seventh bar. Hodges, Carney and Williams play solos that are practically identical to those on the March 1937 recording. Hodges's soprano saxophone decoration of the introduction and coda is noticeably more fluid at Carnegie Hall than on the original recording, which might suggest the impact of interim rehearsals and performances on the piece as a fixed entity. However, an alternate take of "Blue Reverie" from the same March 1937 session demonstrates significant differences from the released version; in particular, Ellington's solo is more harmonically adventurous. Williams's solo is the most consistent across the three versions, but on the alternate take he plays half of a "tag" ending that he adds in full to his rendition of his solo at Carnegie Hall. This evidence confirms that the musicians were clearly accustomed to producing different versions of the piece, but it suggests that Ellington's musicians were asked to work from a transcription of their recording at Carnegie Hall. The photograph of a rehearsal for "Blue Reverie" at Carnegie Hall (Figure 2.3) showing music stands in front of the players suggests that some notation was produced. Ellington's musicians gave a superficial impression of authenticity to the performance of "Blue Reverie" at Carnegie Hall, but in replicating their recorded solos they were asked to indulge in what might be perceived as inauthentic jazz practice.

"JAM SESSION"

The Carnegie Hall "Jam Session" consisted of a performance of "Honeysuckle Rose" by Fats Waller and Andy Razaf, which had been introduced originally in the show *Load of Coal* at Connie's Inn in New York (Peterson 1993: 218). Fletcher Henderson was the first bandleader to record an instrumental version of "Honeysuckle Rose," in 1932. Not surprisingly, then, the number entered Goodman's repertoire at an early stage, before he had a permanent band. He recorded it in February or March 1934 under the pseudonym "Bill Dodge" for the World Broadcasting System, which leased the sides to radio stations (Connor 1988: 42). This version consisted entirely of solos over relatively simple backing figures. By early 1935, Goodman had obtained another arrangement that he first performed on the *Let's Dance* radio show, in which some of the backing figures, and especially the elaborate ensemble melodic paraphrase in the first chorus, strongly suggest a reworking of the Henderson version.

The Carnegie Hall "Jam Session" group consisted of Goodman with Harry James, Vernon Brown and Gene Krupa from his orchestra; Count Basie along with Buck Clayton, Lester Young, Freddie Green and Walter Page from Basie's orchestra; and Johnny Hodges and Harry Carney from Duke Ellington's orchestra. All of the musicians took solos with the exception of Brown and Krupa, making this the longest number in the concert at more than 16 minutes. Fortunately, given the size of the group, the "Jam Session" had been rehearsed earlier in the week. Also, Teddy Wilson recalled that Goodman was "excellent at running a jam session. He would call out: 'You take the next chorus,' 'Now, we're going out,' 'Drum solo,' or 'All right! Piano break, four bars!'" (Wilson et al. 2001: 50). Prior to the concert, most of the group had participated in recordings of "Honeysuckle Rose." Hodges was in the band for Mildred Bailey's 1935 recording, and Basie recorded a version in his first session for Decca in January 1937, at which point his band included Clayton, Young and Page. The interpolation of the melody from Vincent Youman's "Tea for Two" in the latter demonstrates the influence of Henderson's recording, in which this melody was heard in the final chorus. Basie's version uses the same key scheme as "One O'Clock Jump" beginning in F major, also Waller's preferred key, and modulating into D flat for the solos, the key adopted by Henderson and Bailey. Goodman's "jammed" "Bill Dodge" version is in F, but his later arrangement was in D flat. F major seems to have been maintained as the established key for jam session–type performances, including at Carnegie Hall. In general, none of the early arrangements are particularly complex, spotlighting different soloists over repetitive backing riffs, exactly in the manner of a jam session where an arrangement of this type would be made on the stand.

As discussed in Part One, the growing popularity of jam sessions reflected public interest in the informal activities of jazz musicians and also established a core repertoire of "standards" as the basis of improvised performances. In March 1936, "Honeysuckle Rose" was included alongside other early standards such as "Basin Street Blues" and "Tiger Rag" in a WNEW broadcast entitled "A Demonstration of Swing," featuring Bunny Berigan and Teddy Wilson among others. Having already recorded his composition several times, Fats Waller included it alongside "Blues" in "A Jam Session at Victor" in March 1937, which was intended to be a promotional opportunity for the label (Sudhalter 1999: 508). Although it would be natural for Waller to include one of his own compositions in the session, this also suggests that "Honeysuckle Rose" had become standard fare for up-tempo jamming, just as the blues was established as the basis for slower impromptu performances. A year after the Carnegie Hall concert, "Honeysuckle Rose" was performed as part of a jam session organized and broadcast by the British Broadcasting Corporation, which included Harry James and Teddy Wilson.

The Carnegie Hall "Jam Session" on "Honeysuckle Rose" begins with a short introduction from Basie. The head is collectively improvised for two choruses, but Harry James can often be heard playing the melody. The first solo is taken by Lester Young, the first chorus of which is transcribed by Sudhalter, who points out that Young avoids melodic paraphrase and uses familiar one-note "rides" at the end of the first chorus and the beginning of the second (Sudhalter 1999: 258–259). Further, Young uses a triplet motive throughout his solo and incorporates sequential repetition, such as in the excerpts in Examples 2.41a and 2.41b.

EXAMPLE 2.41A "Jam Session," Lester Young's solo, first chorus bridge (Sudhalter 1999: 258–259)

EXAMPLE 2.41B "Jam Session," Lester Young's solo, third chorus, final A section (transcription)

Basie takes three choruses, playing characteristic blues-influenced ideas in the upper register of the piano with a particular preference for the D-A flat tritone, which features heavily in his first and last choruses; an excerpt from the start of the latter is shown in Example 2.42. Basie's trumpeter Buck Clayton also plays three choruses, probably muted, as on his solo in Basie's 1937 recording. Under this solo, the ensemble plays harmonized riffs shown in Example 2.43. The first, introduced by Goodman, is similar to that used in Henderson's 1932 recording (there have been suggestions that this originated with Claude Hopkins; see Magee

EXAMPLE 2.42 "Jam Session," Count Basie's solo, third chorus, bars 1–7 (transcription)

EXAMPLE 2.43 "Jam Session," ensemble riffs under Clayton's solo (transcription)

2005: 287 n219) and in Goodman's full orchestra arrangement. It is reintroduced later under James's solo. In the second chorus of Clayton's solo, Young can be heard introducing two further riffs, which are taken up by the ensemble.

The applause and laughter following Clayton's second chorus suggests that Johnny Hodges was ready to begin his solo but was cut off by Clayton continuing. It may have been that the players had been instructed to take only two choruses each, but after this was disregarded by Basie the other musicians were not prepared to stick to this limit. As Howard Becker has observed of more recent jam sessions:

> If there were, say, four horn players sitting in, in addition to our own, every one of them would play the same number of choruses.... [The] strict etiquette [of jam sessions] told us the number of choruses the first player played set the standard others should follow. To play more would be rude, pushy, self-aggrandizing; to play less hinted that the first player had gone too far and, worse, the following players who played less had less to say. (It usually happened that the first soloist played too many choruses, hoping to get something going even though it had started slowly.) [Becker 2000: 172].

Hodges (on alto) takes a characteristically melodic approach to his solo (but avoids the original melody), sustaining clearly defined phrases over the changes, such as in the final section of his first chorus (Example 2.44). Krupa accompanies Hodges for his three choruses on the bell of the cymbal, and later he introduces subtle punctuation on his small splash cymbal.

Alto saxophone

Walter Page takes the next two choruses, playing to modern ears what barely sounds like a solo, as he maintains the four-beat "walking" bass. However, at the time of the concert this in itself was a relatively recent development in jazz, and moreover extended bass solos were rare. Basie's 1937 recordings of "One O'Clock Jump" and "Honeysuckle Rose" both include a chorus featuring the rhythm section, but more specifically Robinson cites Page's solo on "Pagin' the Devil," recorded in September 1938 with the Kansas City Six, as "one of the earliest [bass solos] on record" (Robinson and Kernfeld n.d.). In any case, the applause that greets Page's progression up the fingerboard at Carnegie Hall is testament to the novelty of the solo. Similarly unusual for the period was Harry Carney's baritone saxophone solo, exploiting the full range of the instrument and integrating different approaches to improvisation—in successive sections of his first chorus, melodic paraphrase, sustained melody (rather like Hodges), sequential broken chords in the low register that also paraphrase the melody, and blues-based phrases (shown in Example 2.45).

Although he attempts to carry on, Carney's solo is cut off after two choruses by Goodman, who plays four choruses in his usual style, often using the flattened third, which is sometimes growled. At the end of the first chorus and the beginning of the second, there are unusual examples of Goodman placing a motive in different parts of the bar, thereby changing its emphasis (Example 2.46a). One of the other musicians responds to this, shouting "pick it up," and Krupa responds with more vigorous drumming. Similarly exceptional is a phrase over the bridge of the second chorus using the same rhythmic pattern, which, as Example 2.46b shows, begins on notes outside Goodman's usual improvising range.

Freddie Green was an important part of Count Basie's rhythm section, but he rarely played solos. One suspects that Goodman had Dick McDonough's contributions to his 1934 "Bill Dodge" version in mind

EXAMPLE 2.45 "Jam Session," Harry Carney's solo, first chorus, excerpts (transcription)

when he asked the guitarist to take the next chorus. Green retains his usual rhythm section strumming, but by voicing the chords high up the fingerboard and incorporating chromaticism he introduces a melodic element. Similarly to Page's solo, Green's chorus demonstrated the integral workings of Basie's rhythm section to the Carnegie Hall audience.

The final solo was taken by Harry James, who uses his full gamut of techniques in his three choruses, including high notes, half-valving, lip trills and several figures that again recall the virtuoso trumpet repertoire, as Example 2.47 shows. At the end of his first chorus, James influences the rhythm section, particularly Krupa, to play more quietly and attentively, and then sets up a motive that Krupa punctuates with his bass

EXAMPLE 2.46A   "Jam Session," Benny Goodman's solo, end of first chorus and beginning of second (transcription)

EXAMPLE 2.46B   "Jam Session," Benny Goodman's solo, second chorus, bars 9–10
(transcription)

EXAMPLE 2.47   "Jam Session," Harry James's solo, third chorus, bars 9–16
(transcription)

drum. Krupa is more directly responsive to the improvisation of Goodman and James than to the other musicians in the "Jam Session."

The number concludes with four collective choruses; although they
are somewhat directionless, they include some interesting features. In
the first of these choruses, the ensemble places heavy accents on the
fourth beat of every other bar, the figure used in the Henderson recording and subsequent Goodman performances. After the bridge, Krupa

places the accent instead on the second beat of the bar, and James leads the rest of the ensemble to conform. James can frequently be heard attempting to lead backing riffs, and Krupa introduces a four-bar crescendo in the penultimate chorus, both in an effort to lend some form to this final section. There is a better sense of specific ownership of the bridge sections in the final three choruses, which are taken by Young, then James and Clayton trading two-bar solos and finally Basie, over a chromatic line in the ensemble again initiated by James.

Although he doesn't take a solo, Krupa's playing in the "Jam Session," transplanted into Basie's rhythm section, is arguably the most interesting of all the musicians who took part. Schuller argues that Krupa intrudes on Basie's rhythm section here (Schuller 1989: 240); I suggest that Basie, Page and Green channel Krupa's enthusiasm with the result that, unlike many of the Goodman band's performances, the "Jam Session" is only fractionally (rather than significantly) faster at the end than the beginning. Krupa demonstrates a lightness of touch rarely observed in the other large ensemble numbers in the concert, and he responds sensitively in accompanying the different soloists. Notably, Krupa's drumming in the closing stages of the "Jam Session" is dominated by the hi-hat, reflecting the technique of Jo Jones in Basie's rhythm section.

TRIO AND QUARTET

JOHN GREEN's "BODY and Soul," with lyrics by Robert Sour and Edward Heyman, is "one of the most recorded tunes in jazz," according to José Bowen, who is working on an exhaustive study of recorded versions (2007). The song was initially popularized in London, where it was published and probably therefore written (Fuld 2000: 148). Goodman alluded to this link with Britain when he included "Body and Soul" on a shortwave broadcast from New York to London in January 1937. "Body and Soul" was recorded in early 1930 by a number of leading British dance bands, including those of Jack Hylton and Bert Ambrose. Later in the year, it was taken up by Paul Whiteman and interpolated by Libby Holman into a show called *Three's a Crowd*, securing similar success in the United States, and it was also recorded by Louis Armstrong (Suskin 2000: 130). Bowen argues that Coleman Hawkins's popular 1939 version, rather than the sheet music or the early performance history, set a standard key (D flat) and tempo (quarter note = 90) for the piece (2007). However, Goodman anticipates this in a series of performances up to and including Carnegie Hall, and they also constitute rare early examples of performances without a vocal.

"Body and Soul" was the second number ever recorded by the Benny Goodman Trio in their first session on July 13, 1935, and there are recordings available of several live performances by the group from 1937. Following Carnegie Hall Goodman did not play it again until 1942, suggesting that the concert performance could mark the end of a phase in its development. There is evidence to suggest that sometime between January and March 1937 Goodman reconceptualized his approach to "Body and Soul," and that this reached its apotheosis at Carnegie Hall, by some measure the slowest available performance from the Trio up to that date. In the live performances in 1937 and 1938, the structure was cut down to two choruses of the 32-bar AABA form, omitting an extra BA that was included presumably to bring the number up to the required length for the side of a record in 1935. In the revised structure, Goodman plays the three A sections of the first chorus and Teddy Wilson takes the bridge; essentially, they swap leads on the second chorus.

Barry Kernfeld uses "Body and Soul" as a case study in the entry on Improvisation in *The New Grove Dictionary of Jazz*, pointing out that in the 1935 Trio recording both Goodman and Wilson use melodic paraphrase as a basis for their performances. Goodman "scarcely alters the theme," and he repeats his rendition consistently on further occurrences of the A section, but in Wilson's solos "notes from the song serve merely as signposts within a florid, largely newly invented line" (Kernfeld n.d.). Goodman and Wilson's performances at Carnegie Hall continue to exemplify these characteristics. Example 2.48 shows that Goodman's

EXAMPLE 2.48 "Body and Soul," Benny Goodman, first chorus, bars 1–8, 1935 (Kernfeld) and Carnegie Hall, showing Teddy Wilson's harmonization (transcription)

rendition of the main theme at Carnegie Hall is very similar to that of his 1935 recording. However, his performance is straighter, as he adheres more strictly to the triplet subdivisions of the beat whereas earlier versions are more flexible rhythmically; he avoids ornamentation (as in bars 4 and 5), and most notably he disregards the blue note at the end of bar 7. When he plays the bridge in the second chorus, Goodman diverts significantly from the melody in bars 3 and 4 and 7 and 8, as shown in Example 2.49. The destinations of these improvisational flourishes, A in bar 3 and C flat in bar 7 (the latter being derived from the original melody), were established and used consistently from March 1937, although they appear individually in performances prior to that. Indeed, Wilson emphasizes Goodman's C flat in bar 7 as if he were expecting it, using a tritone substitution rather than the expected G⁷ at this point, both at Carnegie Hall and previously in October 1937.

Wilson's renditions of the melody of "Body and Soul" are more varied across the available performances than Goodman's are. His capacity for flexibility and inventiveness is clear in the 1935 session, where the melody is much less explicit in his performance on the alternate take than on the released recording. In general, Wilson's solos at Carnegie Hall often demonstrate development of the stride pattern into three-part texture with florid upper line, a more sustained middle part and bass line as in his first solo on the bridge of "Body and Soul," shown in Example 2.50. As in this example, Wilson's solos often have a double-time feel. This is also implied by Krupa's brushes, usually as fills rather than to coincide with the soloists. In all the extant performances, Wilson relies less on the melody in his solos on the

EXAMPLE 2.50   "Body and Soul" Teddy Wilson's solo, first chorus, bars 17–20
(transcription)

A sections than on the bridge, maybe not only because of the difficulties inherent in the modulating progression but also because he is conscious that by the second chorus the main theme has already been stated three times by Goodman. However, Example 2.51 shows that the melody appears in the middle part in Wilson's solo on the second A section in the second chorus, demonstrating that although it is not heard as explicitly it is not far from his mind. Wilson's solos are rich in harmonic substitution, inserting fifth-based progressions in place of stepwise harmonic movement and vice versa. In early versions of "Body and Soul," Wilson is inclined to treat the first three bars of the piece, where he is accompanying Goodman, as a ii-V-I in D flat major, using the altered dominant, A flat augmented, initially for the entirety of the second bar and then for the second half of this bar. The additional altered dominant that Wilson plays in bar 2 at Carnegie Hall (see Example 2.48) can also be heard in an October 1937 broadcast. This creates a circle of fifths–type progression in the second bar, which Wilson often voices distinctively in the upper register of the piano.

EXAMPLE 2.51   "Body and Soul," Teddy Wilson's solo, second chorus, bar 12
(transcription)

Although the coda for "Body and Soul" was evidently formulated at or before the 1935 session, the arrangement of the final A section immediately preceding it developed alongside Goodman's aforementioned alterations to his performance of the melody between January and March 1937. In earlier versions, Goodman begins to play the melody again in this final section, either immediately or from the second bar, but from March 1937 he continues his solo while Wilson reintroduces the melody in octaves for the first four bars. The Carnegie Hall performance of this rearrangement is particularly effective in achieving a sense of climax at the start of the final section, as momentum is achieved through Krupa's double time coinciding with Goodman's solo.

"Avalon" was made famous by Al Jolson, who claimed a writer's credit alongside Vincent Rose and later Buddy DeSylva. No doubt the furor over the plagiarism of the song's melody from "E lucevan le stelle," an aria from the opera *Tosca*, which culminated in the court finding in favor of Giacomo Puccini's publishers in January 1921, helped to increase sales and resulted in the song becoming the equivalent of number one in the same month (Gardner 2000: 188; *New York Times* 1921). The song became popular among jazz musicians from the late 1920s and was the only tune in Crawford and Magee's core repertory that was recorded more often in Europe than in the United States between 1900 and 1942 (1992: xxiii). Avalon, or Avalon Bay, is the main city on Santa Catalina Island, California, which was developed as a holiday resort from the late 19th century. The resurgence of the song coincided with a rise in publicity for the resort under the auspices of William Wrigley, who from 1927 offered large cash prizes for those who swam between the mainland and the island, in preparation for the opening of the Catalina Casino in 1929 (Dean 1980/R1996). "Avalon" was a relatively recent addition to the repertoire of the Goodman Quartet. Having been rehearsed for inclusion in *Hollywood Hotel* (although it did not make the film's final cut), it was broadcast in May and June 1937 and recorded in the studio the following month.[5] It was then featured in two further broadcasts prior to Carnegie Hall. As with "Body and Soul," Goodman did not return to "Avalon" until some time after Carnegie Hall—in this case the 1950s—although he continued to perform it regularly after that time.

The four eight-bar phrases in the melody of "Avalon" are closely related, featuring a similar conjunct melodic shape that resembles the Puccini aria, but each one is different. The basis of the Goodman Quartet's version of "Avalon" is very similar to the published song, and when performed at fast tempi the slow moving melody and relatively straightforward harmonic changes were an ideal vehicle for virtuosic improvisation. Goodman performed it in E flat major, following contemporary jazz practice of Coleman Hawkins and Jimmie Lunceford, who both recorded versions in 1935. As with the Trio's "Body and Soul," the recorded arrangement established the pattern for subsequent live performances of the piece, including the introduction and coda. The introduction loosely resembles "Taps," a bugle call associated with the U.S. military; it was played by Goodman on the first available recorded live performance but allocated to Hampton from the recording session onward. The final chorus, which forms the coda, uses a chromatic descent followed by a blues-inflected figure, shown in Example 2.52, for the first two phrases. The dominant pedal under the chromatic sections was developed sometime before October 1937. The third phrase of this chorus is given over to a pseudo-improvised *tutti*, with the melody on the vibraphone and Goodman playing in his upper register. In the final phrase of the number, the descending chromatic sequence is extended until the cadence. On broadcasts the Quartet was usually joined by the Goodman Orchestra for the blues-influenced figure in the coda, but this did not occur at Carnegie Hall. This coda is similar to the transition passage before the final chorus in Eddie Durham's arrangement for Lunceford, which uses a similar chromatic descent followed by a passage around the flattened third. The arrangement for Michel Warlop's orchestra, which accompanied Hawkins, also uses a descending chromatic sequence to form the brief coda.

EXAMPLE 2.52   "Avalon," coda, bars 1–8 (transcription)

Goodman's performance of the melody of "Avalon" at Carnegie Hall is consistent with previous versions. Although he employs significant rhythmic variation, he retains the original straight rhythm in the third bar of each phrase, to which the word "Avalon" is set (the final line instead has the internal rhyme, "And so I think I'll *travel on* to Avalon" at this point instead). Goodman makes some small alterations to the melody, in particular embellishing (by the time of Carnegie Hall, sacrificing the melody altogether) the final rather predictable descent to the tonic. In previous performances, following the introduction and head, Wilson, Goodman and Hampton each took one solo chorus. The same order of soloists was retained at Carnegie Hall but with each solo doubled in length. In earlier, slower versions such as the studio recordings, Wilson uses more harmonic substitutions; his later solos retain the basic structure of the original harmony and tend to emphasize melodic invention. However, in all the broadcast versions Wilson elaborates the harmony strikingly and consistently in bars 9–12 of his solo. At Carnegie Hall this occurs in his second chorus, in which he uses a rhythmically diminuted sequential repetition of parallel 10ths in the left hand around the V⁷ harmony, as shown in Example 2.53. He also includes more florid playing and is less reliant on the melody than in previous performances. Krupa backs Wilson's solo sensitively using brushes, and also drumming on the rim of the snare drum and on the cymbal stand to create a rhythmic but light accompaniment that alludes to earlier styles of jazz.

Goodman's recorded solos on "Avalon" prior to Carnegie Hall are all significantly different. There are some similarities with the broadcast of just over a month before and some use of melodic notes, but his solo at Carnegie Hall is neither preconstructed nor primarily reliant on the melody. The simplicity of the basic material of "Avalon" allows Goodman to demonstrate his improvisational facility in a combination of melodic paraphrase, licks and playing over changes. Hampton, on the other hand, reuses ideas from previous solos. His earlier solos paraphrase the melody closely, but this is less clear at Carnegie Hall, where he creates new lines through sequential repetition and also develops rhythmic interest in his solo by integrating the rhythmic idea from the coda.

Under the applause following "Avalon," Hampton can be heard beginning to play "Stompin' at the Savoy," which was noticed at the time by the critic George Simon. Reviewing the concert in *Metronome*, he commented

EXAMPLE 2.53   "Avalon," Teddy Wilson's solo, second chorus, bars 9–12

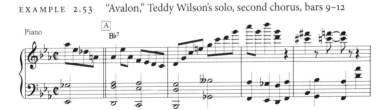

that Hampton "got off to a wrong start on *The Man I Love*, with continued applause for the previous number covering up his mistake" (Simon 1938b: 18). The Goodman Quartet recorded George Gershwin's ballad "The Man I Love" in the same recording session as "Avalon" in July 1937. Gershwin's death on July 11, 1937, might have prompted inclusion of one of his songs. Despite being cut from the shows *Lady Be Good*, *Strike Up the Band* and *Rosalie* (Suskin 2000), "The Man I Love" achieved considerable success, reaching its peak of popularity in May 1928 (Gardner 2000: 202).[6] It was recorded by several popular singers and groups such as Paul Whiteman's Orchestra, Isham Jones's and the Casa Loma Orchestra, but it was not particularly well established as a jazz standard before 1938. Aside from the studio recording, no other performances of this number by Goodman prior to Carnegie Hall are available, though it then remained in the repertoire of Goodman's small groups for the rest of his career. He also performed it in an arrangement for big band from 1940.

The Goodman Quartet's arrangement of the "The Man I Love" was simple: two choruses, with Goodman playing the A sections in the first and Wilson, unaccompanied, on the bridge in the relative minor. Hampton took over for the first half of the second chorus with Wilson again on the bridge and Goodman to finish. Goodman's repetitions of the main theme are virtually identical and based on a consistent rhythmic interpretation. This theme is accompanied by sustained chords from the vibraphone and low-register piano, resulting in a distinctive rich, but decaying, timbre. The harmony of the theme allows a descending bass line to be constructed over the first six bars. At Carnegie Hall, Krupa accents the changes of harmony strongly with cymbal and bass drum, and the low register of the piano is faint, producing quite a different effect from the original recording.

Wilson's solos over the bridge of "The Man I Love" on the 1937 recording and at Carnegie Hall all use a tonic pedal and an inner descending chromatic line, which is in effect a transposition of the bass line of the main theme. Wilson's first solo on the released recording seems both uncharacteristic and incongruous within the overall performance (Example 2.54a). It is played straight without a hint of swing or obvious rhythmic freedom, and the left hand fill in the fourth bar and the harmony at the end of the section sound more like Gershwin himself. Although Wilson's second solo on this recording shows more rhythmic and stylistic freedom, it remains for the most part strongly anchored by the C pedal and the elaboration is somewhat hesitant. At Carnegie Hall, Wilson's first solo (Example 2.54b) paraphrases the melody closely over the aforementioned pedal and chromatic inner line, but the second (Example 2.54c) develops a fragment of this material and inserts a circle of fifths progression into the fourth bar.

EXAMPLE 2.54 "The Man I Love," Teddy Wilson's solo, a. July 1937, first chorus;
b. Carnegie Hall, first chorus; c. Carnegie Hall, second chorus (transcriptions)

Hampton is effective in constructing melodic lines that avoid simply following the obvious descent of the harmony, which he includes as a counterpoint. In the first part of his solo, he uses mainly rising arpeggios to counteract the pull of the harmony, as shown in Example 2.55. Although Hampton's solo is not an obvious paraphrase of the melody, he draws more specifically on its oscillations in the second phrase of this chorus (Example 2.56).

Vibraphone

Vibraphone

A broadcast of "The Man I Love" from March 1938 exposes the Carnegie Hall performance as developmental. In this later version, Goodman's statements of the theme are much more flexible, and Wilson and Hampton play stronger solo lines. Goodman provides a sustained line based on the voice leading of the harmony *sotto voce* behind Hampton, who no longer states this himself. Wilson's solos introduce more variety into the bridge sections, in which the pedal becomes less explicit, pursuing the approach of his second Carnegie Hall solo.

Goodman's tribute to Gershwin and the first half of the Carnegie Hall concert concluded with "I Got Rhythm," which Gershwin wrote for his musical *Girl Crazy* in 1930. Initially the song was recorded as a vocal number, and for two years even the most jazz-influenced versions included at least one vocal chorus. Red Nichols recorded "I Got Rhythm" in October 1930, just over a week after the opening night of *Girl Crazy* on Broadway. Nichols had put the pit band together for the show, including Goodman, who was freelancing at the time. There was a falling out toward the end of the show's run when Goodman used Nichols's best musicians to secure one of his first (albeit short-run) engagements as a bandleader (Firestone 1993: 69). Goodman's main solo contribution to Nichols's "I Got Rhythm" was to growl the melody of the bridge. Crawford posits this recording as indicative of establishment of "I Got Rhythm" as a jazz standard, when other artists presented it as a popular song or used it as a basis for new compositions (Crawford 2004: 157). As discussed earlier, an example of the latter is "Don't Be That Way," and therefore Gershwin's song frames the first half of the Carnegie Hall concert just as it was emerging as a significant aspect of the jazz canon.

"I Got Rhythm" had been in the repertoire of Goodman's Orchestra since at least May 1935, but the first commercially available performance by the Quartet is a broadcast in April 1937. Both Wilson and Hampton recorded their own versions around this time, which might have influenced its inclusion. Whereas all the other small-group repertoire performed at Carnegie Hall was recorded in the years prior to the concert, or in the case of "Dizzy Spells" soon afterward, Goodman did not record "I Got Rhythm" with his own group until 1945 (with a sextet). The Quartet established an arrangement for "I Got Rhythm" in or prior to the April 1937 broadcast that was also the basis for the Carnegie Hall performance. Adopting a fast tempo, Wilson, Goodman and Hampton join at two-bar intervals to play an eight-bar introductory statement of the main theme, suggesting a spontaneous jam session although in fact this was the Quartet's usual practice for the beginning of "I Got Rhythm."

Although ostensibly in the standard 32-bar popular song format, Gershwin's "I Got Rhythm" has an extra two bars in the final section, which are included in Goodman's version. In the first chorus Goodman treats the melody quite freely, in particular improvising new material over the final two bars of each A phrase. Wilson uses a I I° ii⁷ V⁷ progression in place of the usual I vi ii⁷ V⁷ throughout. The bridge is built on the usual circle of fifths progression, enlivened by Wilson's extremely chromatic "walking" bass line, but even with Wilson's additions the A sections remain relatively static harmonically. The three front-line players tackle this in different ways. At points Wilson diverts completely from the original harmony, most significantly at the start of his second phrase, shown in Example 2.57, where he uses a melodic and harmonic sequence to temporarily step outside the key.

EXAMPLE 2.57   "I Got Rhythm," Teddy Wilson's solo, first chorus, bars 9–10 (transcription)

Goodman and Hampton draw on diatonic motivic repetition in their solos. Example 2.58 shows how Goodman uses this technique over the A sections, and his adaptation of a motive to fit with the harmonic progression of the bridge. Hampton also uses small motives in his solo, but unlike Goodman's these are often three beats in length, and therefore when repeated are set in different parts of the bar, as shown in Example 2.59. Wilson deliberately starts playing B flat minor harmony throughout the A sections in the second chorus of Hampton's solo, to which Hampton responds by playing D flats and diminished arpeggios. However, in the final section of this chorus, Hampton remains in the tonic major, and in response Wilson abandons the minor after four bars.

EXAMPLE 2.58 "I Got Rhythm," Benny Goodman's use of motive (transcriptions)

EXAMPLE 2.59 "I Got Rhythm," Lionel Hampton's solo, second chorus, bars 17–22 (transcription)

Following the solos, the arrangement of "I Got Rhythm" performed at Carnegie Hall concludes with four *tutti* choruses, the first of which includes dramatic stop-time at the seventh bar of the first two phrases, followed by two *tacet* bars save for Krupa's bass drum maintaining the beat. There is a further stop-time device in the following chorus, in which the stop halts the repetition of a sixteenth-note turn figure with a crescendo. In the summer of 1937, this was lifted from the arrangement of "I Got

Rhythm" and incorporated into "I've Got a Heartful of Music," which was the Quartet's featured number in *Hollywood Hotel*.[7] Krupa contributes to generating excitement over this sequence of four choruses by increasing his activity and volume. This is particularly noticeable in the successive bridge sections: in the second chorus, he adds cymbal crashes anticipating the first beat of every other bar where the chord change occurs; in the third, he plays a syncopated rhythm on the tom-toms; and finally he plays sixteenth notes throughout at top volume. Ultimately, Goodman wails in his upper register, the same technique he used when he recorded "I Got Rhythm" with Nichols at the start of the decade.

As with "I Got Rhythm," Goodman first recorded "China Boy" with Red Nichols, but at a slightly earlier session in July 1930. Written by Dick Winfree and Phil Boutelje, "China Boy" was published in 1922 but did not become popular with jazz musicians until some years later (Crawford and Magee 1992). The original verse incorporates standard signifiers of exoticism (minor key with open fifths in the bass and the whole tone scale). Interestingly, Wilson uses distinctive parallel fifths in the bass under the third phrase of the head in Goodman's 1936 recording of this number. The lyrics position both singer and audience as observing a lullaby sung by a woman, referred to only in racialized terms as "almond eyes," to her "china boy." The lullaby itself, which is the chorus of the song, is in the form ABCA', with the C phrase in the key of the flattened mediant, relative major of the tonic minor, from which a minor version of the subdominant is also borrowed in the B phrase. The chorus uses a dotted half-note plus quarter-note rhythm to suggest the lilt of the lullaby.

Contrary to many of the other numbers performed by Goodman's Trio and Quartet at Carnegie Hall, "China Boy" had been initially taken up by smaller jazz groups such as McKenzie and Condon's Chicagoans, which included Gene Krupa at the time of their 1927 recording. This constitutes an origin for the stop-time used in Goodman's performances, which originally gave space for a bass solo. The song became popular with larger orchestras later, following the release of Paul Whiteman's version in 1929 (Boutelje worked for Whiteman as a pianist and arranger). This version retained an association with the style of earlier recordings with an extended clarinet solo by Irving Friedman, and it became famous for Bix Beiderbecke's solo. Goodman recorded "China Boy" in 1936, which is the only other Trio performance available, although it was also included on several *Camel Caravan* broadcasts from July 1936, and Goodman continued to perform the piece with various small groups throughout his career.

Goodman treats the rhythm and melody of "China Boy" quite freely in the head, improvising new material around melody notes in two four-bar sections at the end of the second and final phrases. In common with the other up-tempo numbers, the group seems to have planned to take two choruses each in the concert, as opposed to the single chorus solos on the recording. However, the structure is even further elongated with shouted directions to "Take one more [chorus]" for Krupa and Goodman. "China Boy" was the first small-group number in the second half of the concert, and the group seems to be prepared to jam more freely than before the interval. Wilson takes the first solo, which unlike some of his solos on other numbers in the concert is built around the melody and harmony of the original, as in the second phrase of his second chorus, shown in Example 2.60. Goodman largely avoids paraphrasing the melody but introduces two motives, transcribed in Example 2.61, in the second eight-bar section of his

EXAMPLE 2.60 "China Boy," Teddy Wilson's solo, second chorus, bars 9–16 (transcription)

EXAMPLE 2.61 "China Boy," Benny Goodman's solo, first chorus, bars 9–15 (transcription)

solo; they form the basis of his subsequent improvisation. The first (X), an ornamented descent, derives from Friedman, Whiteman's clarinetist. Goodman had included this idea in his solo on the recording he made with Nichols, but it was not in evidence on his own 1936 version. The second (Y) is a common Goodman lick that is used in "China Boy" particularly where the harmony moves back to the tonic chord. Later in the performance, Goodman varies, develops and adapts these ideas within different harmonic settings; Example 2.62 shows his use of versions of Y in his second chorus.

EXAMPLE 2.62 "China Boy," Benny Goodman's solo, second chorus, bars 1–13 (transcription)

Just as Goodman drew on earlier performances of "China Boy" in his solo, so Krupa brought his previous experience of the piece to bear, incorporating the stop-time device from McKenzie and Condon's version as the basis for a drum solo. Krupa plays three solo choruses mainly using brushes, the first on the snare drum, the second incorporating tom-toms working up to continuous eighth notes that are maintained in the third, using one brush on the snare and one stick for the toms and cymbal. Krupa accelerates markedly, particularly in his final chorus, but something approaching the original tempo is regained by the group after his solo. The following chorus is shared between Goodman and Wilson; the latter plays over the third eight-bar section. In the 1936 recording, the coda followed this chorus, but at Carnegie Hall a shout of "Go on, Ben" leads to a further solo chorus. Goodman replicates the phrase that introduced the two motives, and in addition to the continued pervasiveness of motive Y he also draws on X, which appears in part at the start and end of this chorus. A shout of "One more, Ben"

prompts yet another chorus for Goodman, but then "We're going out" directs the group to the coda.

The introduction and coda of the arrangement of "China Boy" feature the piano. Table 2.2 shows the four-bar "tag" progression used at the beginning and end of the arrangement in the 1936 recording, with two chords in each bar. At Carnegie Hall, Wilson extends and adapts this progression to form an eight-bar phrase with one chord per bar for the introduction, as shown in Table 2.3. On the 1936 recording and at Carnegie Hall, the coda consists of eight bars for clarinet and drums, eight bars for solo piano (both of which are "free" harmonically) and then *tutti* for the original tag progression.

Table 2.2 "Tag" progression in "China Boy"

	Gm^7	G#^{o}	F	D^7	Gm^7	C^7	F	C^7
F major:	ii^7	#ii^{o}	I	VI	ii^7	V^7	I	V^7

Table 2.3 Introduction to "China Boy" at Carnegie Hall

	F	F^{o}	Gm^7	C^7	F	D^7	G^7	C^7
F major:	I	I^{o}	ii^7	V^7	I	VI^7	II^7	V^7

"Stompin' at the Savoy," an Edgar Sampson composition originally recorded by Chick Webb in 1934, refers to the Savoy Ballroom in Harlem, where Webb was resident and where he battled other bands, including Goodman's. The number had been in the repertoire of Goodman's Orchestra since at least 1935, but the first documented performance by the Quartet is a broadcast in November 1936. This was followed by a studio recording in December, the first available version. Unusually, and unlike "I Got Rhythm," which passed from Quartet to orchestra repertories, "Stompin' at the Savoy" was used regularly in both formats for the duration of Goodman's career, and some features of the Webb/Goodman big-band version influenced the Quartet arrangement.

The form of the Quartet's "Stompin' at the Savoy" is extended significantly at Carnegie Hall compared with earlier versions, including development of the introduction. The 1936 recording began with the triplet figure introduced by Hampton and then harmonized by Wilson and Goodman, which outlines the falling major third that concludes the melody. At Carnegie Hall an additional eight bars at the start of the piece introduce the rising minor third, which pervades the main theme, over a dominant pedal. This part of the introduction seems to have been developed as the result of including "Stompin' at the Savoy" in two *Camel Caravan* broadcasts in which spoken introductions were made over the start of the number. In March 1937 Goodman introduces the members of the Quartet who then join in with the vamp, and in August 1937 Wilson, Krupa and Hampton improvise under Goodman's dialogue with the host.

The theme of "Stompin' at the Savoy" is inherently antiphonal. Previous big-band arrangements designated one motive to the brass and the other to the saxophones, and in the Quartet arrangement there is a similar split between clarinet and piano. At Carnegie Hall, the vibraphone, which was omitted from these statements of the main theme in previous performances, echoes the clarinet. This provides an additional component, but the texture remains clear as a result of differences in timbre and register, as shown in Example 2.63. Goodman carries the melody in the bridge, accompanied by sustained vibraphone chords and decorative piano fills over the left-hand stride pattern.

"Stompin' at the Savoy" is really a feature for Hampton, with Wilson allotted one solo bridge and Goodman only an occasional break. In his first solo chorus, Hampton introduces some rhythmic interest in a solo that often centers on the tonic pitch. The harmony of the bridge, although following a circle of fifths progression beginning with the subdominant (G flat), reaches keys apparently quite remote from the overall key of the piece (B major, E major, A major). In addition, there are chromatic shifts in the harmony within each key center. Both Hampton and Wilson use melodic paraphrase as a technique for dealing with this harmonic complexity in their solos. In Hampton's second chorus, the accompaniment changes to pre-arranged "stomping" quarter notes for piano and clarinet, and Hampton plays melodic fragments with similar regular rhythm (including a quotation from *William Tell*) that are answered by Krupa.

The format of what was the final ensemble chorus in 1936 is played four times in total at Carnegie Hall, again in response to shouted

EXAMPLE 2.63   "Stompin' at the Savoy," head (transcription)

directions to take "one more." Initially in the first of these choruses Hampton plays the melody in octaves with Goodman improvising above, and then Hampton imitates Goodman, but thereafter the A sections are collectively improvised. Similarly to the breaks for Goodman toward the end of the full-band arrangement, stop-time in the bridge creates the opportunity for two-bar breaks in this final group of choruses in the Quartet version. In the first two ensemble choruses the breaks are taken by Hampton, Goodman and Hampton again; those of the second chorus are shown in Example 2.64. Hampton clearly outplays Goodman on these breaks, principally because he plays in double time, and in the third chorus Goodman suddenly gives up his break, telling Hampton to "take it." In the fourth and final chorus, Krupa solos in the final stop-time passage, although there is some uncertainty between the musicians, with Hampton terminating his break to let him go ahead. On earlier performances where there is only a single chorus in this format, the breaks were taken by Hampton, but they were often accompanied by Krupa.

EXAMPLE 2.64 "Stompin' at the Savoy," second ensemble chorus, bars 17–22 (transcription)

The final small-group number of the concert was a Hampton original, "Dizzy Spells," a late addition to the program of which there are no recorded performances prior to the Carnegie Hall concert. Having included the number in the *Camel Caravan* broadcast immediately prior to the concert, the Quartet made a studio recording of the number in March 1938, with Dave Tough replacing Krupa, and broadcast it again later in the year. At Carnegie Hall, the head is prefaced by an introduction that begins with a 16-bar drum solo setting a breakneck tempo, followed by repetition of a cadential figure.

The head is virtuosic but musically quite straightforward: parallel tonic (E flat major) scales in eighth notes for clarinet, piano and vibraphone beginning on the root, third and fifth of the tonic triad respectively, over tonic and dominant harmony. This part of the melody ends with a passage that descends sequentially. The bridge is based on a series of dominant sevenths beginning on the subdominant, descending chromatically every other bar. Unusually, this phrase is repeated so that the bridge is 16 bars long and the overall form of the head is AABB'A. The entire head is repeated, at which point the piano part can be heard more clearly in the octave above the vibraphone and clarinet, resulting in open rather than closed-position parallel triads.

Goodman, Wilson and Hampton play two solo choruses each. In Goodman's solo, the static harmony of the A sections leads him toward repetition of small motives while deftly negotiating the chromatic harmony in the bridge. Hampton, similarly to Goodman, uses repetition over the A sections of his solo, but his approach to the bridge, like Wilson's, is built strongly on voice leading between the chords. Wilson's solo is richly inventive, beginning with a possible quotation from Gershwin's *An American in Paris* and departing from the expected string of eighth notes to play distinctly separate phrases, as shown in Example 2.65. Having begun the bridge with oscillating spread chords, he then creates a contrapuntal texture as shown in Example 2.66.

Following the solos, the arrangement incorporates a curious section consisting of two 14-bar phrases. Each begins with six bars of collective improvisation on tonic harmony with stop-time on the first beat of the seventh, at which point the augmented dominant chord is built up and reiterated with increasingly shorter note values recalling the introduction. This 14-bar phrase is then repeated and is followed by a further eight bars of collective improvisation before the head proper resumes. Arguably the most significant musical error of the concert occurs after the first A section of this head, as Goodman goes forward to the bridge but Hampton and Wilson repeat the A section. Realizing his error, Goodman immediately switches back to improvising in the tonic key, at the same time as Wilson starts playing the harmony of the bridge, resulting in eight bars of harmonic chaos. Hampton cues the bridge, and the group plays eight bars over the chromatic harmonies before returning to the tonic. Krupa plays what sounds like an "ending" following a further eight bars, but it becomes clear that this section is in fact the start of a new chorus. The ensemble plays a further two choruses incorporating drum breaks in the bridge of the first. Following his mistake, Goodman sounds quieter, suggesting he has moved or turned away from the microphone toward his ensemble to communicate with them more closely.

EXAMPLE 2.65 "Dizzy Spells," Teddy Wilson's solo, first chorus, bars 1–15 (transcription)

EXAMPLE 2.66 "Dizzy Spells," Teddy Wilson's solo, first chorus, bars 9–16 (transcription)

CONCLUSION

The Carnegie Hall performances were often consistent with Goodman's previous renditions of these numbers and the performances leading up to the concert often demonstrate the evolution of standard interpretations. Goodman's studio recordings were generally "safe" performances, from which further development took place. Loren Schoenberg has suggested that this may have been because the sessions took place at 9:00 A.M., when the band had usually just finished playing in the early hours (Levinson 1999: 37). Having established a clear style for the band through the Henderson arrangements, Goodman then applied this to the appropriated numbers, and there is evidence that this was achieved collectively in rehearsal as well as through the work of arrangers. Wilson recalled that Goodman was the arbiter in a similar process with the small groups: "It was Goodman who decided whose idea would be used for the introduction, whose idea would go in the interlude, and whose idea to change key at a certain point would be used, and of course he contributed ideas himself" (Wilson et al. 2001: 50).

Clearly, the situation of the concert had a particular impact on those arrangements which could be opened up for more extended improvisation. The "Jam Session" best exemplifies the striking variety of approaches to improvisation in the concert, but alongside this some of Goodman's sidemen felt sufficiently pressured to reproduce the same solo on successive performances. Goodman is most inventive when improvising on numbers with familiar changes, such as the small-group pieces and the Henderson arrangements, drawing on an emerging core repertory that was already spawning contrafacts in anticipation of bebop. Other items in the concert, notably the killer-dillers "Swingtime in the Rockies" and "Life Goes to a Party," correspond with the advanced harmonic invention shown in Wilson's improvisations. This combination of consistency and innovation epitomizes Goodman's aim when he formed his orchestra: "to get good musicians, work on intonation, a blend of tone and uniform phrasing in rehearsals, then depend on them to take care of themselves pretty much on the stand" (Goodman and Kolodin 1939: 140).

PART THREE

Representation

After the Concert attend the Battle of Swing between Chick Webb and his Orchestra with Ella Fitzgerald and Count Basie and his Orchestra with Billie Holliday [sic] TONIGHT Savoy Ballroom Lenox Ave. & 140th St.

— "CARNEGIE HALL PROGRAM" 1938: 9

REPERCUSSIONS

THIS ADVERTISEMENT IN the Carnegie Hall program directed the audience to the Savoy Ballroom immediately after the concert. According to George Simon in *Metronome*, Krupa, Hampton and "the Benny Goodman family jammed into Harlem's Hot House to see and hear the Count gain a newspapermen's [sic] decision over the famed Chick" (Simon 1938a: 15). The battle had been organized by Helen Oakley, who objected

FIGURE 3.1   Martha Tilton in the Carnegie Hall scene of *The Benny Goodman Story* (1955). "Benny," played by Steve Allen, looks on (Jerry Ohlinger's Movie Material Store).

FIGURE 3.2   Harry James takes a solo on "Sing, Sing, Sing" in the Carnegie Hall scene of *The Benny Goodman Story*. Buck Clayton is seated on James's right and Gene Krupa accompanies on the drums (Jerry Ohlinger's Movie Material Store).

to the way in which Webb was allowing Ella Fitzgerald to "dominate" the band and hoped that being beaten by Basie would help him see the error of his ways (Korall 2002: 36–37). Simon appears to have held a similar view, but the result of the battle was so close that there had to be "an actual vote and a show of hands," rather than the usual approximation of audience enthusiasm by volume, which contradicted the critics (Charters and Kunstadt 1962: 291). The *New York Amsterdam News* (1938a: 16) reported that "Chick Webb and Ella Fitzgerald were declared winners by the popular vote of the 'battle of swing' Sunday night after the ballots were counted. Chick led Count Basie two to one, and Ella polled three times as many votes as Billie Holiday."

The Basie-Webb battle is more than just an interesting footnote to the Carnegie Hall concert. As Stowe points out, the two events can be understood as polar opposites indicative of wider societal issues, but the overlap of performers, repertoire, audience and conventions of reception also helps to place the importance of the Carnegie Hall concert into perspective within its own time (Stowe 1994: 21). In a 1971 anthology of his swing era writing, Simon positions his review of the Carnegie Hall concert among descriptions of various contemporary band battles, which emphasizes that there were other events with perhaps an equal or even stronger claim for inclusion within the history of jazz (Simon 1971). Indeed, before the release of *The Famous 1938 Carnegie Hall Jazz Concert* album in 1950, the concert and the Savoy battle were similarly ephemeral events and the audience and musicians simply moved on, literally in some cases as Simon's account indicates, to the next live experience. Setting aside, then, for the moment, the critical reaction to the concert in 1938 and the effect of the recording on retrospective perceptions of the Carnegie Hall concert, but not discounting the potential for reviews to influence subsequent activities (aspects that I consider at length later), I begin Part Three by discussing the immediate repercussions of the concert for Goodman and his musicians.

Generally speaking, the band returned to its usual activities following the concert, beginning with a *Camel Caravan* broadcast two days later on January 18, 1938. Goodman initially took up residency at the Paramount Theater for three weeks and then, after a short tour, returned to the Madhattan Room in March (Connor 1988: 82–83). In addition to replicating the complete concert or sections from it, which will be discussed in "Re-creation" below, the details of Goodman's broadcasts and recordings over the three-month period following the concert demonstrate the basic congruence of the Carnegie Hall concert within the band's activities. "Don't Be That Way" and "One O'Clock Jump" were recorded at the full band's first studio session after the concert, followed by "Blue Room" in March 1938. "Don't Be That Way" and "Blue Room" were also broadcast prior to these sessions, along with many other numbers from the concert. Omitted from the documented performances following the concert were numbers that the analysis in Part Two demonstrates had reached a stable state: "Sometimes I'm Happy," "Blue Skies," "Swingtime in the Rockies" and "Sing, Sing, Sing" and for the small groups "Body and Soul," "Stompin' at the Savoy" and "Avalon." However, these could well have been included in the performances the band gave at the Paramount, particularly "Sing, Sing, Sing," which was becoming ubiquitous. Anomalies were "I Got Rhythm," the documented reprise of which was not until later in the year, and "Big John Special," which, although it was a longstanding item in Goodman's repertoire, had yet to be recorded and was eventually included in a studio session only in May 1938. In addition, the Quartet broadcast numbers that were programmed but not performed at Carnegie Hall, namely "I'm a Ding Dong Daddy," "Dinah" and "Tiger Rag." Beatrice Lillie was even presented as a special guest on a February broadcast, providing a link to another unrealized possibility from the plans for the concert (Connor 1988: 81–83).

Unsurprisingly, the *Camel Caravan* show on January 18, 1938, makes both implicit and explicit reference to the Carnegie Hall concert. The inclusion of "Don't Be That Way," which had been introduced in the previous week's show (prior to the concert), was explained by the presenter as a response to "a flood of letters from the students [listeners] asking that it be repeated"; and "Honeysuckle Rose," used in the "Jam Session," was performed by the Quartet. This is followed by what Connor terms "the initial example extant of a classical performance by Benny Goodman," the first movement of Mozart's Clarinet Quintet with the Coolidge String Quartet, which created an unusually rarefied atmosphere on the show (Connor 1988: 81). These items exemplify the emergence of different repercussions of the concert for Goodman and his musicians.

MOZART Inclusion of Mozart in the January 18 broadcast is undoubtedly significant as a response to the Carnegie Hall concert, and an indication of things to come for Goodman. In the words of the presenter, it would only be fair to add "a little Carnegie Hall touch to the swing school" because Goodman had "rocked those hallowed walls with *our* music." Later in the broadcast, Goodman announces, over an instrumental introduction, that Martha Tilton will sing "Mama, That Moon

Is Here Again." In a scripted exchange, typical of the *Camel Caravan* shows, Tilton protests:

TILTON: No, Professor; I'm going to sing the "Jewel Song" from Faust.
GOODMAN: You're what?
TILTON: I'm going to sing the "Jewel Song" from Faust. After all, I sang in Carnegie Hall too, I guess I can get fancy.
GOODMAN: This is one time I win. Now, if you can sing the "Jewel Song" to this music then go ahead.
TILTON: Well, it might sound like "Mama, That Moon Is Here Again" but it's the "Jewel Song" to me.
GOODMAN: Well honey, anything you sing is the "Jewel Song" to all of us.
TILTON: Thank you, Professor.

This dialogue makes explicit the contextual framework for Goodman's Mozart performance, as well as a demonstration of gender-based hierarchy in bands of the period. Tilton is shown to be constrained as a performer; she is permitted to sing only in the genre provided for her by Goodman and the band and so cannot attempt the "Jewel Song" from Gounod's opera *Faust*. Goodman believes the fusion of Gounod and swing to be impossible and preserves the stylistic division and hierarchy between swing and classical music.[8] By contrast, Tilton happily assigns equal value to a popular song and an opera aria—an inevitable consequence of the restrictions placed on her. Goodman responds to this with a patronizing tone, since he has shown that he has transcended the need to be content with performing popular songs through his performance of Mozart. Performing at Carnegie Hall potentially gives both Tilton and Goodman the right to "get fancy," performing classical music to thereby establish themselves as artists. However, only Goodman had the power to capitalize on this by asserting his autonomy as a bandleader and soloist, which also enabled him to control the performances of Tilton and other band members. Goodman went on to record the entire Mozart Quintet in April, marking the beginning of the public manifestation of what he termed his "double musical life," which was to define his later career (Firestone 1993: 247). Indeed, he was to return to Carnegie Hall many times to perform classical music as well as jazz, beginning with the premiere of Bela Bartók's *Contrasts*, which he commissioned with violinist Joseph Szigeti, in January 1939 (Hancock 2008: 207).

By contrast, artistic autonomy not being permitted to Tilton in the *Camel Caravan* script was also manifest in reality for Goodman's musicians. Examining the Carnegie Hall concert performances in context demonstrates that maintaining the standards Goodman demanded necessarily had a direct impact on performances. Over a series of performances of a particular number, not only the interpretation but often also the solos develop consistency. Magee points out that "Nowhere in the accounts of Goodman's rehearsals do observers mention improvised solos," but this does not mean that these were not important to Goodman, or indeed that he had no influence on them (Magee 2005: 213). Goodman wrestled with the dichotomy of authenticity to jazz practice and public demand in 1939:

> The most important element is still improvisation, the liberty a soloist has to stand up and play a chorus in the way he feels—sometimes good, sometimes bad, but still as an expression of himself, rather than somebody else who wrote something for him. If you want to put it this way, it's something that is genuinely American, because it's the expression of an individual—a kind of free speech in music.
>
> On the other hand, I always like to have men around me who play as consistently as anyone can reasonably ask. I'd rather have a man who will play good, solid stuff six nights out of seven than the fellow who is brilliant once a week and erratic the other six. That's because I feel that the public has a right to a good performance whenever it comes in to hear us play, rather than considering itself lucky if they happen to catch us on the one night when everybody is feeling right [Goodman and Kolodin 1939: 237–238].

Similarly, tenor saxophonist Art Rollini recalled that at Billy Rose's Music Hall (in 1934):

> I had a lot to play and felt free to improvise any way that I chose but a couple of years later Benny became more critical and would listen carefully to every note a man played. Then I felt restricted and often played the same jazz solos [Rollini 1989: 35].

By late 1937, becoming aware that lack of consistency in his improvising could lose him his job, Rollini

> would get solos written on my sheet [music] but, seeing so many men come and go, I began to hand them over, first to Vido [Musso] and then to Babe [Russin]. I was content with playing what I had, and said to myself, "Let the other guy try to please Benny" [62–63].

This pressure may also explain, in general terms, why musicians began to leave the band in 1938.

"DON'T BE THAT WAY"   Rumors that Gene Krupa might leave Goodman had circulated previously when his contract was up for renewal, but they resurfaced shortly after the concert (Firestone 1993: 219). Al Brackman in wrote *Melody Maker*:

> Although denied many times, indications that Gene Krupa might leave Goodman's band in April to form his own orchestra are stronger than ever. If such a move is made, it is understood that Goodman will sponsor the enterprise and lend assistance in its organisation [Brackman 1938c: 11].

Disagreements had been in evidence previously when Krupa worked under Goodman for the singer Russ Columbo; according to Hammond, Krupa complained that Goodman would only let him play with brushes (Hammond and Townsend 1977: 111). Hammond also identified the concert unequivocally as the point of fracture, citing musical reasons as the basis for the split:

> Contrary to what many think, Gene was not at his best during the Carnegie Hall concert. Benny took a new hard look at him that night. Suddenly he came to the conclusion that the way he was playing disrupted the whole structure of the band. The band had become too tight and tense, too precise. Benny wanted more subtlety within the time feeling—something he felt Gene no longer was capable of bringing to the band [in Korall 2002: 70].

For others, such as pianist Jess Stacy, it was Goodman's jealousy of Krupa's popularity with the fans that was the root of the problem: "I believe Benny did have some problems with the way [Krupa] emerged as the big star and crowd pleaser" (Firestone 1993: 221). The reality was probably something in between these perspectives. Contrary to Hammond's interpretation, Goodman is at pains to praise Krupa's technical ability in his autobiography as a drummer who gave "the rhythm section the lift it needed," although he acknowledges that they had "musical differences" and that Krupa's departure was inevitable as he "wanted to do things his own way" (Goodman and Kolodin 1939: 163–164). A further statement affords greater insight into the nature of these differences: "There was always Gene and his 'showmanship' for the writers to talk about, even if they didn't have any idea of what a great drummer he was" (206). Although he might have been personally jealous of the attention Krupa received, Goodman was clearly professionally concerned about the triumph of style over musical substance.

Undoubtedly performances for icky fans in theaters in the months following the concert contributed to the tension. Hammond reported for *DownBeat*, under the headline "Hysterical Public Split Goodman & Krupa," that

> There have been some harrowing experiences for Gene, trying to follow Benny's desires for him to relax and to play as a member of the rhythm section rather than a soloist, but finding it all impossible to disregard the crowd's pleas for more and more display of technique [Firestone 1993: 222].

Arguably, the beginning of the end can be isolated not only to the Carnegie Hall concert, as Hammond suggested retrospectively, but to Krupa's first drum break in "Don't Be That Way." This provoked an audience response that was entirely consistent with the musical style rather than the surroundings, and that in effect defined the parameters for the audience reception of the concert. By contrast, the crowd grows noticeably quiet at the start of Goodman's solo. This performance is an ideal illustration of Krupa's extroversion as opposed to Goodman's introversion, which is discussed below. According to the documentation of performances between the concert and Gene Krupa leaving the band on March 3, 1938, "Don't Be That Way" was included in three broadcasts and a recording session and therefore played more often than any other piece in this period (Connor 1988: 82). This may have been because it was a new number Goodman was preparing to record, or because it had become extremely popular, but it is possible that Goodman used repetition of the number to further exert his control over Krupa. Certainly, Krupa never plays such virtuosic solos in the subsequent extant performances of "Don't Be That Way" as at Carnegie Hall. In these later versions, the first solo is dominated by bass drum and cowbell, without the continuous sixteenth notes and punctuating cymbal crashes heard at the same point in the Carnegie Hall performance. Although Krupa plays sixteenth notes through the second solo, he doesn't use the cymbals. The restrictions Goodman placed on Krupa are confirmed by Connor's eyewitness account of Goodman and Krupa "feuding openly on stage" at the Earle Theater in Philadelphia in February 1938:

Gene, perched high on his drummer's throne downstage nodded towards Benny, gestured as if to break his sticks, pantomimed "He won't let me." Groans and hoots from the crowd. For his part Benny ignored the audience, appeared totally bored whenever Gene had a drum solo, left no doubt in anyone's mind as to his reaction to the crowd's clamor for Krupa [Connor 1988: 83].

Krupa left the band at the end of the Philadelphia engagement, followed shortly afterward by Allan Reuss and George Koenig and then by Babe Russin and Hymie Shertzer in March and April respectively (Connor 1988: 84).[9] Harry James also left just under a year after the concert, citing another Carnegie Hall number, "Sing, Sing, Sing," as the reason for his departure:

> I don't think I ever told anybody this, but I was going through a real mental thing, and it was all built around "Sing, Sing, Sing." I'd been sick; they gave me some experimental pills—sulpher [sic] pills—only they weren't very refined yet. Well, they wigged me out, and it happened the first time just as I was supposed to get up and play my chorus on "Sing, Sing, Sing." I just couldn't make it. I fell back in my chair. Ziggy said to me, "Get up" but I couldn't, so when he saw what was happening he got up and played my solo. I was completely out of my mind. It happened again another time, too, so that every time the band played "Sing, Sing, Sing" I'd get bugged and scared it would start all over again. You know, that Stravinsky-type thing that the trombones and then the trumpets play just before the chorus? Well, that would really set me off. I tried to explain it to Benny and I'd even ask him to play "Sing, Sing, Sing" earlier in the evening, so I could relax for the rest of the night. But of course that was his big number, and so I couldn't blame him for wanting to hold off. Finally I just left the band. I couldn't trust myself anymore. At least with my own band I could play the tunes I wanted to play [Simon 1968: 535].

The negative effects of repetitions of a piece that initially represented collective creativity but had become a standardized arrangement is striking, as is James's desire for autonomy over the stability Goodman's band offered. This also became clear to Bobby Hackett, whose performance at Carnegie Hall has been considered career-defining: "I got stuck with the assignment which I didn't want to do and I'm sorry I did" (Chilton and Kernfeld; Firestone 1993: 213).

"HONEYSUCKLE ROSE" The Quartet performance of "Honeysuckle Rose" on the January 18 *Camel Caravan* broadcast begins with a rhapsodic rendition of the head by Goodman and Wilson. This might have led Goodman fans to read it as a musical reflection on the concert, particularly being positioned after the Mozart, which framed the performance virtually for radio. Reflection may also be read in performances recorded on the day after the concert by Eddie Condon and his Windy City Seven, which included Bobby Hackett and Jess Stacy.[10] This session, released as "Jam Session at Commodore No. 1," was organized by Milt Gabler for Commodore Records and included medium and fast blues entitled respectively "Carnegie Drag" and "Carnegie Jump." "Carnegie Drag" begins with a two-chorus solo from Stacy in which the turnarounds at the end of the choruses are reminiscent of his introduction to "One O'Clock Jump." But more strikingly, Stacy incorporates oscillating parallel fourths in the upper register, which recall the parallel triplets in his "Sing, Sing, Sing" solo. In general, these performances highlight Stacy's strength as a soloist, but since Goodman rarely featured him on broadcasts or recordings it was the Carnegie Hall concert that established his abilities publicly, both in 1938 and again on release of the recording in 1950. The rarity of a Stacy solo undoubtedly emphasized the apparent spontaneity of his performance on "Sing, Sing, Sing" despite its probable precedents. Further, the Windy City Seven sides show that Stacy's "classical" gestures were not necessarily a specific response to the situation of Carnegie Hall but part of his developing improvisational language. As Stacy himself recalled of the "Sing, Sing, Sing" solo: "I'd been listening to Edward McDowell and [Claude] Debussy, and I think some of their things got in there" (Coller 1998: 57), but this could equally apply to his solo on "Carnegie Drag" and other moments in the session with Condon (such as when comping behind Bud Freeman on "Beat to the Socks").

In addition to reflecting musically on the "Jam Session," Goodman also singled it out for consideration in his autobiography, in which he describes the rehearsal:

> I went down in the hall to get an idea of how it sounded, but before they had done more than five or six choruses on 'Honeysuckle Rose', the thing was jumping so much that I had to rush up and get in on it. We probably would have kept on playing all night if there hadn't been jobs waiting for us. (Goodman and Kolodin 1939: 231–232)

The Carnegie Hall concert is treated proportionately with other events in Goodman's career and without undue emphasis in his autobiography. However, the comments on the concert follow a discussion of Goodman's views on race based on his experiences with the Trio and Quartet ("nobody cares much what colors or races are represented just so long as we play good music") that place it in a particular perspective. This section continues:

> That night at Carnegie was a great experience, because it represented something—a group of musicians going on that stage and playing tunes by Gershwin and Berlin and Kern and arrangements by Fletcher and Edgar Sampson, getting up and playing the choruses the way they wanted to, each of them just being himself—and holding the attention of all those people for two hours and a half [Goodman and Kolodin 1939: 232].

Here the concert is presented as a metaphor for broad social equality ("each of them just being himself") but defined through particular reference to race, identifying presentation of music by Jewish composers and black arrangers as a significant aspect. As discussed in Part One, in addition to Goodman's regular small groups and the one-off collaboration with Ellington's musicians the Carnegie Hall "Jam Session" presented what was in effect a racially integrated big band, and therefore it forms an important part of the long-term progression toward integration in jazz. Indeed, Lionel Hampton temporarily took over on drums after Krupa's departure, and in July 1939 Fletcher Henderson became the first black musician permanently employed to play in the main Goodman band (Connor 1988: 100). However, these and other changes in personnel left Goodman "with only four members who had been there the year before: Chris Griffin, Ziggy Elman and trombonists Vernon Brown and Red Ballard" (Firestone 1993: 261). This contrasts dramatically with the all-important period of stability prior to the concert.

RECORDING

Benny Goodman has returned to Columbia records, the label he left to go to Capitol almost three years ago. Columbia has signed him to a three-year contract under which he'll cut both longhair and pop sides. Deal also gives Columbia rights to records made of Goodman's 1938 concert at Carnegie Hall, which spot many of the top jazzmen of the late 30's. These will be

Following a period with Capitol records during which he experimented with bebop, Goodman disbanded toward the end of 1949. He then spent time focusing on classical music, almost as a catharsis, and recorded Aaron Copland's Clarinet Concerto, another of his own commissions, as well as the Mozart Clarinet Quintet and Darius Milhaud's *La Création du Monde* during his first year back with Columbia. The release of *The Famous 1938 Carnegie Hall Jazz Concert* album on November 13, 1950, brought Goodman back into the public spotlight and contributed significantly to defining a new retrospective direction to his jazz work—the direct opposite of his recordings with Capitol.

The release of the concert on LP was accompanied by discourse predicting a resurgence of swing. In the issue of *DownBeat* in which the album was extensively reviewed, Goodman was featured as the subject of the "Bouquets to the Living" series, apparently implicating himself with a certain degree of irony within a potential revival:

> Despite the relatively low estate to which bands have fallen in recent years, he feels sure that there will be a resurgence. It will not be done by gimmicks or hullaballoo publicity, he thinks. The thing that will bring back bands, he says, will be bands which play good music intelligently [Wilson 1951: 1].

Metronome featured a letter from "Fred Crystal of New York" that specifically identified the release of the concert as a catalyst for a revival:

> We've found that the great music of the 1935–1941 Swing Era has almost disappeared. In its place we have been undergoing the tortures of various types of novelties, hillbillies, etc. But this month the opportunity has come to stage a comeback. We have a splendid chance to lift Old King Swing off his feet and get him back in there punching. The opportunity I refer to is the long awaited release of Benny Goodman's 1938 Swing Concert at Carnegie, on records [Crystal 1951: 28].

Comparisons with the previous revival of New Orleans jazz were inevitable. For Marshall Stearns, writing in *The Story of Jazz* (1956), the reissue of "Benny Goodman's 1938 recordings" proved that the previous revival of New Orleans jazz was not a singular occurrence but a significant trait: "there is practically no era in the history of jazz that does not have the range of appeal to make a revival possible" (Stearns 1956: 217). Bill Grauer was optimistic that a degree of authenticity might be possible:

> Goodman's music was always frankly aimed at the general public rather than at a specialized jazz audience. So it can be offered to today's listeners in its original style, rather than having to undergo the sad dilutions that characterized the late lamented Dixieland revival [Grauer 1951: 3].

Certainly, as Crystal's letter indicates, there had been a desire for a swing revival for some time prior to the release of *The Famous 1938 Carnegie Hall Jazz Concert*. Grauer, writing in the *Record Changer* in June 1951, mentions that WNEW's disc jockey Art Ford "has been conducting an almost single-handed campaign for many long years, trying to bring swing back into the national spotlight" (Grauer 1951: 3). WNEW had been at the forefront of recorded music radio with Martin Block's *Make Believe Ballroom* show and retained a focus on swing as it became nostalgic (Erenberg 1998: 43). Prior to the release of *The Famous 1938 Carnegie Hall Concert*, Columbia issued a 12-inch 78 rpm disc containing recorded introductions by Goodman to the various numbers, accompanied by a script with suggestions for their use (these can be heard on Columbia/Legacy C2K65143).[11] Clearly, radio stations such as WNEW were responsible for the continuation of an audience for swing and would have played a significant part in developing awareness and consumer demand for the release of the 1938 concert.

The presentation of the album undoubtedly influenced its reception and in particular encouraged its canonization. Most significantly, "the first swing concert in the history of Carnegie Hall" had become *The Famous 1938 Carnegie Hall Jazz Concert* for the record release. The effect of this was to recontextualize the event as notable for being the first presentation of a specific style of popular music within the history of the Hall (anchoring it to a particular time and place) and for establishing it as an event of continued significance within the wider history of jazz, at a time when there were successive attempts to understand this better. The change from "first" to "famous" moves the judgment of the importance of the concert from the objective toward the subjective. Positing the concert as famous when this status had been achieved mainly through discourse would create a fundamental demand for hearing the performances when they became available.

The format of the original release on 12-inch LPs was practical, in allowing nearly the whole concert to be presented on two discs, and it also gave *The Famous 1938 Carnegie Hall Jazz Concert* a particular status. Following the "war of speeds" in 1948–49, in 1950 RCA Victor abandoned the 45 rpm extended play format and released their first record at 33⅓ rpm, the speed pioneered by Columbia, and established this as the standard for the LP (the 45 rpm speed was retained for singles) (Gronow and Saunio 1998: 98). Previously, some albums were released on multiple discs in 78 rpm format, including compilations of jazz singles and reissues, and also, in the case of *Chicago Jazz*, produced by George Avakian for Decca in 1939–40, recordings made specifically with an album in mind. The LP was developed mainly to provide a suitable format for the long movements of classical works, but it was launched by Columbia in 1948 in two sizes, 10-inch mainly for popular music (and shorter classical works) and 12-inch for classical (Marmorstein 2007: 165). *The Famous 1938 Carnegie Hall Jazz Concert* was therefore unusual as an early example of a jazz record in the 12-inch LP format (the 1949 Charlie Parker album *Bird Blows the Blues*, on Dial, might be considered the first, but it was produced in very limited numbers). In addition, the album was released on the premium Columbia Masterworks label, which had been associated with classical music since its foundation in 1927. Although Avakian explained that this was primarily an economic decision—"We had to do that for the Goodman album because of the all the extra number of copyrights that were on the program" (Myers 2010: n.p.)—the choice of label and format for the release provided another way in which the performances from the 1938 concert continued to intersect genre-defined modes of production and reception and articulate aspiration to artistic status.

The packaging of the album, boxed in a regal purple with Kolodin's extensive liner notes, lent the discs importance as historical artifacts, but the concert was also packaged metaphorically within a narrative of innocent discovery that belied the commercial motives behind its release. According to Kolodin's liner notes, the discs "turned up in a closet of the Goodman home a few months ago. Daughter Rachel came upon it and asked: 'Daddy, what's this?' Daddy took a look, and wisely decided to have it transferred to tape before listening again" (Kolodin 1950: 13). Although he reasserted this explanation in his recorded introductions on the Columbia promotional disc, Goodman offered another version of the story in a transcription of a radio interview printed in *DownBeat* in 1956, in which the acetates were discovered by his sister-in-law, Rachel Spieden (*DownBeat* 1956: 12). Unlike in Kolodin's story, the adult Rachel realizes the potential value of the records and insists that Goodman takes them away to protect them from her son. The quality of the presentation and production, which enabled a return in spirit to the original performance, against the narrative of the chance recording of the concert and rediscovery of the acetates added value to the discs as material artifacts:

> It was beautifully recorded by CBS, off a direct wire from Carnegie; it's perfectly pressed here [Ulanov 1951: 29].

> And the whole concert has been recorded with a fidelity which belies the almost casual way in which it was accomplished. Columbia deserves an Oscar, a D.S.C. or something for having made available this memorable history-making concert [Archetti 1950: 254].

Bill Savory, who engineered the first release, recalled that Goodman "was really turned on by the music and was playing the acetates around the house. He'd put the needle down casually and say, 'Oh, that's not the beginning,' and drag the arm across the record" (Firestone 1993: 367). This is probably indicative of lack of technical awareness rather than lack of appreciation; after all, Goodman had deliberately kept the discs as an heirloom. According to Savory, it was at his instigation that Goodman had the records copied onto tape, "which he [Goodman] then proceeded to use as a kind of sales number" to secure a contract with Columbia (Firestone 1993: 367). Transferring the recording onto LPs via tape was far from easy, thanks to the limited capacity of the discs on which it was recorded, which meant the concert originally took up 28 sides (Hancock 2008: 149). Savory recalled that "only one record in that whole complete set of seventy-eights ended with applause at the end of the selection. The rest had to be spliced together" (Firestone 1993: 368). But in addition to establishing the continuity of the original performance, decisions were made that more profoundly affected the content of the original release, as Savory recalled:

> There was also a good bit of editing to be done inside the tunes. On some of them I had to cut out a whole chorus, then patch it up so it made sense musically and came out at the right place. There were a lot of clicks and pops. There were also some problems with the material itself. In the long jam session on "Honeysuckle Rose" the tempo

slowed down toward the end because everyone had gotten tired [Firestone 1993: 369].

In Savory's description, there seems to be a fluid distinction between edits done as a result of technical inadequacies ("clicks and pops") and those made on more subjective artistic grounds as a critique of the performance. According to the producer Michael Cuscuna, the latter was standard practice:

> The introduction of ¼" tape in 1949 gave us the ability to edit music freely.... Jazz producers, for the most part, used tape editing judiciously to save a take by editing out a bad chorus or replacing an ensemble section that contained a musical clam. But there were excesses. The released version of "Jumpin' at the Woodside" from Buck Clayton's Jam Session series for Columbia Records [1954] ping pongs between two different takes recorded six months apart with different personnel and instrumentation! [Cuscuna 2005: 66].

In addition to the edits Savory mentions, two complete numbers from the concert were omitted from the original album release ("Sometimes I'm Happy" and "If Dreams Come True"), allegedly because of poor sound quality. However, it can be no coincidence that these numbers were the two sweet ballads of the concert; perhaps they were considered to be incompatible with a retrospectively imposed definition of jazz. Reactions to the preparation of the initial release have informed more recent versions of the album, which are considered under "Re-creation" below.

Just as the Carnegie Hall concert performance is embedded within the development of the jazz concert and audiences listening to jazz in the 1930s, so the release of the concert recording is linked to the contemporary context of jazz in 1950. Bernard Gendron points out that although swing was implicated in the reaction against both New Orleans revivalism (to which it was the modern commercial antithesis) and bebop (where it was aligned *with* Dixieland as "traditional"), by 1947 it was merely caught in the crossfire in debates between the moldy figs and the modernists (Gendron 1995: 32, 49). In other words, swing had reached a position where it could be perceived nostalgically and revived. As we have seen, the desire for reissues of earlier jazz and the capturing of off-air broadcasts as a quest for authentic jazz performance was prevalent among fans from the 1930s, and George Avakian's work in the 1940s had already established reissues as an important part of Columbia's jazz output (Marmorstein 2007: 110). Although *The Famous 1938 Carnegie Hall Jazz Concert* was aesthetically similar since it represented a live, rather than studio, performance (like an aircheck) from the past (like a reissue), it could not be categorized as either of these. Indeed, the album seemed to offer a more direct and potent connection with a bygone age since the sounds captured in 1938 had never been heard by a wider public, and not at all since that date: "It is one of the authentic documents in American musical history, a verbatim report, in the accents of those who were present on 'The Night of January 16 1938'" (Archetti 1950: 254). Therefore, although a further important precedent was established by the release of recordings of Norman Granz's *Jazz at the Philharmonic* concerts as "live albums" in the 1940s, *The Famous 1938 Carnegie Hall Concert* was unusual and important inherently because it was a recording of a quantifiably "historic" event.

RECEPTION

Comparison of the reception of the concert as a live event in 1938 and in response to the 1950 album allows the effects of recontextualization, retrospection and mediation on perceptions of the performances to be evaluated. As a live recording, *The Famous 1938 Carnegie Hall Jazz Concert* is itself a valuable source for the audience reception in 1938 through analysis of audible reactions. Although the recording would only capture a certain level and type of audience response, which then is subject to editing, this sonic evidence can be cross-referenced against written accounts of audience behavior. Triangulating different sources in this way allows audience reception to be studied in some depth rather than restricted solely to the written reaction of specific critics.

At the start of the concert, there was audible background noise and chatter. Joe Hanscom, a *Metronome* reporter who, like Annemarie Ewing for *DownBeat*, focused on supposedly peripheral aspects of the concert as a complement to the main feature article, noted that Goodman deliberately began "Don't Be That Way" before the crowd had settled down: "Still they kept cheering. So he tapped his foot a couple of times, and his band proceeded to drown out his audience. Not polite, but thoroughly expedient" (Hanscom 1938: 18). The noise finally subsided at Goodman's solo. The audience response to Krupa's drum break on the opening number has been discussed, but his extrovert performances throughout the concert received comment in several reviews. In the *New York Herald Tribune*, Francis D. Perkins commented on the contrast between Krupa, whose "gestures and facial expressions proved unusually engrossing for those near enough to note them in detail," and Goodman, who was "the calmest in mien, even when he did incredible work on his clarinet, and he presided over the sessions of the trio and quartet with an air of paternal benevolence" (Perkins 1938: 7). Ewing's analysis illuminates the differences between Krupa's and Goodman's relationships with the audience:

> For the most part, the audience did just what the music indicated. When it was noisy, they were noisy. In fact at one point during "Bei Mir Bist Du Schoen" they all began clapping in time to the music.... And because of the size of the hall, they were inevitably a little off the beat—a circumstance which filled the boys with momentary consternation, until Gene set in on all the drums he had, to drown them out and keep the rhythm intact. And when the music lowered to a quiet passage, folks sat rapt and quiet, too. Sometimes it seemed almost as if Benny were directing the audience [Ewing 1938: 7].

Similarly to the scenario of "Don't Be That Way" and its repercussions, here Ewing describes how Krupa projected his performance to the audience, whereas Goodman drew on the power of introversion to ensure their attention.

In the first half, "One O'Clock Jump" also provoked cheering and applause: "Before the men had completed their job, they had been drowned out by applause and cat-calls" (Simon 1938b: 15). The applause for "Sensation Rag" and "I'm Coming Virginia" in "Twenty Years of Jazz" might be described as polite, especially in comparison with "When My Baby Smiles at Me" and "Shine," which provoked chatter and laughter. However, in general terms there was a more vociferous audience reaction in the second half of the concert in response to performances, especially of the small groups, which were more obviously projected. In the first half Goodman was observed "grinning knowingly at a few ickies who were being overcome" during "I Got Rhythm" (Simon 1938b: 18), but in the second half the Quartet can be heard shouting out directions to each other, as well as making visual gestures:

> This time they were much more relaxed, and even went so far as to kid among themselves as they swung through *China Boy*, *Stompin' at the Savoy*, and an original composition. Strictly upon musical merits, Teddy stole the show, though Lionel and Gene went through plenty of contortions that amused the crowd [Simon 1938b: 44].

> The biggest kick came when Gene concked his cymbal so hard it fell off its stand on to the floor. Lionel picked it up, hit it a few times with his

vibre hammer, and returned it to Gene. Whereupon Gene hit it off the stand again. It was like a ping-pong match [Hanscom 1938: 40].

There was a tendency for the audience (or a section of it) to clap to the beat in several numbers, including, as previously mentioned, "Bei Mir Bist Du Schön": "The Gothamites commenced to do all sorts of clapping here and seemed to enjoy immensely Ziggy Elman's Ghetto Get-off." The finale of "Sing, Sing, Sing" was received similarly to "One O'Clock Jump": "Everybody started to applaud, stamp, cheer, yell, as the band went into the number's final outburst. And long after it was complete they kept on yelling, until Benny satisfied them with a couple of encores" (Simon 1938b: 44). Before both of the encores, voices can be heard shouting out, probably suggesting the names of numbers they would like to hear.

Other than "Sing, Sing, Sing," it was "Loch Lomond" that received the most sustained applause, which "held up the proceedings for almost five full minutes," leading Goodman to apologize for not having an encore prepared (Simon 1938b: 18). The audience may have been influenced by Tilton's strength in the face of the adversity of the failed microphone, and for those in the audience who were not jazz fans this would be the number they were most likely to be familiar with. Also, on three occasions ("When My Baby Smiles at Me," the first stop-time in "I Got Rhythm" and in the middle of "Big John Special") early applause is indicative of the audience's unfamiliarity with "trick" ending devices. This reception corresponds to the mixed composition of the audience, identified primarily through age and behavior, as recalled by Goodman himself and reported in contemporary reviews in *Metronome*, *DownBeat*, and *Melody Maker*:

The Carnegie Hall concert we gave came along about this time and went well despite the highbrows who saw things in the music we never intended putting in it—and the hoodlum jitterbugs. A noisy minority, they blasted out the horns, yelled and stomped a dozen smooth passages of the trio into oblivion and wrecked a few numbers with trick ends completely [Goodman and Shane 1939: 13].

Several thousand bristling and whistling swing cats and...several hundred long-haired symphony hounds who deigned to put in a rather smug appearance [Simon 1938b: 15].

The audience was undoubtedly the strangest assortment ever gathered within the sturdy walls of Carnegie; adolescent schoolboys, attired like misprints in Esquire, who applauded everything, including the klinkers, to baggy-eyed pseudo-sophisticates who applauded nothing—including several enjoyable spots [H.E.P. 1938: 1].

Only fault to be found with the concert, strangely enough, was the audience. Those near-maniacs who act like they have St. Vitus dance or ants in their pants were very much in evidence, and their stupid habit of whistling and clapping vociferously each time one of the boys took a hot chorus very soon became objectionable. Another mania cultivated by these idiots was that of tapping heavily and clapping out rhythm along with the band. These "ickies" were counter-balanced by a few intelligent listeners who "shushed" them (one man actually stood up in his seat and shouted "Shut up, you punks!") [Scholl 1938: 11].

Perceptions of the overall reception of the concert vary considerably. Olin Downes, classical music critic for the *New York Times*, wrote that "the audience remained applauding and cheering till a late hour" (Downes 1938: 11). Hobe Morrison (who was more likely to be acquainted with Goodman's performances) suggests a less enthusiastic reception in his report for *Variety*: "The band got away after only two encores—filing off the platform after the applause had died" (Morrison 1938: 51). The audible reactions suggest that the audience was similarly polarized in terms of experience and knowledge of Goodman's music. The applause was often as much in reaction to familiar personalities as for features of the music itself, such as at the start of Harry James's solo on the opening number; as the various guests came onto the stage for "Blue Reverie" (receiving a "grand ovation," according to Simon, 1938b: 18) and the "Jam Session"; and then for Teddy Wilson and Lionel Hampton for the small groups and Martha Tilton in the second half.

The reviews of the concert are significant not only as a gauge of reception but also in provision of discourse that disseminated the event to a wider "audience" than the few thousand people present in Carnegie Hall on the night of the concert. Essentially, as discussed in Part One, the principal feature of swing in the concert hall had already been established and was reiterated in many of the reviews, often using the metaphor of the effect that swing could have on the fabric of the Hall:

…the candy kid of jazz turning on the heat in the temple of the classics [Morrison 1938: 46].
Short-Hairs Shag, Long-Hairs Wag, Walls Sag, as Goodman's Gang Transforms Ancient Hall Into Modern Swing Emporium [Simon 1938b: 15].
The staid Carnegie Hall…was recently shaken by the invasion of Benny Goodman and his band [*Rhythm* 1938: 41].
Carnegie Hall's Walls Bulge as 3800 Klinkers and Sophisti-cats Hear B.G. [H.E.P. 1938: 1].

Initially, the basic premise of repositioning Goodman's usual music into concert hall surroundings contributed to a distinct atmosphere in the Hall. Bob Bach, a Goodman fan who knew the band well, recalled that "the atmosphere was like having someone in your family bar mitzvahed or doing the valedictory at commencement" (in Balliett 1978: 158). William Shawn remembered that "the atmosphere was very highly charged in the hall. In fact, I can't remember any other musical event quite like it, unless it was a particular Toscanini concert or Oistrakh's first appearance here" (158). Even Downes described "a quivering excitement in the air, an almost electrical effect" (1938: 11). Further to this, descriptions of the nervousness of the musicians from Hanscom and particularly Ewing, as she had backstage access, added to the sense of occasion for the majority who were reliant on the reportage as a basis for their perceptions of the event.

The audience was inevitably, and perhaps unusually, a focus for the critics, as this was where any clash between genre and venue would be played out. Downes wrote: "We went to discover, a new, original, thrilling music. We stayed to watch a social and physical phenomenon" (1938: 11). In *DownBeat* Ewing mentioned that several well-known classical musicians were in the audience (1938: 7). Inevitably though, it was the ickies who attracted the attention of observers, their audible presence on the recording perpetuating their reactions for more recent analysts. Both *DownBeat* and *Melody Maker* reported that "during the interval the balcony and gallery audience went into complete disregard for Carnegie Hall etiquette and amused itself by throwing small paper aeroplanes through the hall and, in general, turning the occasion into a Mardi Gras atmosphere" (Brackman 1938b: 11). These were likely made from Kolodin's program notes, adding to the subversion of this activity. In the *Herald Tribune*, Perkins observed that "the great majority were well acquainted with the music of Mr. Goodman and his colleagues in the field, and indulged in some swinging of their own in their seats in response to the persistent and infectious rhythms" (Perkins 1938: 7). However, for Morrison in *Variety* this behavior demonstrated a victory for the traditions of the concert hall: "In the end it was the illustrious old brick pile, Carnegie Hall, which turned out the winner. It even subdued the Goodman jitterbugs, who did no shagging or big-appling in the aisles... [the] chief fly in the rhythmic ointment were the sedate surroundings. It gradually wore down the cats" (Morrison 1938: 46, 51). Uniquely, Kolodin suggested that "ordinary concert hall criteria did not apply. Informality reigned supreme," noting the applause during numbers (Kolodin 1938a: 15). Simon's observations suggest that compromises were made in the behavior of both extremes of the audience: "One kid after another commenced to create a new dance: trucking and shagging while sitting down. Older penguin-suited men in traditional boxes on the sides went them one better and proceeded to shag standing up" (Simon 1938b: 44).

However, once the "noisy minority" of "hoodlum jitterbugs" and the "several adults [who] left before the concert was over, some before intermission" are discounted, the reactions to the concert were generally muted (Goodman and Shane 1939: 13; Morrison 1938: 51). H.E.P. explained in *DownBeat* that for the Goodman fans the concert was disappointing, "a duplication of what had been heard so often, previously, on recordings, stage and at the Penn Hotel" (1938: 1). Bob Bach commented:

> We knew what we'd hear at Carnegie—the trumpet riffs of "Sing, Sing, Sing" and the ride-outs in the last chorus of the hot numbers and Gene Krupa wrapping everything up with a solo, but we didn't know what would get the biggest applause, what would blow the roof off. Truthfully, nothing really did [in Balliett 1978: 158].

H.E.P explained that for the music critics "the fact that the music made no startling excursions into new fields to be explored was a disappointment that seemed to incense their reaction with ire, rather than cordiality" (1938: 1). Similarly, *Metronome* summarized the responses under the title "Benny's Barrage Baffles Critics—Dailies' Music Editors Beat Around the Bush in Review of Music They Do Not Know" (*Metronome* 1938: 18). A 1938 editorial in the *New York Herald Tribune* highlighted the problems of developing a critical framework for assessing the concert: "The trouble with bringing a critical judgement to bear on such a performance is that the commentator is likely to be placed in the position of a man who, upon examining an orange, remarks: 'This is not a very good apple.'"

Not surprisingly, then, many of the music critics founded their comments on comparisons with classical music, with instrumental timbre and rhythm as particular points of focus. Perkins perceived "a notable range of instrumental sonorities and colors, from proclamative, ear-filling plangence and rousing brilliance to mellow smoothness" (1938: 7); but for Downes, "the tone of the brass instruments, almost continually overblown, is hard, shrill and noisy. The other instruments add what they can to swell the racket" (1938: 11). With regard to rhythm, several reviewers were in agreement with the opinion that "Unchanging Tempo of Concert was Cause of Boredom" (H.E.P. 1938: 6). H.E.P. suggested that greater variety was required for concert presentations of swing, but for others the prominence of the unvarying rhythm pointed to the inadequacy of improvisations: "Nor did we hear a single player, in the course of a solid hour of music, invent one interesting or original musical phrase, over the persistent basic rhythm" (Downes 1938: 11).

The "Jam Session" was particularly criticized in reviews of the concert, especially having been established, including in Kolodin's program notes, as the archetype for swing performance. Fundamentally, it was considered to be too long, to the extent that most critics (apparently) timed it, recording a range from 10 minutes to "about thirty minutes" in the *New York Amsterdam News* (1938b). Even Simon was forced to admit that the "Jam Session" was "the weakest part of the program" although he blamed the setting, whereas H.E.P. asserted that the problem was "the enormity of this type of band (eleven musicians!)" (Simon 1938b: 18; H.E.P. 1938: 6). Simon reported that "the listeners, including the most thoroughbred cats, were quite obviously restless and didn't tend the jammers any smaller ovation than they deserved." Even Kolodin, despite a more favorable assessment of the "Jam Session," concluded "Wisely, no encore was attempted" (Kolodin 1938a).

None of the reviews explicitly mention racial integration, although this is implied in the African American newspaper the *New York Amsterdam News* in an article (1938b) focused on inclusion of the work of black arrangers and performers in the concert. The contributions of Ellington's sidemen were particularly highlighted in several reviews, although H.E.P. noted that the format of the "Twenty Years of Jazz" section implied that Ellington's music was passé and "precedent to Goodman's year" (H.E.P. 1938: 6). Ewing noted Goodman was "sitting happily in the back row like one of the boys" in the "Jam Session." (Ewing 1938: 7). The potential for broad social equality in swing was more explicitly articulated in an editorial in the *New York Times*: "If the individual has his unhampered say in music, he may manage to have it in other fields. Dictators should be suspicious of swing" (1938).

The judgments of the main specialist periodicals were divergent, with George Simon in *Metronome* heralding the concert as a triumph for swing but H.E.P. in *DownBeat* concluding indifferently that "when the debit and credit sides are added and subtracted, the total indictor will probably point to 'So What?'" (H.E.P. 1938: 6). However, there was actually considerable consistency in their assessment of the positive and negative aspects of the concert. Although "Loch Lomond" received an ovation, Simon noted that Tilton was "plainly even more nervous than the band" and H.E.P. felt that her appearance and stage presence saved the day. "One O'Clock Jump" and "Swingtime in the Rockies" were considered highlights, in concordance with the audience reaction, and Krupa's contribution to these numbers was noted. The solos on "Sing, Sing, Sing" by Krupa, Goodman and Stacy were singled out for particular praise. Stacy's solo was described as "soft church music" by Simon; H.E.P. noted its "expert phrasing and imaginative improvisation, melodically beautiful and completely apart from his usual style," demonstrating how Stacy was known only for his few solos with Goodman at this time, rather than his contributions elsewhere (Simon 1938b: 18; H.E.P. 1938: 6).

Ultimately, in 1938 there was already some sense that the concert had attained historic status. In addition to Ewing's comment to this effect, which I cited in the Preface, several reviewers offered a comparison with Paul Whiteman's "Experiment in Modern Music" concert. Morrison, Downes and Perkins acknowledged the difference between Whiteman's overt attempts to show that "jazz had progressed beyond the limitations implied in the term" and Goodman's presentation of "music which serves his orchestra's purpose in the regular course of its activities" in the concert hall (Perkins 1938: 7). Acknowledging Whiteman, Grofé and Lopez as predecessors, Morrison "figured this was probably the first straight jazz concert by a name band in symph hangout" (Morrison 1938: 51). However, the concert made little impact in jazz literature prior to the release of *The Famous 1938 Carnegie Hall Concert*. This is unsurprising not only because of the lack of a recording but also with reference to the attempts of early jazz writers to establish, in Panassie's terms, "the real jazz," which often led to a focus on black musicians. In *The Real Jazz* Panassie attributes his revisionism (from an earlier stance in *Hot Jazz*, 1934) to his deeper understanding of jazz as black music. Although he notes Goodman's incorporation of black musicians, Carnegie Hall is not mentioned as a particular incidence of integration (Panassie 1942/R1946: 198). Ramsey and Smith's *Jazzmen* (1939) cites Goodman's Congress Hotel engagement as significant in the history of jazz; Carnegie Hall is mentioned only as a venue for the *From Spirituals to Swing* concerts (1939: 256). However, there are notable consistencies in the stylistic analysis of Goodman in the pre-1950 literature, which may be indicative of Goodman's image following the concert:

> An even more detestable clarinet style was brought into favor by another white clarinettist of Chicago, Benny Goodman. This style makes the clarinet a "precious" instrument. The refined phrases which are generally played legato, remind one more of the birds twittering in the trees than of jazz music. Naturally these ethereal melodies

are sprinkled with blue notes and occasionally give place to inter-rupted phrases which are supposed to swing [Panassie 1942/R1946: 104].

[Goodman] brought to jazz a concert-hall beauty of tone and fluidity of technique [Finkelstein 1948: 50].

The clarinet, its fine reedy timbre gone, has acquired a cloying quality and its melodic line flows in a drooping, decorative pattern like that of Artie Shaw and much of Benny Goodman's playing. Gone is the flash-ing, elastic, whip-like quality of Dodd's phrases, his blue and surging tone, his swinging stresses. So this music sings, not in the African tones of jazz, but in bathetic and sentimental accents. It is salon music [Blesh 1946: 266].

Panassie's imagery is particularly vivid in presenting the unearthly quali-ties of Goodman's music as the antithesis of the "real jazz" and alluding to the stereotypical features of classical music in terms of pretension, refine-ment and lack of swing. Clearly, Goodman had developed strong associa-tions with the concert hall or salon, signified through the timbre of his clarinet even in his jazz performances, especially against the new backdrop of bebop in which the instrument was much less prevalent. At the least, the 1938 Carnegie Hall concert provides the roots of this dimension of Good-man's musical persona; at most it is implicit in these critical appraisals. However, writing from a post-bop perspective, André Hodeir identifies similar characteristics in Goodman's playing and also Teddy Wilson as the roots of "cool" in his chapter "Miles Davis and the Cool Tendency," recall-ing earlier descriptions of Goodman's introverted performances:

Wilson's touch was unusually delicate and Goodman replaced his predecessors' thick vibrato with a more discrete timbre. Sharp at-tacks, rough timbre, hard touch and vibrato had for a long time been regarded as essential characteristics of the Negro's sonority, whereas they were actually just characteristics of the hot idiom. Lester Young deserves the credit for showing that it is possible to avoid almost all these features and still produce authentic jazz [Hodeir 1956: 119].

Significantly, Hodeir's work is not only written in the light of subse-quent developments in jazz but follows his compatriot Panassie in con-structing his account of jazz through recordings, now out of necessity (typified by the early European experience of jazz) but also as a deliber-ate methodological choice:

The judgements of jazz in this book are based on recordings, which have reached a stage of technical perfection that makes such an approach valid. Besides, the recording is the most trustworthy witness we have in dealing with an art form of which nothing that is essential can be set down on paper. The reader should not be surprised, therefore, if the words *work* and *record* are used interchangeably throughout [Hodeir 1956: 2].

DeVeaux has identified the 1950s as a significant juncture in establishing "the jazz tradition" as a paradigm for jazz writing, whereas previously "historical narrative only gradually emerged from criticism" (1991: 531). Sherrie Tucker notes:

[In the 1950s] "Jazz tradition" historiography took several forms, including historical surveys, such as Barry Ulanov's *A History of Jazz in America* (1952), "great man" histories, sometimes in the shape of collected interviews, such as Nat Shapiro and Nat Hentoff's *Hear Me Talkin' to Ya: the Story of Jazz by the Men Who Made it* (1955), and musical analyses, usually of recordings. André Hodeir was perhaps the first to periodize jazz history, and to canonize pivotal performances in his... *Jazz: Its Evolution and Essence* (1956) [Tucker n.d.].

The tendency to construct jazz history through recordings at this time was fueled by reissues, particularly the re-release of recordings in the new LP format. In this context, *The Famous 1938 Carnegie Hall Jazz Concert* was well placed to achieve canonical status. Barry Ulanov's view on Goodman in *A History of Jazz in America* (1952) is distinct from Hodeir's, as Ulanov draws on his experience of hearing the band live to provide a comparative perspective for assessing recordings. Although this is by no means a guarantee of objectivity, Ulanov's position allows him to state that "no single record caught the enormous impact of that band" (1952/R1958: 204). Moreover, as an audience member at the 1938 concert Ulanov could also place *The Famous 1938 Carnegie Hall Jazz Concert* in a position of representative dominance within not only Goodman's career but the entire "swing era" with a degree of legitimacy.

Most of that concert is on those records, which capture with remarkable fidelity the band itself, Jess Stacy's five lovely choruses in "Sing, Sing, Sing" and the inspired collaboration of musicians from the Count Basie, Duke Ellington and Benny Goodman bands, and Bobby Hackett—a collaboration that thrilled all of us present that glittering night. This was Benny's achievement, the matching of equal talents on all jazz instruments with little concern for box office and much for musicianship. To a greater or lesser degree, insofar as they matched that achievement, other bands and musicians made a permanent or transient impression during the swing era [Ulanov 1952/R1958: 204].

The position of the two main specialist periodicals in relation to *The Famous 1938 Carnegie Hall Jazz Concert* was similar to their response to the concert in 1938, with Ulanov reviewing the album in broadly positive terms for *Metronome*, and Michael Levin demonstrating a more critical stance in *DownBeat*. In both cases, is clear that the album was regarded as inherently historical at the time of its release, which was due to its musical style, and therefore it had value within different constructions of jazz history. For Ulanov it is "the most meaningful memento possible" of the swing era, and Levin comments that "as a historical index, this album is a valuable possession." Ulanov values the performances themselves, as they enable his nostalgic desire to "return in spirit to the memorable evenings of Swing." From this perspective, he particularly notes "Twenty Years of Jazz" as "one of the delightful sections of the bill," with terminology referencing variety shows within which humor plays a significant part. Levin, however, suggests that the performances on the album have value only as representations of a profoundly outdated style, which he summarizes negatively as commercial appropriation of black music: "the big-money aping of the great middle-30s Negro swing bands by Goodman, Shaw, Miller, and all the rest." Levin sustains this fundamental point throughout his review, criticizing Goodman's commercial repertoire and "crowd-pleasing devices." In particular, he uses his assessment of the small groups, the "Jam Session" and "Twenty Years of Jazz," to demonstrate the originality of the contributions of the black musicians in contrast to Goodman and James's formulaic improvisation. Both critics continue the familiar criticism of the "Jam Session," but Levin attributes "the difference between the swinging feeling here and the synthetic slamming which goes on during much of the rest of the LP" to the guest players and blames any weakness on the "Goodmanites" (Levin 1951: 14–15; Ulanov 1951: 29).

Responding in their reviews to the growing sense of a swing revival, both critics were in agreement that re-performing swing was undesirable. For Ulanov, this represented "a kind of infantile regression which is more important psychologically than musically" and upholds the authenticity of records of earlier swing performances. Levin argues that revivalism is not only impossible but potentially of little worth as the resulting music is profoundly inadequate compared to more recent styles: "A man playing 1938 jazz in 1950 just can't do it convincingly—because he himself has heard and perhaps prefers other things." In summary, Ulanov presents a relativist perspective, using the album to celebrate the jazz tradition where manifestations can be valued in their own right. By contrast, Levin uses the album primarily to illustrate a narrative of evolutionary progress whereby modern jazz can be valued. A further essential difference between the two reviews is the comparative perspective each draws on in assessing the performances. As in *A History of Jazz in America,* Ulanov compares the recording to his memory of the concert within the context of the swing era, whereas Levin compares the performances to Goodman's studio recordings and acknowledges an outsider retrospective position: "It must be remembered that to some extent a 1938 concert is being judged by 1950 standards" (Levin 1951: 14–15; Ulanov 1951: 29).

Once the ideological differences between Ulanov and Levin are put to one side, the commonalities between the two reviews can be understood as the result of mediation of the concert through a recording. Krupa was noted by many of the 1938 reviewers but was not mentioned by Ulanov and criticized throughout Levin's review:

> Time and time again, Krupa's drumming is revealed as loud, wobbly, and too often completely out of sympathy with what the band or soloist is doing. Bassist Harry Goodman was probably a good road manager; here once again his bassing shows up as weak and completely lacking in rhythmic push [Levin 1951: 14].

The acoustic properties of the hall and placement of the microphone (as well as possible post-production decisions) seem to favor the drums, as Krupa's relative volume is not representative of contemporary Goodman performances, whether in the studio or on broadcasts. The 1938 audience, even the classical critic Francis Perkins, understood Krupa's performance with reference to his physical gestures and as a response to the audience, which Ulanov would also have experienced. However, the recording essentially presents disembodied performances that seemed overly projective taken out of context. Harry Goodman's bass was usually under-represented, and a similar point could be made in respect to Allan Reuss's guitar. However, Bill Savory recalled that balance problems with bass and drums were interlinked on the Carnegie Hall recording: "Harry Goodman's bass was…a little weak on the big band numbers.

From time to time I was able to bring that up, but if I brought it up too high, all you got was Krupa's foot" (Firestone 1993: 368).

Just as Krupa could be criticized for being overly projective, Jess Stacy's "Sing, Sing, Sing" solo was not only suitable for dissemination on record but congruent with the newly emergent cool aesthetic of 1950s jazz. Ulanov and Levin agree that Stacy's contributions were superlative. According to Ulanov, "Those of us who were there that night didn't realize" that Stacy's solo on "Sing, Sing, Sing" was the "high spot of the evening" (1951:29). In 1938 reviews this solo was noted only by the specialist critics, since the judgment depended on understanding this as unique among Stacy's recorded performances with Goodman, which itself depended on wide knowledge of contemporary recordings. In 1951 Levin appraised Stacy's solo in similar terms: "His work all the way through this album is of a much higher level than he usually put on records during any of the short solos given him on Goodman's commercial releases in the same period" (Levin 1951: 14).

Evaluation of *The Famous 1938 Carnegie Hall Jazz Concert* within the body of recorded jazz in 1950 is fundamental to understanding its success. There is no reference in the 1950s reviews to the idea of swing in the concert hall, which had previously been used to explain the importance of the concert; instead, critics ultimately assess the album against Goodman's other recorded performances. Despite Levin's reservations, he judges many of the performances to be better than Goodman's contemporary studio recordings; Ulanov describes "Goodman standards of the time, definitively performed." *The Famous 1938 Carnegie Hall Jazz Concert* had value not only for representing performances from 1938 that had a place within the history of jazz, but also specifically as a live album within the *recorded* history of jazz, although this aspect was only loosely implied in the first reviews. "There is no comparable record of the time before our time that made the music of today possible," wrote Ulanov in *Metronome* (1951: 29), and Levin said in *DownBeat* that "the factor that is currently exciting so many people about this LP is that it has enthusiasm, large energetic chunks of it" (1951: 14).

The release of *The Famous 1938 Carnegie Hall Jazz Concert* led to reassessment of the 1938 performances that was influenced by the perspective of time and also by the record as mediator. In 1938, the concert could be historicized only in relation to previous events. Its historical importance therefore hinged on circumstantial factors such as the unusual mix of the audience and the presence of jazz in the concert hall, so the performances were assessed primarily through gauging the audience reaction.

The audience is notably absent from the 1951 reviews; instead, the performances are compared with other recordings, against which they were often demonstrably unique. Twelve years after the original concert, placing swing in the concert hall was no longer so radical, and different elements of the concert come to the fore, particularly the "cool" aesthetic and the construction of jazz history. Reviews demonstrate that *The Famous 1938 Carnegie Hall Jazz Concert*, and by association the Carnegie Hall concert, had become implicitly canonized within the interlinked dimensions of the "jazz tradition," a developmental lineage of jazz and the history of jazz recording.

RE-CREATION

> Swing continues to reassert itself, reaching new audiences but always cloaked in nostalgia.
>
> —STOWE 1994: 244

Following Goodman's concert, Carnegie Hall was further established as a venue for popular music performance, with concerts by W. C. Handy and Paul Whiteman and a recital by Ethel Waters in 1938 alone, involving a large number of swing musicians. At the end of the year, John Hammond staged his first *From Spirituals to Swing* concert at Carnegie Hall, dedicated to Bessie Smith, with a second concert a year later involving Goodman's sextet. Goodman had already returned to Carnegie Hall twice by this time, for the premiere of Bartók's *Contrasts* and then with his full band in October 1939 for a concert celebrating the 25th anniversary of the performing rights organization the American Society of Composers, Authors and Publishers (ASCAP) alongside the bands of Fred Waring, Paul Whiteman and Glenn Miller. Goodman's part of the program opened with "Don't Be That Way," ended with "Sing, Sing, Sing" and included "One O'Clock Jump." The *From Spirituals to Swing* concerts reflected those aspects of Goodman's 1938 concert on which Hammond was clearly influential, namely promotion of Basie's band, presentation of the history of the music and principles of racial equality and integration. Hammond also drew on earlier models of concerts in the Hall, especially in his fundamental aim to present "Negro music from its raw beginnings to the latest jazz" (Hammond and Townsend 1977: 199). The second *From Spirituals to Swing* concert exemplified the principle of racial equality with an integrated jam session and Goodman's sextet. The number of jazz concerts in Carnegie Hall in 1938–39 solidified the perception of Goodman's January 1938 appearance as a "first," and to an extent it established playing at the Hall as a rite of passage for jazz musicians.

Although Goodman would never attempt to replicate the 1938 concert exactly in Carnegie Hall itself, it was re-created in various forms both in the immediate aftermath of January 16, 1938, and following the release of *The Famous 1938 Carnegie Hall Jazz Concert* in 1950, which itself became the most pervasive "re-creation" of the live event. These re-creations would contribute significantly to perpetuating and disseminating the 1938 Carnegie Hall concert beyond the limitations of the audience members who were present on the night. Having established a successful formula at Carnegie Hall, Goodman's management proposed to reuse it, following the precedent of Whiteman with his "Experiment in Modern Music" concert tour in 1924. *DownBeat* reported prior to the concert that "Benny Goodman goes on a concert tour this year...keeping away from theatres and ballrooms," attributing the idea to John Hammond. The concerts were to feature a "special jazz piano concerto" by Mary Lou Williams, with the possibility of involving further guests (*DownBeat* 1938: 2). In the end, the concert tour was restricted to a single performance at Symphony Hall in Boston on May 1, 1938.[12] Bobby Hackett reprised his role as Beiderbecke in "I'm Coming Virginia," and although Williams did not appear, the idea of a piano concerto, suggesting an attempt to parallel Gershwin's *Rhapsody in Blue* in Whiteman's concert, anticipates her work with symphony orchestras from the 1940s. The Boston concert was in fact concluded by Williams's composition "Roll 'Em," which was already well established in Goodman's repertoire.

As at Carnegie Hall, the audience reaction was a significant determinant of the success of the Boston Symphony Hall concert. George Frazier reported for *DownBeat*:

[The audience reaction] was flattering, of course, and, in several instances, nothing short of idolatrous, but it was damned distracting too. The 3,000 odd who jammed every available inch of Symphony Hall behaved so bastardly that some magnificent jazz was completely drowned out. The wrong things—that is, the items that inclined to killer-diller and the exhibitionistic—were the popular successes of the evening, while the genuine thrills were accorded hardly more than a smattering of polite applause. Musically, the affair failed to maintain the standard set at Carnegie in January, but that, as I say, was largely due to the differences between the two audiences [quoted in Baron 1979: n.p.].

Goodman similarly recalled that "the thing turned into such a nightmare of mass hysteria I lost my temper, turned, faced the audience of 3,000 and shouted: 'For heaven's sake, shut up!'" (Goodman and Shane 1939: 13). There are several possible reasons for the difference in reception between Carnegie Hall and Symphony Hall. In New York, ickies were able to hear Goodman regularly at other venues, but in Boston they would undoubtedly be willing to pay for a one-off chance to hear Goodman wherever he was playing and may have dominated the Symphony Hall audience to a greater degree than at Carnegie Hall. Geoffrey Wheeler explains that the concert was advertised to students of the Massachusetts Institute of Technology (MIT) as part of an Interfraternity Council weekend, which might also explain the high spirits (Wheeler 2008: 36). The Carnegie Hall concert had already demonstrated that it was possible to present swing in the concert hall, so there may have been a sense that the music and associated icky behavior was now accepted in these surroundings. In addition, as Goodman's concert took place a few days prior to the beginning of the Boston Pops Orchestra season, it was likely to be aligned with the lighter program and more informal atmosphere of these concerts, further mediating the tension between genre and venue that had been so influential on behavior at Carnegie Hall (36).

The program for the Boston concert, recently reproduced by Wheeler, contained revised notes by Kolodin reflecting the changes in repertoire (39–40). The structure was similar to that of the Carnegie Hall concert, with the main difference being that the first half concluded with the full orchestra playing "Sing, Sing, Sing," which may also have led to increased excitement early in the evening. "Sometimes I'm Happy" was retained as the second number, and other numbers from the Carnegie Hall concert ("Don't Be That Way," "Big John Special" and "One O'Clock Jump") were performed at different points in the program. The items performed by the small groups were not listed in the printed program. The "Jam Session" was omitted, but the "Twenty Years of Jazz" demonstrates the closest replication of a particular section from the concert, for which the *Camel Caravan* show on February 15, 1938, was a precedent. Members of the Original Dixieland Jazz Band (Eddie Edwards, trombone; Larry Shields, clarinet; and Tony Sbarbaro, drums) were guests on this broadcast, performing "Dixieland One-Step" with Jess Stacy and Bobby Hackett. Following "I'm Coming Virginia" and "When My Baby Smiles at Me," Duke Ellington's "Blue Reverie" was replaced by "Mood Indigo," which, because it avoided individualistic solos and featured clarinet and piano primarily, was more easily replicated without Ellington's musicians. "Shine" was repositioned to follow the Ellington number, and the full-band "Roll 'Em" was used as the culmination of the historical sequence, replacing "Life Goes to a Party" as representative of Goodman's current style. In the Boston concert (according to the printed program), "Blue Reverie" was replaced by an Edgar Sampson arrangement of Ellington's "I Let a Song Go Out of My Heart," which a contemporary recording shows to be overwhelmingly in the Goodman style with muted brass alluding to Ellington. This version of "Twenty Years of Jazz" concluded with the harmonically adventurous "Lullaby in Rhythm," by Edgar Sampson and pianist Clarence Profit.

Re-creating "Twenty Years of Jazz" was a convenient way of representing and thereby perpetuating the Carnegie Hall concert. Re-performing the full-band numbers from the 1938 program would suggest generalized retrospection rather than evoking Carnegie Hall specifically, as they were drawn from Goodman's usual repertoire. The "Jam Session" could not be easily re-staged without numerous guests, but the historical section could be performed by Goodman's usual personnel. Replication of this particular part of the Carnegie Hall concert would also allow Goodman's place in the historical lineage of jazz to be continually reinforced, and especially as the culmination could simply be updated to reflect his current style. Bill Savory recalled Goodman's enthusiasm for this part of the concert when he was working on the Carnegie Hall recordings in preparation for the album: "The 'Twenty Years of Jazz' thing worked okay on the stage but didn't really fly when you listened to it. Benny and I had a big discussion about that, but he insisted I do it" (Firestone 1993: 369).

As well as live performances, the practice of re-creating the Carnegie Hall concert through recording was established immediately. The final part of H.E.P.'s review of the 1938 concert in *DownBeat* suggested that readers could "Run a Benny Goodman Concert—At Home!": "If your own hot club or swing group would like to duplicate the concert on a phonograph machine, the following program as given by Benny Goodman at Carnegie Hall, can be obtained on disks:..." (1938: 6). A listing of the program followed, with indications of substitutions for items not recorded by Goodman. Versions by the original artists were suggested for "Twenty Years of Jazz," and for the "Jam Session" "Victor's twelve inch platter, made this last year, titled 'Jam Session at Victor'" featuring Fats Waller, as discussed in Part One (6). Live performances provided re-creations authentic to the original concert as they were essentially embodied, albeit not always by all the "correct" bodies, while remaining ephemeral. In 1938, records could only offer a typically disembodied but also simulated experience of the concert using related performances, and only some small sense of objectifying the event. However, *The Famous 1938 Carnegie Hall Concert* was a sounding object that allowed the original performances to be both re-created and reified. As an unusual live jazz recording, the album had importance and relevance for younger listeners, as well as those with a retrospective or nostalgic relationship with the performances. However, this prime re-creation remained fundamentally disembodied; as a result, as John Hammond put it, "there was a new public eager to hear that [Carnegie Hall] band in person" (Hammond and Townsend 1977: 313).

In the years following release of *The Famous 1938 Carnegie Hall Concert*, Goodman's activities were rooted in reification and embodiment of the past. In a direct extension of fetishist fan behavior, an album of airchecks from the 1930s, originally recorded by Bill Savory, was released on Columbia Masterworks in 1952, entitled *Jazz Concert No. 2*, despite George Avakian's objections to the title (Firestone 1993: 371). A Columbia advertisement demonstrates how this format was used to give these performances an apparent coherence and value commensurate with, or even surpassing, *The Famous 1938 Carnegie Hall Concert* in their authenticity to Goodman's performance practice in the 1930s:

> Jazz concert no. 2 includes a series of the most authentic performances ever made of the original Goodman orchestra, trio and quartet. AUTHENTIC because here's the original all-star Goodman organization as it actually supplied its great new music before entranced dancers and listeners in the ballrooms, hotels and clubs of the nation when swing was at its height! [*Billboard* 1952: 30].

Goodman also began making new big-band recordings in the studio that referenced the past through repertoire consisting mainly of arrangements by Fletcher Henderson, but these were recordings that aspects of the performance (and particularly the production) rendered demonstrably of the present. The original Goodman Trio was reunited for a broadcast, the recording of which was sold to raise money for Henderson, who was seriously ill (Firestone 1993: 373). In April 1953, Goodman returned to Carnegie Hall with a big band as part of a tour with Louis Armstrong's All Stars. Howard Taubman noted approvingly in the *New York Times* that "Benny's effort to recapture the past has gone a long way" (1953), but in the opinion of others who were present, including Hammond, Goodman "played atrociously" (Hammond and Townsend 1977: 316). Ultimately, it was Goodman's collapse, withdrawal from the tour and subsequent recriminations rather than a narrative of triumphant comeback that dominated the press (Firestone 1993: 380).

In 1956, this problematic performance at Carnegie Hall was supplanted by a widely disseminated re-creation of the original Carnegie Hall concert as part of the film *The Benny Goodman Story*. Goodman did not appear in the film but recorded the soundtrack with several musicians who had taken part in 1938. Hymie Shertzer, Babe Russin, Chris Griffin, Gene Krupa, Allan Reuss, Lionel Hampton and Teddy Wilson also played themselves in the film, and Martha Tilton, Ziggy Elman and Harry James appeared in the Carnegie Hall sequence (see Figures 3.1 and 3.2). Following the model of *The Glenn Miller Story*, with which the film shared producer and scriptwriter (Valentine Davis, who also directed), *The Benny Goodman Story*'s primary narrative is the romance between Benny (which name I use here to differentiate from the real Goodman) and John Hammond's sister Alice (who married Goodman in reality in 1942), alongside the depiction of aspects of Goodman's career. Glenn Miller's early, unexplained and tragic death set an obvious end point for the film of his life, but the 1938 Carnegie Hall concert was chosen as the triumphant conclusion for the Goodman film. As such, even though the depiction of the concert is loosely modeled on the original, it was adapted to function as a culmination of personal and professional strands of Benny's story, as well as in accordance with pragmatic concerns such as the need for star billing for Harry James, Goodman's sideman in 1938 but by 1950 a famous bandleader in his own right. Presentation of numbers still familiar to audiences in the 1950s was important, as the film's musical director Joe Gershenson revealed in an interview in *Metronome*: "We checked the sale of all the Goodman records from the time they were made to the present, to find which ones the public would really prefer, finally arriving at the twenty-five tops" (Kelley 1956: 20). The re-creation of the Carnegie Hall concert in *The Benny Goodman Story* uses an equal mix of numbers that were actually played in 1938 ("Shine," "Sensation Rag" and "Sing, Sing, Sing") and interpolations ("And the Angels Sing," "Moonglow" and "Memories of You").

In addition, "Don't Be That Way" is the source of contrivance throughout the film. The phrase is used in reference to Benny on several occasions when he pursues his inclination against the advice of those around him. At a rehearsal in Carnegie Hall, this advice comes from his brother Harry, who warns Benny against taking a chance on the concert in which his reputation would be at stake. It is Benny who appends the title to "that Edgar Sampson thing" in this rehearsal because, as he puts it in regard to the expression, "that is what I've heard all my life." The rehearsal of the number prior to the Carnegie Hall concert and Benny's authorial appropriation reflects actuality. In the film, "Don't Be That Way" is not only selected as the opening number of the concert but also represents the ultimate fulfillment of Benny's artistic autonomy. We also know that the concert has the potential to reunite Benny and Alice, who have been temporarily estranged; her journey by airplane and car to Carnegie Hall is shown as the concert progresses. The relationship has been dysfunctional throughout the film, with Benny unable to articulate his feelings for Alice unless through his clarinet, while she has maintained that her idea of a real musician is someone who plays at Carnegie Hall. Prior to the concert, Benny's mother, portrayed as a stereotypical Jewish matriarch, objects to the romance, arguing in one of the more memorable lines from the film "you don't mix caviar with bagels." But present at the concert, she is shown to be condoning precisely this mixture of high and low culture and social class as well as Jewish and non-Jewish identities, circumstances that enable Benny to finally propose to Alice from the Carnegie Hall stage.[13]

Consistent with previous re-creations, the film's version of the concert focuses on "Twenty Years of Jazz." The Carnegie Hall sequence begins with Harry James making his first appearance in the film to reprise his 1938 version of "Shine." By 1955 James had adopted this as a feature with his own band, and his ownership of the performance, as distinct from signifying Armstrong, is made clear in *The Benny Goodman Story*. In the film, "Shine" is actually no longer part of the "Twenty Years of Jazz" (which follows), so the reference to Armstrong is minimized. The camera is often focused on James, establishing his physical presence, and he is name-checked in a shot of a replica program book. James's solo is very similar to that in the 1938 concert, demonstrating that it had become canonized in its own right, but he is accompanied by sustained saxophones, commensurate with the smooth style for which he had become known, rather than the rhythmic figures typical of earlier hot jazz that were played in 1938.

The inclusion of "Sensation Rag" is explained to the film's audience by Mrs. Hammond (John's mother): "This part seems to be historical. It's called 'Twenty Years of Jazz.'" Just as the original "Twenty Years of Jazz" reflected Goodman's biography, in *The Benny Goodman Story* the "Twenty Years of Jazz" is directly synonymous with Benny's history. As the band plays "Sensation Rag," images from earlier in the film of Benny's teenage encounter with Kid Ory when working on a riverboat are shown. In that scene, the music of Ory's all-black band, performed standing up and without notation, contrasts with the white band in which Benny is playing, uniformed and seated behind music stands. Despite any previous indication of his jazz credentials, Benny asks to sit in with Ory and can instantly play jazz. The film positions black musicians as the roots of jazz, and in the film's version of the concert Buck Clayton is part of the small group for the performance of this number. Inclusion of "Sensation Rag" in this "Twenty Years of Jazz" has little to do with the ODJB's recording and the corresponding history of jazz. Instead, it has become a metaphor for Benny's unmediated experience of jazz, which authenticates him as a jazz performer.

In effect, the confluence between jazz history and Benny's history, having been established so explicitly, persists throughout the remainder of the Carnegie Hall sequence; it is not clear if, or when, the "Twenty Years of Jazz" sequence ends. Next, Martha Tilton and Ziggy Elman join the band for "And the Angels Sing," shown in a replica program as the number following "Bei Mir Bist Du Schön" (which is not heard). This song was based directly on a Jewish tune, "Der Shtiller Bulgar" (The Quiet Bulgar), associated with klezmer bandleader Harry Kandel, which Elman had recorded in a jazz version under his own name with the title "Fralich in Swing" in December 1938. This was then taken up by Goodman as a vocal for Tilton with lyrics by Johnny Mercer. Inclusion of this number served to remind the film's audience of Benny's Jewishness at this crucial point in the narrative. A Quartet performance follows, in which there is a flashback through Hampton's eyes to jamming with Benny, Teddy Wilson and Gene Krupa in a café on the West Coast (in which Lionel is chef, waiter and entertainer, so portraying Benny in the role of liberator). Appropriately enough, "Avalon" was played at this point in the film since the Trio had just returned from playing a benefit on Santa Catalina Island. Although "Avalon" was performed at the 1938 concert, it is not reprised in the film and is substituted by a performance of "Moonglow," referencing the Quartet's recorded history (it was the first number the combination recorded) rather than the reality of their 1938 appearance.

As the finale, the full band plays "Sing, Sing, Sing," which implicitly references Goodman's history on film (having been used in *Hollywood Hotel*) as well as the 1938 concert itself. The camera focuses here on Goodman's manager, Willard Alexander, and images of the Palomar Ballroom success.[14] Following a rapturous reception, Benny turns to Krupa and Wilson and begins an encore, "Memories of You," a song used as a leitmotiv in the film for Benny's developing relationship with Alice. Although the number was not included in the 1938 concert, Goodman performed it with his sextet in Carnegie Hall as part of the *From Spiritu-als to Swing* concert in 1939. The impression is that it is unplanned be-cause Benny projects the introduction toward Teddy Wilson, rather than the audience, so that he can pick up the number. Since it is "their song," Alice recognizes this as a marriage proposal. Ultimately though, it seems the concert has had little impact on Benny and Alice's relationship; Benny still speaks to Alice through his clarinet and Alice fully respects Benny only when he is on the Carnegie Hall stage.

The Benny Goodman Story presents a beguiling re-creation of the Car-negie Hall concert through a veneer of authenticity that actually results in a distorted perception of the original event. This idea may be illus-trated with reference to the distinctive large double door with pediment in the back wall of the stage behind the band, a copy of those at the side of the stage at Carnegie Hall in 1938 (see Figure 3.1). In *The Benny Good-man Story*, the door was repositioned where it would be in shot as an effective signifier of Carnegie Hall, but presenting an inaccurate percep-tion of how the stage actually looked. Similarly, a replica of the concert program is used as a visual device in the film to authenticate the repertoire of the concert and to position the film's audience alongside the concert audience. Despite sustained criticism of *The Benny Goodman Story*, as an embodied representation (albeit with the wrong bodies in many cases) this film has had a pervasive influence on perceptions of the album and the original 1938 event.

Embodiment is also used as an authenticating device in the film, most obviously with the presence of many 1938 alumni. The appearance of Ziggy Elman for "And the Angels Sing" gives visual authenticity to Mannie Klein's performance on the soundtrack of what was, after all, material strongly associated with Elman. The idea of Goodman's sound authenticating Steve Allen's embodiment is more problematic. Allen's miming underlines Goodman's absence, and at points in "Sing, Sing, Sing" Goodman can clearly be heard on the soundtrack when Benny is not actually playing. More significantly, the physical presence of Wilson, Hampton and Clayton authenticates Benny's performances, especially in the context of how the roots of jazz are presented in the film, but it exag-gerates the state of racial integration in 1938. By this date, Wilson and Hampton appeared in Goodman's small groups, which were in effect presented as "special features," but not as members of his main band; Clayton's participation in the 1938 concert was limited to the "Jam Ses-sion." Although Wilson and Clayton appear as part of the main orchestra throughout the film, including at Carnegie Hall, there is no explicit ref-erence to related racial issues in the script. Moreover, in the final stages of the film alone, Benny claims responsibility for the title of Edgar Sampson's composition, and Harry James's presence obliterates Armstrong.

Ultimately, as Gabbard points out, culminating the film with the Carnegie Hall concert sequence elevates white jazz in a final gesture typical of the white jazz biopic (1996: 80). Nevertheless, the extensive associated press coverage of the film seized on Goodman's contributions to integration in jazz. This included a feature in the *New York Post* entitled "The OTHER Benny Goodman Story," which presented a chronological overview of "how Benny Goodman broke the color line in the big band business," noting that "the climax of Goodman's integration campaign came at the history-making Carnegie Hall concert in 1938, when the Goodman crew was augmented by Negro musicians from Duke Ellington's and Count Basie's orchestras" (Gruenberg 1956: 5). Arguably more significant moments occurred previously, with the first public performances of Goodman's integrated Trio in 1936, and later, when Henderson was employed as a permanent member of Goodman's main band in 1939.

Although some of the publicity for the 1938 concert suggested that presenting swing in the concert hall would primarily serve to legitimize the music as art in its own right, contemporary accounts of the event itself more consistently describe that the surroundings served to acculturate the behavior of swing fans to the norms of the concert hall. There is no reference to the idea of swing in the concert hall in the 1950s reviews of the album, with critics simply tending to assess the concert performances against Goodman's other recordings, but the theme of legitimization is made prominent again in *The Benny Goodman Story*. When the idea of the concert is suggested to Benny in an earlier scene, he responds, "It would be a landmark, not just for us but for all hot music, a sign of recognition." A focus throughout the concert sequence is the reaction of the Hammond parents, whose fine clothes demonstrate that they, along with the rest of the audience, "belong" in Carnegie Hall. Eventually, in "Sing, Sing, Sing," the Hammond feet begin to tap. With few signs of the young icky fans, the film emphasizes acceptance of swing by the establishment rather than the effect of the surroundings on the swing audience as described most prominently in the 1938 reviews.

The (re-)canonization of repertoire heard in *The Benny Goodman Story* was ensured not only by the film itself but also through "remarkably similar discs released by five recording companies" in 1956 that left consumers with aesthetic choices about how they wished to listen to the "soundtrack." John S. Wilson described these differences in the *New York Times*. Victor provided "polish and studio sound quality" on *The Benny*

Goodman Story soundtrack. Columbia drew on airchecks for *The Great Benny Goodman*, which was "rougher, looser, and frequently more suggestive of the excitement projected by the Goodman band in those days." Decca's album of new recordings with the convoluted title *Music of the Soundtrack of The Benny Goodman Story* had a "slightly different flavor" due to the contributions of musicians who had not previously associated with Goodman (Wilson 1956). Similarly, audiences had more choice about how they wanted to experience the 1938 Carnegie Hall concert through the availability of various live performances and recorded versions.

The decennial anniversaries of the Carnegie Hall concert have been marked with live events since 1968, when Goodman held a party that reunited many of the Carnegie Hall alumni. The event was sponsored by WNEW, which broadcast interviews and a jam session by the some of the guests (Connor 1988: 254). In 1978 Goodman gave a concert at Carnegie Hall that deliberately bore little resemblance to the original event. The 1938 repertoire was represented only by "Loch Lomond" (in a new arrangement) and "Sing, Sing, Sing;" "Don't Be That Way" and "Stompin' at the Savoy" were heard as part of a medley. Otherwise the program was a mix of old and new, ranging from the Dixieland number "That's a Plenty" to Beatles hits. This concert involved only two of the performers from 1938 in addition to Goodman: Lionel Hampton and Martha Tilton. The concert was considered too long and the program poorly planned; the band was under-rehearsed and plagued by poor amplification, and Goodman struggled to fulfill the bandleader role. In the words of *DownBeat* critic Arnold Jay Smith, "This night, it seemed that not only was Goodman himself not up to his previous standards, but that whatever else could have gone wrong did" (Morgenstern et al. 1978: 21).

Goodman attempted to reinvent the concert in 1978, but following his death in 1986 the 50th anniversary concert exhibited the opposite response, presenting a replication of the original program with Bob Wilber in the role of Goodman. The principal alteration was to position "One O'Clock Jump" at the end of the concert, which allowed the guests from Basie and Ellington's bands to be included in the finale (Kanzler 1988). This change may have been made to highlight the collaborations and particularly the racial integration of the original event, although Wilber's small groups were apparently all white (1988). At the interval of the concert, one of Goodman's clarinets was presented to Carnegie Hall by William Hyland, the executor of his will. Hyland performed "Memories of You" on the instrument, providing a clear link with *The Benny Goodman*

Story. Used in the film as a theme for the love between Benny and Alice, this song now directed similar emotions toward Goodman's memory. Presenting the instrument emphasizes the importance of artifacts in jazz history, especially since *The Benny Goodman Story* had established Benny as being able to make his most profound utterances (such as a marriage proposal) through his clarinet.

Wilber had presented successful tributes to Goodman since at least 1980, when Goodman himself visited Michael's Pub in New York and "sat delighted as the musicians [Wilber's sextet] re-created the historic Goodman Carnegie Hall jazz concert of 1938." Goodman even joined in with the group himself, effectively endorsing their efforts (Cummings and Krebs 1980). Wilber also organized a 75th birthday concert for Goodman in 1984 in which he used arrangements from Goodman's library (Wilber and Webster 1989: 189). Similarly, use of the original arrangements helped to ensure a faithful re-creation of the concert in 1988, but the solos presented a more complex problem. Rather than copying the original solos, the group adhered to jazz practice by improvising new material, "basing solo ideas (and lengths) on the original recordings" (Kanzler 1988). For example, pianist Mark Shane signified on Stacy's original "Sing, Sing, Sing" solo by introducing material variously identified as Chopin, Ravel and Debussy (Simon 1980; Wilson 1988). Wilber's approach was congruent with the rise of the jazz repertory orchestra from the 1970s, to which, as Gary Kennedy points out in his useful survey, "the practice of re-creation from classic recordings" was integral (Kennedy n.d.). However, as Kanzler commented, "Atavism, even the most inspired atavism, has its limits, and the soft glow of nostalgia can't equal the bright, vibrant beam of the original creative moment" (Kanzler 1988: 42). With the re-creation of an authentically embodied version of the 1938 concert now impossible, owing to the death of Goodman and many of his original sidemen, Wilber's concert reinforced *The Famous 1938 Carnegie Hall Jazz Concert* as a definitive source to which all live re-creations would necessarily be secondary.

As a result, debate persists as to which recording best represents the 1938 concert, focusing particularly on the related issues of completeness and sound quality. "Sometimes I'm Happy" and "If Dreams Come True," the numbers missing from the 1950 release, were issued on Sunbeam Records alongside airchecks in 1973. In 1977, John McDonough prepared liner notes for a 40th anniversary reissue, but the original discs could not be found at Columbia and the project was abandoned (McDonough 2006: 11). Meanwhile, the album was remastered "directly from the original analog tapes" and released on CD under the Columbia Jazz Masterpieces brand in 1986. The new title, *Benny Goodman Live at Carnegie Hall*, foregrounded "liveness" as a defining feature of the recording, which 1950s commentators had expressed only in broad terms of "enthusiasm" but could now be understood in the context of a longer history of live recording. After a long search, the original discs from 1938 were found to be in the possession of Howard Scott, the producer of the 1950 album, who said he had been given them as a present by Goodman (McDonough 2006: 12). In 1999 Sony released *The Famous 1938 Carnegie Hall Jazz Concert* on the reissue label Columbia Legacy, thus highlighting the historical nature of the recording. This new version, produced by Phil Schaap, included the two missing numbers, material previously edited from "Honeysuckle Rose," additional applause and Goodman's only announcement (after "Loch Lomond").[15] This was coupled with material from the promotional disc supplied to radio stations. Although the release used the original 1950s artwork, the spine of the CD case bears the text "Benny Goodman at Carnegie Hall—1938—Complete," and the newly added items are highlighted in the notes on the back cover.

A full-page advertisement for the 1999 release printed in *DownBeat* (a condensed version of the text on the back of the CD itself), headed "The Most Legendary Concert in Jazz History," recalls the rhetoric of the handbill for the original concert:

> On the night of January 16 1938, American music was changed forever when Benny Goodman, The King of Swing, brought jazz to the rarefied concert setting of Carnegie Hall for the very first time—and presented what many consider the most famous live show in jazz history.
>
> On this night, Goodman and his band of jazz giants and very special guests conquered the classical music mecca and won a new respectability for "America's indigenous art form."
>
> Originally issued on LP in 1950, this 2-CD set presents the groundbreaking event in its entirety for the first time ever. It includes 5 bonus tracks taken from newly discovered sources [the famous "lost acetates"], both original and new liner notes, and stunning previously-unpublished photos.
>
> Featuring performances by some of the great jazzmen of the century including Count Basie, Harry James, Lionel Hampton, Lester Young, Johnny Hodges, Cootie Williams, Harry Carney, Gene Krupa and many others [*DownBeat* 1999: 70].

The advertisement text makes obvious reference to the "great men" model of jazz historiography. Similarly, the "Jam Session" was valued by reviewers not only for its supposed completeness on the new release (which actually made it longer, with the potential of compounding earlier criticisms), but as a "once-in-a-lifetime public jam"; and a complete listing of the players involved was often given (Sohmer 2000: 130). Many reviews rely on the presence of the "great men" of jazz to quantify the importance of the event; for example, John McDonough in *DownBeat* wrote that the concert is primarily "an astonishing assembly of the period's greatest modern players, all at their height, in a vigorous and sustained concert performance" (2000a: 76). Sohmer is unusual in defining the importance of the concert as "an unprecedented coup for jazz and racially integrated public performance," since race receives scant mention in the body of reviews (2000: 129). In accordance with the advertisement, the concert has continued to be represented in entries in jazz record guides primarily as a site for acceptance of jazz as "America's indigenous art form," a motive often presented as Goodman's own.

> Goodman felt the need to legitimize the jazz side of his music by fronting a jazz concert in Carnegie Hall [Shadwick 1997: 205, *Gramophone Jazz Good CD Guide*].
> Considered the single most important jazz or popular music concert in history: jazz's "coming out" party to the world of "respectable" music, held right in that throne room of musical respectability, Carnegie Hall [Bogdanov et al. 2002: 487, *All Music Guide to Jazz*].
> This was one of those events—like Ellington at Newport nearly two decades later—when jazz history is spontaneously changed, even if Goodman had clearly planned the whole thing as a crowning manoeuvre [Cook and Morton 2006: 520, *Penguin Guide to Jazz Recordings*].

In fact, legitimization was more clearly demonstrated in *The Benny Goodman Story* (remember the Hammonds tapping their feet) than in the compromises made by both ickies and longhairs in 1938.

By 1999, the place of the Carnegie Hall concert in the history of jazz had been long assured, but nuance was still achievable. "The first swing concert in the history of Carnegie Hall," having become "*The Famous 1938 Carnegie Hall Jazz Concert*," was now "The Most Legendary Concert in Jazz History." The semantic difference between "famous" and "legendary" implies that rather than canonical status of the concert being achieved *through* discourse and representations, including the recording, it is now not only the concert that is canonized but its legend, of which the recording is a fundamental part. This is analogous to and compatible with ongoing construction of the jazz tradition through recordings. The previously cited advertisement in *DownBeat* incorporates photographs from the 1938 concert, the record sleeve from 1950 and the "Live at Carnegie Hall" strap line used for the first CD release to illustrate the legendary nature of the recording. Similarly, the product itself includes numerous photographs, reproduction of a concert program and the reminiscences of its owner, Turk Van Lake, who attended the 1938 concert, in the accompanying booklet. There are also a number of references to the 1950 release, most notably reuse of the cover design, even extending to a cardboard sleeve around the plastic CD case mimicking an LP, and the inclusion of Kolodin's original liner notes. Moreover, the first disc begins with Goodman's retrospective spoken introduction, which places the listener more firmly in 1950 than 1938. Each stage of the recorded mediation of the concert had been marked with a narrative of discovery, the latest chapter of which was the story of the "lost acetates," related by producer Schaap in the liner notes in sensationalist terms, but at the same time elevating the legend itself to the status of high art:

> The truth about the discs and their history can be the basis of a four act opera that would include a lover's triangle, a grand larceny, a high stakes shell game, a great detective story, several charlatans, and no heros [sic] [Schaap 1999: 38].

The reissued album not surprisingly attracted significant attention, both as a result of the inherent canonicity of the concert, which made a complete recorded version attractive, and also in its potential capacity to serve as a sonic icon of the past. This was especially relevant within the profoundly retrospective period at the turn of the millennium that led to a "decade of retrospection" in which the jazz record market was saturated with reissues (McDonough 2000b). The material accompanying the 1999 release presents it as the ultimate representation of the concert, incorporating and improving on all previous manifestations. However, Schaap had an uncompromising and controversial attitude toward producing the recording in which he re-created the complete concert by including as much of the sound captured by the original discs as possible, which meant a corresponding reduction in overall sound quality:

> How you listeners react to the residual disc noise heard on the original 78 RPM discs will be a matter of personal taste. You would not be hearing the new material at all were it not for their recent uncovering. Still, many will find the nicks and scratches discomforting.

Furthermore, they are heard throughout the two CDs.... The greatest noise reduction device is your brain. Trust it to work with your ears to hear music that would otherwise have been excised if a computer did the work. This is the truth [Schaap 1999: 38].

The text on the back of the CD states optimistically, "Schaap's liner notes do acknowledge the process of locating, then remastering, this epochal program, though the focus is always on the stars and the music they created." Conversely, as Schaap himself indicates, far from the original materials simply offering an unmediated experience of the concert, the listening experience was profoundly unlike that of the original concert audience. Schaap's decision to incorporate not only missing musical material but other sounds captured on the original recordings detracted from the performances for some, as the results contradicted expectations of listening to recorded jazz:

> A dozen times on this set in instances ranging from 21 to 74 seconds, the somewhat fanatical producer Phil Schaap has added additional applause and the awkward silence that often took place between songs. This slows down the momentum of the performance and is a waste [*Cadence* 2000].

However, for others, this material provided an experience analogous with being at the concert itself, the aura of the performers and the audience transcending the technological limitations:

> I do vigorously applaud Schaap's decision to give us the entirety of the recordings, audience reaction, between tune waits, announcement of "no encores", clicks, pops, scratches and all [Klee 2000: 40].
>
> Certainly, a very live atmosphere is captured, including full applause and setting-up breaks; the crackling is not constant and can be ignored by concentrating on the exciting music that was played by a gathering of greats [Tomkins 2000: 25].

Tomkins does not particularly differentiate between how additional sounds from the concert and the "crackling" from the recording foster "atmosphere." Indeed, in general terms the extraneous noise can be a constant reminder that one is listening to a recording of a live performance, and it emphasizes the album's status as a historical artifact. In pursuing an agenda of completeness, Schaap's version highlights the limitations of using original recordings to fully re-create past performances in the present, rather than maintaining an illusion of immediacy, which could be achieved by editing, as with the 1950s LPs. Schaap's inherent reification of the original sound source as the most complete representation of the concert was echoed in the final judgment of the majority of reviewers on the new version, which they recommended for its importance as an artifact of jazz history, whereas the 1950 version was preferred for content.

> This concert is essential for every serious Jazz collection. But those of you who still have the LP version would be well advised to keep it! [*Cadence* 2000].

> This is essential music that belongs in every jazz record collection, even if, like me, you retain the previous reissues for sentimental reasons [Klee 2000: 40].

> Although this concert belongs in every historically-minded jazz fan's collection, first time purchasers should be advised that, even with the most advanced remastering techniques available today, complete removal of the never-really-intrusive clicks and pops on the original acetates would have compromised the frequency spectrum governing such aural essentials as harmonic, overtones, tonal brilliance and, not the least, the incomparable acoustics of the Hall itself [Sohmer 2000: 132].

> Presumably to compensate for the "residual" aspect, this is out at midprice. So no excuse for not adding it to your collection [Tomkins 2000: 25].

Aesthetic judgments aside, a particular sound for the concert established over the previous fifty years of *The Famous 1938 Carnegie Hall Jazz Concert* on LP has also had an impact on perceptions, as McDonough suggests:

> To many who had grown up with the LP version, [Schaap's version] sounded shrill and shallow, cluttered with excessive surface scratches and abrasions that could have been avoided without compromising the music.... We have no doubt that anyone with an interest in the seminal jazz concert will want both the Columbia/Legacy and the Jasmine versions [McDonough 2006: 12].

These assessments clearly demonstrate the ultimate canonization of least two recordings as representative of the concert and indeed its "legend." This is further typified by inclusion of both Schaap's version and the previous CD reissue in the *All Music Guide to Jazz: The Definitive Guide to Jazz* (Bogdanov et al. 2002).

The Schaap reissue has been followed by a number of other complete versions of the concert, notably on Jasmine, Avid and Definitive, all of which emphasize their "complete" nature but take different approaches to mastering the material to present a compromise between completeness and sound quality.[16] For example, the Avid notes state, "We believe noise reduction and de-clicking techniques, applied with sensitivity, can enhance the listening experience" ("Liner Notes" 2006: 9). Just as the limited time span of the original two-LP release led to editing that affected perceptions of the performances, so the expanded length of two CDs required consideration of how to fill the remaining space, a decision that also had the potential to influence perceptions as with Schaap's inclusion of Goodman's 1950 announcements. The latest Avid 4-CD set contextualizes the 1938 concert with "classic material from 1954–1955," including *The Benny Goodman Story* soundtrack, positioning the listener within the context of the period of the initial release of the recording. Conversely, the latest Definitive version couples the concert with the *Camel Caravan* show from January 18, 1938 (discussed earlier). The Jasmine release presents only the material of the 1938 concert, but it includes a version of an essay by John McDonough that comprehensively summarizes both the circumstances of the concert and its subsequent dissemination on record (McDonough 2006).

On January 16, 1938, Carnegie Hall presented a unique, if not completely unprecedented, performance situation that resulted in unique, if not completely unprecedented, performances from Goodman and the other musicians. Prior to release of *The Famous 1938 Carnegie Hall Jazz Concert*, these performances remained essentially ephemeral, and the impact of the event was limited to those who were most closely involved. Representation of the concert on record in the 1950s, again unique but not completely unprecedented, gave not only the concert but the album itself canonical status. *The Famous 1938 Carnegie Hall Jazz Concert* has both provoked and enabled subsequent embodied re-creations of the concert in live performance and film as well as in further recordings. It thereby dominates perceptions of the 1938 event. This study has demonstrated both the authority and the inadequacy of recording in representing live jazz performance and mediating between performer and listener.

APPENDIX 1

IV

"Tiger Rag" Nick LaRocca
"Body and Soul" John Green

V

"Avalon" Al Jolson, Vincent Rose
"The Man I Love" (from *Strike Up the Band*) George and Ira Gershwin
"I Got Rhythm" (from *Girl Crazy*) George and Ira Gershwin
    Intermission

VI

"Blue Skies" Irving Berlin
"Loch Lomond" Traditional Scotch

VII

"Blue Room" (from *The Girl Friend*) Richard Rodgers and Lorenz Hart
"Swingtime in the Rockies" James Mundy
"Bei Mir Bist du Schoen" Jacobs, Secunda, Cahn, Chaplin

VIII

"Who" (from *Sunny*) Jerome Kern, Otto Harbach
"Dinah" Harry Akst
"Stompin' at the Savoy" Edgar Sampson
"I'm a Ding Dong Daddy" Phil Baxter

IX

"Sing, Sing, Sing" Louis Prima

X

Reprise

Appendix 2

MEMBERS OF THE ORCHESTRA

Benny Goodman, *Clarinet*
Reeds: Babe Rusin [*sic*], George Koenig, Herman Shertzer and Arthur Rollini
Trumpets: Harry James, Ziggy Elman and Gordon Griffin
Trombones: Red Ballard and Vernon Brown
Harry Goodman, *Bass*; Allan Reuss, *Guitar*; Jess Stacy, *Piano*; Gene Krupa, *Drums*; Martha Tilton, *Vocalist*
Cornet soloist in "I'm Comin' Virginia": Bobby Hackett
Soloists in "Blue Reverie". Johnny Hodges, *Soprano Saxophone*; "Cootie" Williams, *Trumpet*; and Harry Carney, *Baritone Saxophone*

Guest soloists in the Jam Session:
Count Basie, *Piano*
Lester Young, *Tenor Saxophone*
"Buck" Clayton, *Trumpet*
Freddie Green, *Guitar*
Walter Page, *Bass*
Johnny Hodges, *Alto Saxophone*
Harry Carney, *Baritone Saxophone*
and
Members of the Goodman Orchestra

NOTES

INTRODUCTION

1. Full details of repertoire and personnel are given in Appendices 1 and 2.

PART ONE

2. Schuller proceeds to note that Ellington's small groups predate Goodman and Pollack, but only on record (Schuller 1989: 811).
3. In *Really the Blues* Mezzrow recalled that the Harlem Uproar House was closed after an incident when blue swastikas were painted on the dance floor and on a poster at the club (Mezzrow and Wolfe 1999: 289). However, Leonard Feather claims that this was a publicity stunt by the club owner Jay Faggen: "A friend of mine, Mike Gould, who was in the club, saw Faggen at work on the alleged vandalism: nevertheless, Mezzrow recalled the incident in his book as if it had been genuine" (Feather 1986: 29–30).

PART TWO

4. In the following discussion, I use the terms "Goodman's version" and "James's version" for ease of reference, although James was probably primarily responsible for both arrangements.
5. The introduction and coda only were part of a medley by the Goodman Orchestra and Quartet, which was included in the short film *For Auld Lang Syne*, released in April 1938. Leading personalities of the day took part in the film, waiving their fees, and when the film was shown in cinemas patrons were asked to contribute to the Will Rogers Memorial Fund (n.a. 2011).
6. Although Goodman played in the pit for *Strike Up the Band*, this was in 1930 (Firestone 1993: 63). "The Man I Love" was cut from the 1927 production and not included in the 1930 rewrite (Suskin 2000: 68).

7. A melodic quotation from an unknown source at the end of the final bridge was transferred in a similar way.

PART THREE

8. In an interview in 1963, Goodman commented: "To me, the idea of merging jazz and classical music has always seemed to be one of the most difficult things in the world. You might get something good, but you would probably destroy the character of both" (Dance 2001: 262). Incorporation of Alec Templeton's "Bach Goes to Town" into his repertoire in 1938 might be indicative of what he perceived to be a successful fusion at around the time of the Carnegie Hall concert.

9. Just as Goodman and Krupa quickly reestablished their friendship and played together again later in their careers, so Krupa seems to have quickly forgotten his last recording date with Goodman. Connor recalls that Krupa delighted in telling the story of listening to "Don't Be That Way" on the radio and exclaiming in response to the drum break, "Man, that'll never make it." Connor continues: "Not until the record ended did the announcer identify it as Benny Goodman's newest release; Gene thought it was another band and another drummer's!" (Connor 1988: 83). It is significant also that Krupa did not recognize his own playing, which resulted from this latter stressful period with Goodman.

10. Stacy, along with Reuss, was also in the studio on January 18, 1938, with Lionel Hampton and some of Ellington's musicians (among them Cootie Williams and Johnny Hodges, who played at Carnegie Hall). Hampton recorded a laid-back version of "Don't Be That Way" on which the composer, Edgar Sampson, solos on baritone saxophone.

11. Jessup has suggested that these discs were recorded in spring 1951, after the release of the album (2010: 22).

12. Joe Klee recalled that the program for a Goodman concert at Ravinia Park outside Chicago in summer 1938 "listed the selections as played at Carnegie Hall." Therefore, it seems likely that the repertoire and reference to Carnegie Hall endured in Goodman's live performances even though the concert tour did not occur as planned (Klee 2000: 40).

13. Krin Gabbard identifies *The Benny Goodman Story* as part of a series of remakes of the 1927 film *The Jazz Singer* in which these themes are prominent (1996: 39).

14. Goodman wanted Jess Stacy to reprise his piano solo in the film, but although Stacy got as far as the studio the reunion was short-lived:

> I get out there and I discover that they have given most of the things I did with the band to Teddy Wilson, who was never actually a member of the band. And I was supposed to do just some little thing on one number—for flat scale for one session. Then Benny, trying to be funny, said I was playing like I needed a blood transfusion. I told him ---- ----, and walked out [Emge 1955: 39].

15. Although Buck Clayton's final solo chorus was restored, there are still some beats missing from the bridge on this and other reissues.

16. I refer to the most recent versions from these companies: *The Complete Famous 1938 Carnegie Hall Jazz Concert Plus 1950s Material* (2006, Avid AMBX 151); *Benny Goodman Carnegie Hall, January 16th 1938 The Complete Concert* (2006, Jasmine, JASCD 656); and *Benny Goodman The Complete Legendary 1938 Carnegie Hall Concert* (2008, Definitive, DRCD11378). An earlier version from Avid was incomplete. Curiously, Schaap and subsequent reissues omit a portion from the first and second choruses of collective improvisation at the end of "I Got Rhythm" that was included on the original album (and pre-Schaap versions on CD). Therefore, the extent to which these reissues can be considered "complete" is questionable.

REFERENCES

n.a. "For Auld Lang Syne," Internet Movie Database <http://www.imdb.com/title/tt0317520/>, accessed 15 March 2011.

—— (1919), *The One Hundred and One Best Songs* (Chicago: Cable).

Aitch, N. H. (1915), *The Golden Book of Favorite Songs* (Chicago: Hall and McCreary).

Archetti, Enzo (1938a), "Swing Music Notes," *American Music Lover*, 3 (9), p. 362–363.

—— (1938b), "Swing Music Notes," *American Music Lover*, 3 (12), p. 477.

—— (1950), "Review of the Benny Goodman Carnegie Hall Concert (Columbia)," *American Record Guide*, 17, pp. 253–254.

Badger, R. Reid (1989), "James Reese Europe and the Prehistory of Jazz," *American Music*, 7 (1), pp. 48–67.

Balliett, Whitney (1978), "Fortieth," in Whitney Balliett (ed.), *Barney, Bradley and Max: Sixteen Portraits in Jazz* (New York, Oxford: Oxford University Press), pp. 154–165.

Baron, Stanley (1979), *Benny, King of Swing: A Pictorial Biography Based on Benny Goodman's Personal Archives* (London: Thames and Hudson).

Barthes, Roland, and Heath, Stephen (1977), *Image, Music, Text* (London: Fontana).

Becker, Howard S. (2000), "The Etiquette of Improvisation," *Mind, Culture & Activity*, 7 (3), pp. 171–176.

"Benny's Barrage Baffles Critics" (1938), *Metronome*, February, p. 18.

Billboard (1952), "Benny Goodman's Jazz Concert No. 2 [Advertisement]," *Billboard*, November 15, 1952, p. 30.

Blesh, Rudi (1946), *Shining Trumpets: A History of Jazz* (New York: Knopf).

Bogdanov, Vladimir, Woodstra, Chris, and Erlewine, Stephen Thomas (2002), *All Music Guide to Jazz: The Definitive Guide to Jazz Music* (San Francisco: Backbeat Books).

Bordman, Gerald (1982), *Days to Be Happy, Years to Be Sad: The Life and Music of Vincent Youmans* (New York, Oxford: Oxford University Press).

Bowen, José (2007), "Who Plays the Tune in *Body and Soul*?" paper given at RMA/CHARM Conference: Musicology and Recordings, 2007, Royal Holloway, University of London.

Brackman, Al (1938a), "New York by Storm," *Melody Maker*, January 8, 1938, p. 9.

—— (1938b), "New York Also Has Terrific Swing Concert," *Melody Maker,* February 5, 1938, p. 11.

—— (1938c), "New York," *Melody Maker,* January 29, 1938, p. 11.

Brooks, Tim (2004), *Lost Sounds: Blacks and the Birth of the Recording Industry, 1890–1919* (Urbana: University of Illinois Press).

Brown, T. Dennis (n.d.), "Drum Set," in Barry Kernfeld (ed.), *The New Grove Dictionary of Jazz, 2nd ed.* (Grove Music Online, Oxford Music Online).

Butterfield, Matthew (2002), "Music Analysis and the Social Life of Jazz Recordings," *Current Musicology* (71–73), pp. 324–352.

Cadence (2000), "Benny Goodman at Carnegie Hall—1938—Complete," *Cadence,* June 2000, pp. 25–26.

"Carnegie Hall Program—Sunday Evening, January 16th, at 8:30" (1938), (MSS 53, the Benny Goodman Papers in the Irving S. Gilmore Music Library of Yale University).

Charters, Samuel Barclay, and Kunstadt, Leonard (1962), *Jazz: A History of the New York Scene* (Garden City, NY: Doubleday).

Chilton, John (1999), *Ride, Red, Ride: The Life of Henry "Red" Allen* (London: Cassell).

——, and Kernfeld, Barry (n.d.), "Hackett, Bobby," in Barry Kernfeld (ed.), *The New Grove Dictionary of Jazz, 2nd ed.* (Grove Music Online, Oxford Music Online).

Coller, Derek (1998), *Jess Stacy: The Quiet Man of Jazz* (New Orleans: G H B Jazz Foundation).

Collier, James Lincoln (1989a), *Benny Goodman and the Swing Era* (New York, Oxford: Oxford University Press).

—— (1989b), *Duke Ellington: The Life and Times of the Restless Genius of Jazz* (London: Pan Books).

Connor, D. Russell (1988), *Benny Goodman: Listen to His Legacy* (Metuchen, NJ, London: Scarecrow and Institute of Jazz Studies).

Cook, Richard, and Morton, Brian (2006), *The Penguin Guide to Jazz Recordings,* 8th ed. (London: Penguin).

Crawford, Richard (2004), "George Gershwin's 'I Got Rhythm' (1930) (1993)," in Robert Wyatt and John Andrew Johnson (eds.), *The George Gershwin Reader* (Oxford: Oxford University Press), pp. 156–171.

——, and Magee, Jeffrey (1992), *Jazz Standards on Record, 1900–1942: A Core Repertory* (Chicago: Center for Black Music Research, Columbia College Chicago).

Crystal, Fred (1951), "Letter," *Metronome,* March 1951, p. 28.

Cummings, Judith, and Krebs, Albin (1980), "Notes on People," *New York Times,* August 8, 1980, sec. A, p. 20.

Cuscuna, Michael (2005), "Strictly on the Record: The Art of Jazz and the Recording Industry," *The Source: Challenging Jazz Criticism,* 2 (1), pp. 63–70.

Dance, Stanley (2001), *The World of Swing* (New York: Da Capo).

Dean, Penny Lee (1980/R1996), "A History of the Catalina Channel Swims Since 1927," <http://swimcatalina.com/index.php/about/catalina-channe-lhistory-free-book>, accessed March 1, 2012.

Deffaa, Chip (1989), *Swing Legacy* (Folkestone, UK: Scarecrow Press).

DeVeaux, Scott (1989), "The Emergence of the Jazz Concert, 1935–1945," *American Music,* 7 (1), pp. 6–29.

—— (1991), "Constructing the Jazz Tradition: Jazz Historiography," *Black American Literature Forum,* 25 (3), pp. 525–560.

Dodge, Roger Pryor (1940), "Roger Pryor Dodge on Bubber Miley," in Mark Tucker (ed.), *The Duke Ellington Reader* (Oxford: Oxford University Press), pp. 454–458.

DownBeat (1938), "B. G. Invades Sanctum of Long-Hairs," *DownBeat,* January 1938, p. 2.

—— (1950), "Goodman Back with Columbia," *DownBeat,* August 25, 1950, p. 2.

—— (1956), "Radio Interview with Benny Goodman," *DownBeat,* February 8, 1956, pp. 12–13.

—— (1999), "The Most Legendary Concert in Jazz History [Advertisement]," *DownBeat,* November 1999, p. 70.

Downes, Olin (1938), "Goodman Is Heard in 'Swing' Concert," *New York Times,* January 17, 1938, p. 11.

Driggs, Frank (n.d.), "Sampson, Edgar," in Barry Kernfeld (ed.), *The New Grove Dictionary of Jazz,* 2nd ed. (Grove Music Online, Oxford Music Online).

Edwards, Brent Hayes (2002), "Louis Armstrong and the Syntax of Scat," *Critical Inquiry,* 28 (3), pp. 618–649.

Emge, Charles (1955), "Ex-BG Sidemen Evince Mixed Emotions at Biofilm Selections," *DownBeat,* October 19, 1955, p. 39.

Erenberg, Lewis A. (1998), *Swingin' the Dream: Big Band Jazz and the Rebirth of American Culture* (Chicago, London: University of Chicago Press).

Ewing, Annemarie (1938), "Carnegie Hall Gets First Taste of Swing," *DownBeat,* February 1938, pp. 5, 7.

Feather, Leonard (1986), *The Jazz Years: Earwitness to an Era* (London: Quartet).

Ferguson, Otis (1937), "Piano in the Band," in Malcolm Cowley (ed.), *In the Spirit of Jazz: The Otis Ferguson Reader* (New York: Da Capo).

Ferguson, Otis, Chamberlain, Dorothy, and Wilson, Robert (1997), *In the Spirit of Jazz: The Otis Ferguson Reader* (New York: Da Capo Press).

Finkelstein, Sidney (1948), *Jazz: A People's Music* (New York: Citadel Press).

Firestone, Ross (1993), *Swing, Swing, Swing: The Life and Times of Benny Goodman* (London: Hodder & Stoughton).

Fuld, James J. (2000), *The Book of World-Famous Music: Classical, Popular, and Folk* (New York: Dover).

Gabbard, Krin (1996), *Jammin' at the Margins: Jazz and the American Cinema* (Chicago, London: University of Chicago Press).

Gardner, Edward Foote (2000), *Popular Songs of the Twentieth Century: A Charted History* (St. Paul, MN: Paragon House).

Gendron, Bernard (1995), " 'Moldy Figs' and Modernists: Jazz at War (1942–1946)," in Krin Gabbard (ed.), *Jazz Among the Discourses* (Durham, NC, and London: Duke University Press), pp. 31–56.

Giddins, Gary (2001), *Satchmo: The Genius of Louis Armstrong* (New York: Da Capo).

Gilbert, Gama (1938), "Swing It! And Even in a Temple of Music," *New York Times Magazine,* January 16, 1938, sec. 8 (Magazine), pp. 7, 21.

Goodman, Benny (1937), "Letters to the Editors—"Life Goes to a Party," *Life,* November 15, 1937, p. 6.

Goodman, Benny, and Kolodin, Irving (1939), *The Kingdom of Swing* (New York: Stackpole Sons).

Goodman, Benny, and Shane, Ted (1939), "Now Take the Jitterbug," *Collier's Magazine,* February 25, 1939, pp. 11–13, 60.

Grauer, Bill (1951), "Benny Swings Again," *Record Changer,* June, p. 3.

Gronow, Pekka, and Saunio, Ilpo (1998), *An International History of the Recording Industry* (London: Cassell).

Gruenberg, Charles (1956), "The Other Benny Goodman Story," *New York Post,* March 11, 1956, sec. Magazine, p. 5.

Hammond, John, and Townsend, Irving (1977), *John Hammond on Record: An Autobiography* (New York: Ridge Press).

Hampton, Lionel, and Haskins, James (1989), *Hamp: An Autobiography* (London: Robson, 1990).

Hancock, Jon (2008), *Benny Goodman: The Famous 1938 Carnegie Hall Jazz Concert* (Shrewsbury, UK: Prancing Fish).

Handy, William Christopher (1941), *Father of the Blues: An Autobiography* (New York: Da Capo).

Hanscom, Joe (1938), "Pickets, Cameras Attend Concert," *Metronome,* February 1938, pp. 15, 40.

H.E.P. (1938), "Goodman Came, Saw, and Laid a Golden Egg!" *DownBeat,* February 1938, p. 1, 6.

Hodeir, Andre (1956), *Jazz: Its Evolution and Essence* (London: Secker & Warburg).

Horn, David (2000), "The Sound World of Art Tatum," *Black Music Research Journal,* 20 (2), 237–257.

Howland, John (2009), *"Ellington Uptown": Duke Ellington, James P. Johnson, and the Birth of Concert Jazz* (Ann Arbor: University of Michigan Press).

Hurok, Sol (1938), "Letter to Willard Alexander" (New York: MSS 53, the Benny Goodman Papers, in the Irving S. Gilmore Music Library of Yale University).

—— (Salomon), and Goode, Ruth (1947), *Impresario: A Memoir by S. Hurok in Collaboration with Ruth Goode* (London: Macdonald).

Jessup, David (2010), *Benny Goodman: A Supplemental Discography* (Lanham, MD: Scarecrow Press).

Kanzler, George (1988), "Benny Goodman Recalled with Exactness and Uneven Results," *Star Ledger,* January 18, 1988, p. 42.

Kelley, Fran (1956), "Joe Gershenson: Musical Director," *Metronome,* March 1956, p. 20.

Kennedy, Gary (n.d.), "Repertory Band," in Barry Kernfeld (ed.), *The New Grove Dictionary of Jazz,* 2nd ed. (Grove Music Online, Oxford Music Online).

Kernfeld, Barry (n.d.), "Improvisation," in Barry Kernfeld (ed.), *The New Grove Dictionary of Jazz,* 2nd ed. (Grove Music Online, Oxford Music Online).

Klee, Joe H. (2000), "Benny Goodman: The 1938 Carnegie Hall Concert," *Mississippi Rag,* 27 (9), p. 40.

Kolodin, Irving (1938a), "Swing Concert Fills Carnegie," *New York Sun,* January 17, 1938, p. 15.

—— (1938b), "Notes on the Program," in Jon Hancock (ed.), *Benny Goodman: The Famous 1938 Carnegie Hall Jazz Concert* (Shrewsbury, UK: Prancing Fish), pp. 193–204.

—— (1950), "Liner Notes (Reprinted)," *"The Famous Carnegie Hall Jazz Concert,"* Columbia/Legacy C2k 65143.

Korall, Burt (2002), *Drummin' Men: The Heartbeat of Jazz—The Bebop Years* (Oxford: Oxford University Press).

Krasner, David (1997), *Resistance, Parody, and Double Consciousness in African American Theatre, 1895–1910* (Basingstoke: Macmillan).

Lacasse, Serge (2000), "Intertextuality and Hypertextuality in Recorded Popular Music," in Michael Talbot (ed.), *The Musical Work: Reality or Invention?* (Liverpool: Liverpool University Press).

Levin, Michael (1951), "Mix Reviews the Goodman Carnegie LP," *DownBeat,* January 12, 1951, pp. 14–15.

Levinson, Peter (1999), *Trumpet Blues: The Life of Harry James* (New York: Oxford University Press).

Library of Congress (1934), *Catalog of Copyright Entries, Part 3, Musical Compositions* (New Series vol. 29 no. 9; Washington, DC: U.S. Government Printing Office).

—— (1935), *Catalog of Copyright Entries, Part 3, Musical Compositions* (New Series vol. 29 for the Year 1934; Washington, DC: U.S. Government Printing Office).

—— (1938), *Catalog of Copyright Entries, 1938, Part 3, Musical Compositions* (New Series vol. 33 no. 1; Washington, DC: U.S. Government Printing Office).

Life (1937a), "Life Goes to a Party to Listen to Benny Goodman and His Swing Band," *Life,* November 1, 1937, pp. 120–124.

—— (1937b), "Life Goes to a Party (at the Veiled Prophet's Ball)," *Life,* October 25, 1937, pp. 123–126.

—— (1937c), "Life Goes to a Party at a Corn-Husking Bee in Kent, Conn." *Life,* November 8, 1937, pp. 122–125.

—— (1938), "The Story of a Song: 'Bei Mir Bist Du Schön' Now Heads Best-Sellers," *Life,* January 31, 1938, p. 39.

"Liner Notes" (2006), *The Complete Famous* 1938 *Carnegie Hall Jazz Concert Plus* 1950s *Material* (Avid Ambx 151).

Lopes, Paul Douglas (2002), *The Rise of a Jazz Art World* (Cambridge: Cambridge University Press).

Magee, Jeffrey (2000), "Irving Berlin's 'Blue Skies': Ethnic Affiliations and Musical Transformations," *Musical Quarterly,* 84 (4), pp. 537–580.

—— (2005), *The Uncrowned King of Swing: Fletcher Henderson and Big Band Jazz* (New York, Oxford: Oxford University Press).

Marmorstein, Gary (2007), *The Label: The Story of Columbia Records* (New York: Thunder's Mouth Press).

Marx, Albert (1987), "Conference Panel with Albert Marx and Jess Stacy," IAJRC Annual Conference (Los Angeles).

McDonough, John (2000a), "Carnegie Cavalcade," *DownBeat,* June 2000, pp. 76–77.

—— (2000b), "A Decade of Retrospection: The Reissue Trend," *DownBeat,* January 22, 2000, pp. 22–23.

—— (2006), "Benny Goodman at Carnegie Hall: The Story of the Session," *IAJRC Journal,* 39 (4), pp. 29–40.

Mezzrow, Mezz, and Wolfe, Bernard (1999), *Really the Blues* (Edinburgh: Payback Press).

Moore, Allan (2002), "Authenticity as Authentication," *Popular Music*, 21 (2), pp. 209–223.

Morgenstern, Dan, et al. (1978), "Benny Goodman Returns to Carnegie Hall: Four Views," *DownBeat*, June 1, 1978, pp. 20–23.

Morley, Sheridan (2004), "Lillie, Beatrice Gladys [Married Name Beatrice Gladys Peel, Lady Peel] (1894–1989)," *Oxford Dictionary of National Biography*, <http://www.oxforddnb.com/view/article/39938>, accessed April 16, 2010.

Morrison, Hobe (1938), "Goodman's Vipers Slay the Cats, but Salon Crix Don't Savvy Jive," *Variety*, January 19, 1938, pp. 46, 51.

Myers, Marc (2010), "Interview: George Avakian," <http://www.jazzwax.com/2010/03/interview-george-avakian-part-1.html>, accessed May 15, 2010.

New York Amsterdam News (1938a), "Chick, Basie Battle It out in Swingtime," *New York Amsterdam News*, January 22, 1938, p. 16.

—— (1938b), " 'Swing Jam Session' Terrific and Torrid as Masters Exhibit Stuff at Carnegie," *New York Amsterdam News*, January 22, 1938, p. 5.

New York Herald Tribune (1938), "Swing in Carnegie Hall," *New York Herald Tribune*, January 18, 1938, p. 18.

New York Times (1921), "Court Finds Jolson Song Like Tosca Air," *New York Times*, January 29, 1921. *New York Times Article Archive* <http://www.nytimes.com/ref/membercenter/nytarchive.html>, accessed March 1, 2012.

—— (1928), "Handy, Jazz Pioneer, Gives Famous 'Blues,' " *New York Times*, April 28, 1928. *New York Times Article Archive* <http://www.nytimes.com/ref/membercenter/nytarchive.html>, accessed March 1, 2012.

—— (1937a), "Ferde Grofe Gives a Jazz Concert," *New York Times*, January 20, 1937, p. 19.

—— (1937b), "Opera and Concert Asides," *New York Times*, December 12, 1937, sec. 10, p. 9.

—— (1938), "Hot Music at Carnegie," *New York Times*, January 18, 1938, p. 22.

Norton, Pauline (n.d.), "Foxtrot," *Grove Music Online* (Oxford Music Online).

Oakley, Helen (1937), "Call out Riot Squad to Handle Mob at Goodman-Webb Battle," *DownBeat*, June 1937, pp. 1, 3.

Panassie, Hugues (1942/R1946), *The Real Jazz*, trans. Anne Sorelle Williams (New York: Smith & Durrell).

Parsonage, Catherine (2005), *The Evolution of Jazz in Britain, 1880–1935* (Aldershot: Ashgate).

Perkins, Francis D. (1938), "Benny Goodman 'Swings It Out' in Carnegie Hall," *New York Herald Tribune*, January 17, 1938, p. 7.

Peterson, Bernard L. (1993), *A Century of Musicals in Black and White: An Encyclopedia of Musical Stage Works by, About, or Involving African Americans* (Westport, CT, London: Greenwood Press).

Ramsey, Frederic, and Smith, C. E. (1939), *Jazzmen* (New York: Harcourt, Brace).

Rasula, Jed (1995), "The Media of Memory: The Seductive Menace of Records in Jazz History," in Krin Gabbard (ed.), *Jazz Among the Discourses* (Durham, NC, and London: Duke University Press), pp. 134–162.

Rhythm (1938), "The Benny Goodman Swing Concert," *Rhythm*, April 1938, p. 41.

Robinson, J. Bradford, and Kernfeld, Barry (n.d.), "Walter Page," in Barry Kernfeld (ed.), *The New Grove Dictionary of Jazz, 2nd ed.* (Grove Music Online, Oxford Music Online).

Rollini, Arthur (1989), *Thirty Years with the Big Bands* (Oxford: Bayou).

Russell, Tony, and Pinson, Bob (2004), *Country Music Records: A Discography, 1921–1942* (Oxford, New York: Oxford University Press).

Schaap, Phil (1999), "Reissuing Benny Goodman at Carnegie Hall," liner notes, *The Famous Carnegie Hall Jazz Concert*, Columbia/Legacy C2k 65143, pp. 37–38.

Schiff, David (1997), *Gershwin: Rhapsody in Blue* (Cambridge: Cambridge University Press).

Schoenberg, Loren (1997), "Liner Notes" for *The Complete RCA Victor Small Group Recordings*, RCA Victor RCA 68764-2.

Scholl, Warren (1938), "Concert from a Human Angle," *Melody Maker*, February 5, 1938, p. 11.

Schuller, Gunther (1986), *Early Jazz: Its Roots and Musical Development* (New York, Oxford: Oxford University Press).

—— (1989), *The Swing Era: The Development of Jazz, 1930–1945* (New York, Oxford: Oxford University Press).

Secunda, Victoria (1982), *Bei Mir Bist Du Schön: The Life of Sholom Secunda* (Weston, CT: Magic Circle Press, and New York, distributed by Walker).

Shadwick, Keith (1997), *The Gramophone Jazz Good CD Guide: Reviews of the Best Jazz CDs You Can Buy* (London: Omnibus Press).

Shaw, Arnold (1983), *52nd Street: The Street of Jazz* (New York: Da Capo).

Shaw, Artie (1992), *The Trouble with Cinderella: An Outline of Identity* (Santa Barbara, CA: Fithian Press).

"S. Hurok Presents Benny Goodman and His Swing Orchestra" (1938), promotional flyer (New York: MSS 53, the Benny Goodman Papers, in the Irving S. Gilmore Music Library of Yale University).

Simon, George T. (1938a), "Basie's Brilliant Band Conquers Chick's," *Metronome*, February 1938, pp. 15, 20.

—— (1938b), "Benny and Cats Make Carnegie Debut Real Howling Success," *Metronome*, February 1938, pp. 15, 18, 44.

—— (1968), *The Big Bands* (New York: Macmillan).

—— (1971), *Simon Says: The Sights and Sounds of the Swing Era, 1935–1955* (New Rochelle, NY: Arlington House).

—— (1980), "The Night When Carnegie Hall Swung," *New York Times*, January 10, 1988, sec. H, pp. 25, 37.

Sohmer, Jack (2000), "Benny Goodman at Carnegie Hall 1938: Complete," *JazzTimes*, May 2000, pp. 128, 130, 132.

Southern, Eileen (1978), "Black-Music Concerts in Carnegie Hall, 1912–1915," *Black Perspective in Music*, 6 (1), pp. 71–88.

Stearns, Marshall (1956), *The Story of Jazz* (New York: Oxford University Press).

——, and Stearns, Jean (1994), *Jazz Dance: The Story of American Vernacular Dance* (New York: Da Capo Press).

Stowe, David W. (1994), *Swing Changes: Big-Band Jazz in New Deal America* (Cambridge, MA, London: Harvard University Press).

Sudhalter, Richard M. (1999), *Lost Chords: White Musicians and Their Contribution to Jazz, 1915–1945* (New York, Oxford: Oxford University Press).

Suskin, Steven (2000), *Show Tunes: The Songs, Shows, and Careers of Broadway's Major Composers* (rev. and expanded 3rd ed.; New York, Oxford: Oxford University Press).

Tackley, Catherine (2010), "Jazz Recordings as Social Texts," in Amanda Bayley (ed.), *Recorded Music: Performance, Culture and Technology* (Cambridge: Cambridge University Press), pp. 167–186.

Taubman, Howard (1953), "Atom Bomb on Carnegie Hall? No, Man! Goodman and Satchmo Armstrong's All Stars Beat It Out," *New York Times,* April 18, 1953, Amusements Section, p. 16.

Time (1936), "Music: Whoa-Ho-Ho-Ho-Ho-Ho!" *Time,* January 20, 1936. <http://www.time.com/time/magazine/article/0,9171,755686,00.html>, accessed March 1, 2012.

Tomkins, Les (2000), "Benny Goodman the Famous 1938 Carnegie Hall Jazz Concert," *Jazz Rag,* 60, p. 25.

Tucker, Sherrie (n.d.), "Jazz Historiography," in Barry Kernfeld (ed.), *The New Grove Dictionary of Jazz, 2nd ed.* (Grove Music Online, Oxford Music Online).

Tyler, Don (2007), *Hit Songs, 1900–1955: American Popular Music of the Pre-Rock Era* (Jefferson, NC, London: McFarland).

Ulanov, Barry (1951), "BG: 1938," *Metronome,* February, p. 29.

—— (1952/R1958), *A History of Jazz in America* (London: Hutchinson).

Vaché, Warren W. (2005), *Sittin' in with Chris Griffin: A Reminiscence of Radio and Recording's Golden Years* (Lanham, MD, Oxford: Scarecrow Press; [New Brunswick]: Institute of Jazz Studies, Rutgers—State University of New Jersey).

van de Leur, Walter (2002), *Something to Live For: The Music of Billy Strayhorn* (Oxford: Oxford University Press).

Werb, Brett (n.d.), "Jewish Music—Composed Music and Yiddish Theatre," *Grove Music Online* (Oxford Music Online).

Wheeler, Geoffrey (2008), "The Boston Version: Benny Goodman's Second 'Carnegie Hall' Concert," *IAJRC Journal,* 41 (1), pp. 34–47.

Wilber, Bob, and Webster, Derek (1989), *Music Was Not Enough* (Oxford: Bayou).

Wilson, John S. (1951), "BG Gave Much to Dance Biz," *DownBeat,* January 12, 1951, p. 1.

—— (1956), "Benny's Story: Goodman Retrospect Brought to LP Discs," *New York Times,* February 12, 1956, sec. X, p. 18.

—— (1968), "The Angels Sing for '38 Goodman Band," *New York Times,* January 17, 1968, p. 40.

—— (1988), "Jazz: Big Band Revival at Carnegie," *New York Times,* January 18, 1988, n.p.

Wilson, Teddy, Van Loo, Humphrey, and Ligthart, Arie (2001), *Teddy Wilson Talks Jazz* (New York, London: Continuum).

DISCOGRAPHY

Notes: RHJ = The Red Hot Jazz Archive
* = Goodman's studio recording closest in date to January 16, 1938

BENNY GOODMAN CARNEGIE HALL CONCERT, JANUARY 16, 1938

Benny Goodman: The Famous 1938 Carnegie Hall Jazz Concert (Columbia SL 160; 1950, LP)

Benny Goodman Live at Carnegie Hall (Columbia Jazz Masterpieces G2K 40244; 1986, CD)

Benny Goodman: The Famous 1938 Carnegie Hall Jazz Concert [produced by Schaap] (Sony/Columbia Legacy C2K 65143; 1999, CD)

The Complete Famous 1938 Carnegie Hall Jazz Concert plus 1950s material (Avid AMBX 151; 2006, CD)

Benny Goodman Carnegie Hall, January 16th 1938 The Complete Concert (Jasmine, JASCD 6562006; 2006, CD)

Benny Goodman The Complete Legendary 1938 Carnegie Hall Concert (Definitive, DRCD113782008; 2008, CD)

THE ORCHESTRA

"Don't Be That Way"
November 19, 1934, Chick Webb (*Spinnin' the Web*, Membran/Documents)
February 19, 1936, Chick Webb (*Count Basie and His Orchestra 1937/Chick Webb and His Orchestra 1936*, Forlane UCD 19007)
January 18, 1938, Lionel Hampton (*Complete Jazz Series 1938–1939*, Chronological Classics 534)
January 18, 1938, Benny Goodman (*The Complete Legendary 1938 Carnegie Hall Concert*, Definitive, DRCD113782008)

*February 16, 1938, Benny Goodman (*The Harry James Years Volume 1*, RCA Bluebird 661552)

February 16, 1938, Benny Goodman alternative take (*The Harry James Years Volume 1*, RCA Bluebird 661552)

April 25, 1938, Benny Goodman Quartet (*When Swing Was King*, Mr Music MMCD 7014)

"Sometimes I'm Happy"

1927, Louise Groody and Charles King (*Broadway*, Body and Soul)

c. March 23, 1927, The Six Hottentots, Red Nichols (*Complete Jazz Series 1927–1928*, Chronological Classics 1241)

April 14, 1927, Roger Wolf Kahn (Victor 20599-A, RHJ)

January 24, 1930, Red Nichols (*Complete Jazz Series 1929–1930*, Chronological Classics 1369)

*June 6, 1935, Benny Goodman (*50 Tracks in One Day*, Jasmine JASCD 409)

*July 1, 1935, Benny Goodman (*Complete Jazz Series 1935*, Chronological Classics 769)

January 27, 1937, Benny Goodman (*A Jam Session with Benny Goodman 1935–37*, Sunbeam 149; although the date given on the record sleeve is "August or September 1935," Connor attributes this performance to this later date; Connor 1988: 65)

March 3, 1937, Benny Goodman (*Benny Goodman on the Air, 1937–1938*, Columbia SP)

August 24, 1937, Benny Goodman (*Benny Goodman's Golden Era, More Camel Caravans*, Phontastic 8841/8842)

April 21, 1938, Benny Goodman (*Swingtime*, Sunbeam 152)

September 27, 1938, Benny Goodman (*Complete Camel Caravan Shows 1938*, Jazz Hour, JH 1025)

"One O'Clock Jump"

July 7, 1937, Count Basie (*Complete Jazz Series 1936–1938*, Chronological Classics 503)

October 20, 1937, Benny Goodman (*The Complete 1937 Madhattan Room Broadcasts Volume 2*, Viper's Nest VN 172)

November 3, 1937, Count Basie (*Count Basie and His Orchestra 1937/Chick Webb and His Orchestra 1936*, Forlane UCD 19007)

December 16, 1937, Benny Goodman (*At the Madhattan Room 1937; Encores from Carnegie Hall*, Sunbeam 127)

January 5, 1938, Harry James (*Complete Jazz Series 1937–1939*, Chronological Classics 903)

*February 16, 1938, Benny Goodman (*The Harry James Years Volume 1*, RCA Bluebird 661552)

February 16, 1938, Benny Goodman, alternative take (*The Harry James Years Volume 1*, RCA Bluebird 661552)

May 10, 1938, Benny Goodman (*The Best of Newhouse: Jerry Newhouse Presents Benny Goodman, His Orchestra, Trio and Quartet 1938–39*, Blu-Disc T5001/5002)

September 27, 1938, Benny Goodman (*Complete Camel Caravan Shows 1938*, Jazz Hour, JH 1025 DL)

December 18, 1938, Benny Goodman (*The Best of Newhouse: Jerry Newhouse Presents Benny Goodman, His Orchestra, Trio and Quartet 1938–39*, Blu-Disc T5001/5002)

March 6, 1939, Harry James, Two O'Clock Jump (*Complete Jazz Series 1937–1939*, Chronological Classics 903)

"Life Goes to a Party"

November 4, 1937, Benny Goodman (*The Complete 1937 Madhattan Room Broadcasts Volume 4*, Viper's Nest VN174)

November 6, 1937, Benny Goodman (*The Complete 1937 Madhattan Room Broadcasts Volume 5*, Viper's Nest VN175)

*November 12, 1937, Benny Goodman (*The Harry James Years Volume 1*, RCA Bluebird 661552; and *Complete Jazz Series 1937–1938*, Chronological Classics 899)

December 1, 1937, Harry James (*Complete Jazz Series 1937–1939*, Chronological Classics 903)

*December 2, 1937, Benny Goodman (*The Harry James Years Volume 1*, RCA Bluebird 661552; and *Complete Jazz Series 1937–1938*, Chronological Classics 899)

December 22, 1937, Benny Goodman (*The Complete 1937 Madhattan Room Broadcasts Volume 6*, Viper's Nest VN176)

"Blue Skies"

1927, Al Jolson (*Music of the Movies: The Jazz Singer*, Vanilla One Media Publishing)

August 18, 1933, Fletcher Henderson, "Can You Take It?" (*Complete Jazz Series 1932–1934*, Chronological Classics 535)

January 26, 1935, Benny Goodman (*The Let's Dance Broadcasts 1934–35 Volume 3*, Sunbeam 150)

February 9, 1935, Benny Goodman (*The Let's Dance Broadcasts 1934–35 Volume 2*, Sunbeam 104)

*June 25, 1935, Benny Goodman (*Complete Jazz Series 1935*, Chronological Classics 769)

January 6, 1936, Benny Goodman (*The NBC Broadcasts from Chicago's Congress Hotel 1935–1936 Volume 1*, Circle CCD-171)

November 6, 1937, Benny Goodman (*The Complete 1937 Madhattan Room Broadcasts Volume 5*, Viper's Nest VN 175)

September 13, 1938, Benny Goodman (*Complete Camel Caravan Shows September 1938*, Jazz Hour 1038)

January 9, 1939, Chick Webb (*Chick Webb The Golden Swing Years*, Polydor 423248)

"Loch Lomond"

December 18, 1933, Benny Goodman, "Riffin' the Scotch," Billie Holiday, vocal (*Complete Jazz Series 1931–1933*, Chronological Classics 719)

August 6, 1937, Maxine Sullivan, vocal (*Complete Jazz Series 1937–1938*, Chronological Classics 963)

October 16, 1937, Benny Goodman (*The Complete 1937 Madhattan Room Broadcasts Volume 1*, Viper's Nest VN171)

*November 12, 1937, Benny Goodman (*Complete Jazz Series 1937*, Chronological Classics 879)

November 23, 1937, Woody Herman (*Complete Jazz Series 1937–1938*, Chronological Classics 1090)

January 12, 1938, Wingy Manone (*Complete Jazz Series 1937–1938*, Chronological Classics 952)

August 11, 1938, Teddy Wilson (*Teddy Wilson—His Piano and Orchestra 1938–1939*, Jazz Unlimited)

"(The) Blue Room"

September 27, 1928, Joe Venuti's Blue Four (Okeh 41144, RHJ)

December 13, 1932, Bennie Moten's Kansas City Orchestra (*Complete Jazz Series 1930–1932*, Chronological Classics 591; also released as Don Benjamin y su orquesta de jazz puro as curatito de dichas)

October 17, 1933, Dorsey Brothers Orchestra (Brunswick 6722, RHJ)

July 16, 1934, Isham Jones (Bluebird 6449, RHJ)

August 31, 1934, Isham Jones (Decca 493 B, RHJ)

February 4, 1935, Glen Gray and His Casa Loma Orchestra (*Glen Gray and His Casa Loma Orchestra Volume 1*, Nostalgia Arts 3002)

*March 9, 1938, Benny Goodman (*Complete Jazz Series 1937–1938*, Chronological Classics 899)

March 9, 1938, Benny Goodman (*The Alternative Takes in Chronological Order Volume 2*, Neatwork RP2049)

February 10, 1939, Chick Webb (*Chick Webb The Golden Swing Years*, Polydor 423248)

"Swingtime in the Rockies"

October 27, 1933, Earl Hines, "Take It Easy" (*Complete Jazz Series 1932–1934*, Chronological Classics 514)

*June 15, 1936, Benny Goodman (*Complete Jazz Series 1936 Volume 1*, Chronological Classics 817)

October 27, 1937, Benny Goodman (*The Complete 1937 Madhattan Room Broadcasts Volume 3*, Viper's Nest VN 173)

November 20, 1937, Benny Goodman (*The Complete 1937 Madhattan Room Broadcasts Volume 5*, Viper's Nest VN 175)

June 14, 1938, Benny Goodman (*The Best of Newhouse: Jerry Newhouse Presents Benny Goodman, His Orchestra, Trio and Quartet 1938–39*, Blu-Disc T5001/5002)

March 28, 1939, Benny Goodman (*Camel Caravan Broadcasts 1939, Volume 3*, Phontastic NCD8819)

"Bei Mir Bist Du Schön"

February 2, 1934, Benny Goodman, "Georgia Jubilee" (*Complete Jazz Series 1934–1935*, Chronological Classics 744)

November 24, 1937, The Andrews Sisters (*Greatest Hits*, Air Music)

December 18, 1937, Benny Goodman (*The Complete 1937 Madhattan Room Broadcasts Volume 6*, Viper's Nest VN 176)

December 21, 1937, Ella Fitzgerald (*Complete Jazz Series 1937–1938*, Chronological Classics 506)

*December 21, 1937, Benny Goodman (*The Complete RCA Victor Small Group Recordings*, RCA 68764-2)

*December 29, 1937, Benny Goodman (*The Complete RCA Victor Small Group Recordings*, RCA 68764-2)

"Sing, Sing, Sing"

February 28, 1936, Louis Prima (*Complete Jazz Series 1935–1936*, Chronological Classics 1077)

March 18, 1936, Benny Goodman (*B.G. On the Air!* Sunbeam 105)

July 6, 1937, Benny Goodman, part 1, alternative take (*The Alternative Takes in Chronological Order Volume 2*, Neatwork RP2049)

*July 6, 1937, Benny Goodman, part 1 (*Complete Jazz Series 1936–1937*, Chronological Classics 858)

July 6, 1937, Benny Goodman, part 1, alternative take (*The Alternative Takes in Chronological Order Volume 4*, Neatwork RP2067)

July 6, 1937, Benny Goodman, part 2, alternative take (*The Alternative Takes in Chronological Order Volume 2*, Neatwork RP2049)

*July 6, 1937, Benny Goodman, part 2 (*Complete Jazz Series 1936–1937*, Chronological Classics 858)

July 6, 1937, Benny Goodman, part 2, alternative take (*The Alternative Takes in Chronological Order Volume 4*, Neatwork RP2067)

August 10, 1937, Benny Goodman (*Benny Goodman's Golden Era, More Camel Caravans*, Phontastic 8841/8842)

November 8, 1938, Benny Goodman (*The Best of Newhouse: Jerry Newhouse Presents Benny Goodman, His Orchestra, Trio and Quartet 1938–39*, Blu-Disc T5001/5002)

"If [When] Dreams Come True"

January 15, 1934, Chick Webb (*Spinnin' the Web*, Membran/Documents)

February 19, 1936, Chick Webb; Charles Linton, vocal (*Count Basie and His Orchestra 1937/Chick Webb and His Orchestra 1936*, Forlane UCD 19007)

*December 3, 1937, Benny Goodman (*Complete Jazz Series 1937-1938*, Chronological Classics 899)

December 3, 1937, Benny Goodman, alternative take, New York (*The Alternative Takes in Chronological Order Volume 4*, Neatwork RP2067)

December 17, 1937, Chick Webb; Ella Fitzgerald, vocal (*Complete Jazz Series 1937–1938*, Chronological Classics 506)

December 18, 1937, Benny Goodman (*The Complete 1937 Madhattan Room Broadcasts Volume 6*, Viper's Nest VN 176)

December 22, 1937, Benny Goodman (*The Complete 1937 Madhattan Room Broadcasts Volume 6*, Viper's Nest VN 176)

January 4, 1938, Benny Goodman (*Performance Recordings 1937–1938 Volume 2*, MGM 3789)

January 6, 1938, Teddy Wilson Orchestra; Billie Holiday, vocal (*The Quintessential Billie Holiday Volume 5*, Columbia CK44423)

February 15, 1938, Artie Shaw (*The Complete Rhythm Makers Sessions 1937–1938 Volume 3*, Jazz Band TMCD2194/95-2)

March 24, 1938, Duke Ellington; Ivie Anderson, vocal (*Cotton Club Nights*, Music Memoria 40392-2)

August 13, 1940, "When Dreams Come True," Horace Henderson/Fletcher Henderson (*Complete Jazz Series 1940–1941*, Chronological Classics 648)

"Big John Special"

September 11, 1934, Fletcher Henderson (*Complete Jazz Series 1932–1934*, Chronological Classics 535)

January 13, 1936, Benny Goodman (*The NBC Broadcasts from Chicago's Congress Hotel 1935–1936 Volume 1*, Circle CCD-171)

February 19, 1936, Chick Webb (*Count Basie and His Orchestra 1937/Chick Webb and His Orchestra 1936*, Forlane UCD 19007)

September 8, 1936, Erskine Hawkins (*Complete Jazz Series 1936–1938*, Chronological Classics 653)

April 29, 1937, Benny Goodman (*When Swing Was King*, Mr Music MMCD-7014)

November 16, 1937, Benny Goodman (*Benny Goodman Performance Recordings 1937–1938*, MGM E3789)

December 18, 1937, Benny Goodman (*The Complete 1937 Madhattan Room Broadcasts Volume 6*, Viper's Nest 176)

*May 28, 1938, Benny Goodman (*Complete Jazz Series 1938 Volume 1*, Chronological Classics 925)

September 13, 1938, Benny Goodman (*Complete Camel Caravan Shows September 1938*, Jazz Hour 1038 DL)

"TWENTY YEARS OF JAZZ"

"Sensation Rag"

May 12, 1919, Original Dixieland Jazz Band (*The Creators of Jazz*, Avid AMSC 702)

June 25, 1918, Original Dixieland Jazz Band (Columbia 736, RHJ)

"I'm Coming Virginia"

September 18, 1926, Ethel Waters with Will Marion Cook's Singing Orchestra (*The Very Best of Ethel Waters, 1921–1947*, Master Classic Records 2009)

April 29, 1927, Paul Whiteman (*The King of Jazz 1920–1927*, Timeless Records CBC 1093)

April 29, 1927, Paul Whiteman, take 2 (*The King of Jazz 1920–1927*, Timeless Records CBC 1093)

May 11, 1927, Fletcher Henderson (*Complete Jazz Series 1927*, Chronological Classics 580)

May 13, 1927, Frankie Trumbauer, featuring Bix Beiderbecke (*Complete Jazz Series 1927–1928*, Chronological Classics 1188)

December 13, 1935, Bunny Berigan and His Blue Boys (*Complete Jazz Series 1935–1936*, Chronological Classics 734)

April 23, 1937, Teddy Wilson and His Orchestra, featuring Harry James (*Teddy Wilson Volume 4*, Membran Records)

"When My Baby Smiles at Me"

December 9, 1919, Ted Lewis (Columbia A2908 RHJ)

January 25, 1921, Art Hickman (*From Ragtime to Jazz Volume 1 1896–1922*)

September 13, 1923, Ted Lewis (special promotional recording; N/A)

November 22, 1926, Ted Lewis, take 1 (Columbia 922-D RHJ)

November 22, 1926, Ted Lewis, take 3 (Columbia 922-D RHJ)

May 4, 1935, Benny Goodman (1935 *Let's Dance Broadcasts*, Circle CCD-50)

July 16, 1938, Ted Lewis (Decca 2054)

"Shine"

March 9, 1931, Louis Armstrong (*Complete Jazz Series 1930–1931*, Chronological Classics 547)

August 2, 1935, Putney Dandrige, including Teddy Wilson (*Complete Jazz Series 1935–1936*, Chronological Classics 846)

February 19, 1936, Chick Webb with Ella Fitzgerald (*Count Basie and His Orchestra 1937/ Chick Webb and His Orchestra 1936*, Forlane International UCD19007)

November 19, 1936, Ella Fitzgerald; small group with Webb (*Complete Jazz Series 1935–1937*, Chronological Classics 500)

March 9, 1937, Benny Goodman (*Air Play*, Dr Jazz WGK 40350)

August 10, 1937, Benny Goodman (*Benny Goodman's Golden Era, More Camel Caravans*, Phontastic 8841/8842)

April 21, 1938, Benny Goodman (*Swingtime—1938*, Sunbeam 152)

September 6, 1938, Benny Goodman (*The Best of Newhouse: Jerry Newhouse Presents Benny Goodman, His Orchestra, Trio and Quartet 1938–39*, Blu-Disc T5001/5002)

"Blue Reverie"

March 8, 1937, Cootie Williams and His Rug Cutters (*Complete Jazz Series 1937 Volume 1*, Chronological Classics 675)

March 8, 1937, Cootie Williams and His Rug Cutters, alternative take (*The Alternative Takes in Chronological Order Volume 5 1936–1937*, Neatwork RP 2039)

"Jam Session" ("Honeysuckle Rose")

December 9, 1932, Fletcher Henderson (*Complete Jazz Series 1932–1934*, Chronological Classics 535)

February/March 1934, "Bill Dodge" [Benny Goodman] and His Orchestra (*Benny Goodman—the Early Years*, Biography BCD109)

January 5, 1935, Benny Goodman (*Let's Dance*, Sunbeam 100)

December 6, 1935, Mildred Bailey and Her Alley Cats, including Johnny Hodges and Teddy Wilson (*Complete Jazz Series 1932–1936*, Chronological Classics 1080)

January 20, 1936, Benny Goodman (*The NBC Broadcasts from Chicago's Congress Hotel 1935–1936 Volume 2*, Circle CCD 172)

January 21, 1937, Count Basie, including Lester Young, Buck Clayton, Walter Page (*Complete Jazz Series 1936–1938*, Chronological Classics 503)

September 5, 1937, Teddy Wilson Quartet, including Harry James (*Complete Jazz Series 1937–1938*, Chronological Classics 548)

January 18, 1938, Benny Goodman (*The Complete Legendary 1938 Carnegie Hall Concert*, Definitive, DRCD113782008)

January 20, 1939, BBC Jam Session (*Alistair Cooke's Jazz Letter from America*, Avid AMSC 855)

TRIO AND QUARTET

"Body And Soul"

Note: Benny Goodman Trio unless stated

*July 13, 1935, Benny Goodman (*Complete Jazz Series 1935–1936*, Chronological Classics 789)

July 13, 1935, Benny Goodman, alternative take (*The Alternative Takes in Chronological Order Volume 1*, Neatwork RP2041)

January 6, 1937, Benny Goodman, duet with Teddy Wilson (*Air Play*, Dr Jazz WGK 40350)

March 16, 1937, Benny Goodman (*Air Play*, Dr Jazz WGK 40350)

October 20, 1937, Benny Goodman (*The Complete 1937 Madhattan Room Broadcasts Volume 2*, Viper's Nest VN 172)

October 11, 1939, Coleman Hawkins (*Complete Jazz Series 1939–40*, Chronological Classics 634)

"Avalon"

Note: Benny Goodman Quartet unless stated

February 27, 1928, Red Nichols (*Complete Jazz Series 1927–1928*, Chronological Classics 1241)

March 2, 1935, Coleman Hawkins with Michel Warlop (*The Essential Sides Remastered, 1934–1936*)

September 30, 1935, Jimmie Lunceford (*Complete Jazz Series 1934–1935*, Chronological Classics 505)

June 29, 1937, Benny Goodman (*Performance Recordings 1937–1938 Volume 2*, MGM 3789)

July 30, 1937, Benny Goodman, alternative take (*The Alternative Takes in Chronological Order Volume 2*, Neatwork RP2049)

*July 30, 1937, Benny Goodman (*Complete Jazz Series 1937*, Chronological Classics 879)

October 13, 1937, Benny Goodman (*The Complete 1937 Madhattan Room Broadcasts Volume 1*, Viper's Nest VN 171)

December 22, 1937, Benny Goodman (*The Complete 1937 Madhattan Room Broadcasts Volume 6*, Viper's Nest VN 176)

"The Man I Love"

*July 30, 1937, Benny Goodman (*Complete Jazz Series 1937*, Chronological Classics 879)

March 31, 1938, Benny Goodman (*Swingtime*, Sunbeam 152)

"I Got Rhythm"

Note: Benny Goodman Quartet unless stated

October 23, 1930, Red Nichols, including Benny Goodman (*Complete Jazz Series 1930–1931*, Chronological Classics 1462)

April 26, 1937, Lionel Hampton, entitled "Rhythm, Rhythm" (*Complete Jazz Series 1937–1938*, Chronological Classics 524)

April 29, 1937, Benny Goodman (*Performance Recordings 1937–1938 Volume 2*, MGM 3789)

"China Boy"

Note: Benny Goodman Trio unless stated

December 8, 1927, McKenzie and Condon's Chicagoans, including Gene Krupa (*Eddie Condon Complete Jazz Series 1927–1938,* Chronological Classics 742)

May 3, 1929, Paul Whiteman (*Bix Beiderbecke with Whiteman in Chronology, Complete Jazz Series 1928–1929,* Chronological Classics 1235)

July 2, 1930, Red Nichols, including Benny Goodman (*Complete Jazz Series 1929–1930,* Chronological Classics 1369)

*April 24, 1936, Benny Goodman (*Complete Jazz Series 1936 Volume 1,* Chronological Classics 817)

"Stompin' at the Savoy"

Note: Benny Goodman Quartet unless stated

June 6, 1935, Benny Goodman, orchestra (50 *Tracks in One Day,* Jasmine JASCD 409)

January 20, 1936, Benny Goodman, orchestra (*The NBC Broadcasts from Chicago's Congress Hotel 1935–1936 Volume 2,* Circle CCD 172)

January 24, 1936, Benny Goodman, orchestra (*Complete Jazz Series 1935–1936,* Chronological Classics 789)

December 2, 1936, Benny Goodman (*The Alternative Takes in Chronological Order Volume 1,* Neatwork RP2041)

*December 2, 1936, Benny Goodman (*Complete Jazz Series 1936–1937,* Chronological Classics 858)

March 23, 1937, Benny Goodman (*Air Play,* Dr Jazz WGK 40350)

August 24, 1937, Benny Goodman (*Benny Goodman's Golden Era, More Camel Caravans,* Phontastic 8841/8842)

"Dizzy Spells"

*March 25, 1938, Benny Goodman (*Complete Jazz Series 1938 Volume 1,* Chronological Classics 925)

November 15, 1938, Benny Goodman, with Harry James on drums (*The Best of Newhouse: Jerry Newhouse Presents Benny Goodman, His Orchestra, Trio and Quartet 1938–39,* Blu-Disc T5001/5002)

FILMOGRAPHY

Rhapsody in Black and Blue (Louis Armstrong)

Hollywood Hotel (featuring Benny Goodman and His Orchestra; Warner Brothers)

The Benny Goodman Story (Eureka EKA40278)

INDEX

·

Printed in Great Britain
by Amazon

86508222R00144